THE HAUNT OF HOME

Cemetery, Starkenburg, Montgomery County, MO. From Historic American Buildings Survey, Library of Congress, HABS MO,70-STABU.1-, https://www.loc.gov/item/mo0815/.

The Haunt of Home

A Journey through America's Heartland

Zachary Michael Jack

Northern Illinois University Press
an imprint of Cornell University Press
Ithaca and London

First published 2020 by Cornell University Press

Printed in the United States of America

Library of Congress Cataloging-in-Publication Data

Names: Jack, Zachary Michael, 1973– author.
Title: The haunt of home : a journey through America's heartland / Zachary Michael Jack.
Description: Ithaca, [New York] : Northern Illinois University Press, An imprint of Cornell University Press, 2020.
Identifiers: LCCN 2020002991 (print) | LCCN 2020002992 (ebook) | ISBN 9781501751790 (paperback) | ISBN 9781501751806 (epub) | ISBN 9781501751813 (pdf)
Subjects: LCSH: Place (Philosopy). | Fate and fatalism. | Middle West—Biography—Anecdotes. | Middle West—Social life and customs | Middle West—In literature.
Classification: LCC F351 .J33 2020 (print) | LCC F351 (ebook) | DDC 977—dc23
LC record available at https://lccn.loc.gov/2020002991
LC ebook record available at https://lccn.loc.gov/2020002992

To Grant Wood,
and to Mom,
maestros both
in my book

Life was not a valuable gift, but death was. Life was a fever-dream made up of joys embittered by sorrows, pleasure poisoned by pain; a dream that was a nightmare-confusion of spasmodic and fleeting delights, ecstasies, exultations, happinesses, interspersed with long-drawn miseries, griefs, perils, horrors, disappointments, defeats, humiliations, and despairs—the heaviest curse devisable by divine ingenuity; but death was sweet, death was gentle, death was kind; death healed the bruised spirit and the broken heart, and gave them rest and forgetfulness; death was man's best friend.

—MARK TWAIN, *Letters from the Earth*

Contents

Part III: Resurrections

INTRODUCTION

Middle American Gothic
and the Haunt of Home

We come from people who brought us up to believe that life is a struggle.
And if you should ever feel really happy, be patient: this will pass.
—GARRISON KEILLOR

In his 1997 book *The Undertaking: Life Studies from a Dismal Trade*, funeral director Thomas Lynch recalls what it was like to grow up in Middle America with a father and a family immersed in such a macabre profession. "The worst seemed always on the brink of happening, as his daily rounds informed him," Lynch remembers of his childhood in Milford, Michigan. "For my father, even butterflies were suspect." He learns from his father to perceive in the unrelenting stream of calamites evidence of a merciless God. "Car wrecks and measles and knives stuck in toasters, household poisons, guns left loaded, kidnappers, serial killers, burst appendices, bee stings, hard-candy chokings, croups untreated"—all these, Lynch writes, came to signify "the aberrant disasters" of a small-town Midwestern childhood.

My own childhood, and the childhoods of many Middle American children, passed under a similar pall. In fact my family's stock and trade—farming—was a particularly lethal profession. In 1971, the year my father began reaping and sowing our five hundred acres full-time with my grandfather, farming ranked as the third most dangerous occupation in America. Although agriculture accounted for only 4.4 percent of the workforce back then, it accounted for nearly 10 percent of the disabling injuries. Life in the place we called home could be uniquely challenging, so much so that our hometown was featured as the first chapter in Osha Gray Davidson's nationally popular nonfiction *Broken Heartland: The Rise of America's Rural Ghetto*. Davidson's book exposed to the rest of the nation many of our town's darkest and best-kept secrets, alleged skeletons in the closet that ranged from hunger, to disease, to poverty and premature death.

We could be forgiven, then, if we did not want to watch the many slasher movies set in our part of the country, with their full complement of grim reapers and farm implement–wielding madmen. Most years we did not celebrate Halloween at all, in fact, not for any particular religious objections but for the simple reason that we knew too many men and women with missing limbs, work-disabled bodies, or disfigured faces. It came as no surprise to us when, in 1984, scouts chose our rural region as the location for Stephen King's horror classic *Children of the Corn*.

On the page, Minnesota's Jim Heynen expressed the well-grounded fears of rural and small-town families in popular tales in which rambunctious kids face mortal danger when they disavow their elders' stern warnings. In the aptly named "That Could Have Been You," Heynen recalls:

> In town on Saturday nights, the grown-ups would point out the terrible things that happened to other people.
> See those farmers with all those missing fingers? Cornpickers did that.
> See that boy who doesn't have an arm in his sleeve? Power takeoff did that.
> The evidence was everywhere. Missing thises and thats.

Death was mother's milk for us. Our ancestors slept in their Civil War–era graves in the pioneer cemetery just down the gravel road from where we lay our heads each night—cemeteries we mowed, string-trimmed, and decorated in an agrarian version of Day of the Dead. There we communed with our long-gone kin as naturally as neighbors. While we were friendly with our dead, we took pains not to court disaster or evoke their displeasure, refusing to count our chickens. Each and every October my grandfather served as our unofficial spokesman, expressing our esprit de corps in ruefully predicting that he would not live to see another harvest. In the ultimate paradox, what city friends occasionally derided as his "negativity" or "pessimism" turned out to be a recipe for a long and successful life lived in community.

Fatalism positively infuses the nation's midlands, creeping into its folkways and social mores, feeding a homegrown sense of duende. For many the prairie Gothic connotes a Lake Woebegone–styled stoicism informed by School of Hard Knocks experience: realism leavened by pessimism coupled with a healthy dose of Middle American Murphy's Law. For others the term signifies a darkly déclassé, sky-is-falling world view espoused by the gray and aged living out their days in an interminable flyover country. In *Tales from Lake Woebegone* Minnesotan Garrison Keillor creates a cast of stoical characters that seem to exist almost entirely within the fatalistic limits of their insular town. In a 2012 interview he describes how the ostensible domesticity of his small-town Midwestern upbringing created in him a compensatory taste for life's darker notes. "I had no sorrows," he recalls, "beyond what any normal . . . Minnesotan would go through—scarce money, absurd self-consciousness, cold weather—and so I needed the bitter cigarette and the sting of alcohol to create a little drama for myself. In the movies, a man lights a cigarette before he goes off to face death, and after he has faced it, he pours himself a drink." The young Keillor resorts, metaphorically speaking, to lighting fires where there were none naturally occurring, perhaps to melt the ice of what fellow Minnesota writer Carol Bly in *Letters from the Country* calls the "chill" of a region inhabited by "God's frozen people."

For the poet Federico Garcia Lorca, the death instinct of a place, whether Andalusia or Minnesota, emerges from its duende. Lorca describes the process by which a particular region manifests its own unique love of, and penchant for, "black sounds." In "Play and the Theory of the Duende," the poet maintains that such dark notes are born of

> the mystery, the roots fastened in the mire that we all know and all ignore, the fertile silt that gives us the very substance of art. . . . The duende, then, is a power, not a work. It is a struggle, not a thought.

A region animated by death-and-life struggles, the poet maintains, is a country uniquely conversant with life's end. Duende gestures at precisely

the regional haunt that happens when place-based theologies, patholo-
gies, and artistries coalesce into folkways grounded in trial and tribula-
tion. While the conventions of Southern Gothic popularized by Flannery
O'Connor, William Faulkner, and Carson McCullers—the grotesque, the
macabre, and the fantastical—receive far greater fanfare, Middle American Gothic exerts an equally powerful influence. The Iowa Regionalists
of the 1920s and 1930s, Grant Wood and poet Jay G. Sigmund prominent among them, applied a European Gothic sensibility to the American Heartland long before Southern Gothic became a literary calling of
what O'Connor called the "Christ-haunted" South. For Wood, his native
region's Gothic impulse resided in the artful repressions of its people, a
trademark laconism that left much tragically unsaid or sadly understated,
but never unfelt.

Wood's popular depictions may be more subtle than the grotesques of
the Southern Gothic, and yet the secrets they hold are no less disquieting. A "Gothic, romantic flair" marks Wood's work, insists critic Edward
Ferreter in "Grant Wood Meets Jay G. Sigmund," adding, "It surfaced
with a freakish fascination for an oddly placed Gothic window in a little
farm house in southern Iowa." The painting, Ferreter argues, conveys "an
aura of mystery, horror, despair, and longing" that characterizes the Corn
Belt. The woman in the painting is the real Gothic, he notes, calling her a
"Gothic prisoner" to a repressive culture with "despair, discontent, and
defeatism written in her eyes."

In 1919's short story collection *Winesburg, Ohio*, Wood contemporary Sherwood Anderson crafts arguably the first and finest example of
the literary Middle American Gothic, creating a series of defining grotesques to suit the region's claustrophobic towns and villages. In "Sherwood Anderson and the Gothic Tradition," critic Brian Kornell argues
that Anderson's short story "The Untold Lie" offers the best example
of Midwest Gothic style, in part because the cornfields of Ohio are
used as dark symbols of the "oppression of a disappointed man in a
life he can't escape." In "The Untold Lie" Ray's personal unhappi-
ness amounts to a painful secret kept from the community, "hidden
behind the jovial, monotonous routine of his days." Kornell describes
the character's carefully damned subconscious as a sort of Midwestern
Dorian Gray or Mr. Hyde. Ray's inner world resembles "the corner
of a pretty tapestry being pulled back to reveal something sad, dark,

and neglected underneath," causing the narrator to conclude that "the masks of genial tranquility everyone wears keeps each man alone with his discontent—a discontent that is at once ordinary and unbearably sad."

The paradox apparent in Wood's and Anderson's Gothic portrayals is poignant: How can such a beating-heart section of the country, the very cradle of Regionalism, psychically ground and spiritually anchor a nation while simultaneously serving as its ultimate cautionary tale? Those who chose to leave Middle America sometimes hear in its minor chords and macabre portrayals a chilling message: Middle America is a place to avoid getting stuck in, a place whose fatalistic machinations the monied and mobile do well to escape. Wood, Anderson, and many of their Regionalist brethren present Middle Americans as a Gothic people, from cradle to grave as mindful of death and dying as of living and thriving. Their stories and canvases illuminate an almost funereal life-art practiced with fidelity in the Heartland, where fictional characters and real-life citizens alike undertake the difficult task of living passionately and purposefully against a backdrop of finite and sometimes tragic limits. For true Regionalists, however, the homegrown Gothic amounts to much more than mere pessimism or fatalism; it's an homage to Death, Life's less heralded twin, an animating force no less instructive and no less worthy of its own pages.

From the beginning many of America's most iconic writers represented the nation's midsection not just as a sunny breadbasket brimming with the promise of fertility, but as something unaccountably entombed and sad, strange fruit dead on the vine as fly-by-nighters by the hundreds of thousands abandoned the Midwest and Great Plains for the perceived greater riches of California and the West. Meanwhile, on the Plains, dreams died gruesome deaths in a succession of frontier wars, blistering droughts, agricultural busts, and grasshopper plagues. Indeed, early narratives bespeak the ever-haunt of the region's high lonesome plains and preternatural prairies and grasslands alongside a morbid fascination with its backwaters and fetid cataracts. So richly diverse was the region the pioneers encountered that while the dry Plains became known by the macabre appellation the "Great American Desert," the swampy, nutrient-rich meeting of the Ohio and Mississippi Rivers earned the moniker Little Egypt. Visiting the Little Egypt region of downstate Illinois in 1842 Charles Dickens came away deeply impressed not only by the region's legendary fecundity but by its

distinctly Gothic character. In *American Notes* the Englishman renders a
miasmic region positively steeped in haunt:

> A breeding-place of fever, ague, and death; vaunted in England as a mine
> of Golden Hope, and speculated in, on the faith of monstrous reputations,
> to many people's ruin. A dismal swamp, on which the half-built houses rot
> away . . . teeming . . . with rank unwholesome vegetation, in whose baleful
> shade the wretched wanderers who are tempted hither, droop, and die, and
> lay their bones; . . . a hotbed of disease, an ugly sepulcher, a grave uncheered
> by any gleam of promise: a place without one single quality, in earth or air
> or water to commend it.

The Mississippi River Dickens encountered on his tour of America wasn't
the charmingly lazy waterway of Mark Twain's local color stories, but
something more dastardly: "running liquid mud . . . choked and ob-
structed everywhere by huge logs and whole forest trees . . . rolling past
like monstrous bodies." Even Twain succumbed, late in life, to a darker
view of his native region, bottling native sardonicism and dark irony in
commentaries posthumously published in *Letters from the Earth*. Written during a period in which the region's most iconic scribe found himself mired in debt and grieving the loss of his wife and daughter, Twain
portrays the dashed and delusional hopes of the New World in a decidedly Old World Gothic lens, rendered as "a fever-dream made up of joys
embittered by sorrows, pleasure poisoned by pain; a dream that was a
nightmare-confusion."

In the early 1900s Indiana's Gene Stratton Porter followed Dickens's
and Twain's dark tributary to her own literary wellspring, translating the
Gothic allures of her state's great Limberlost Swamp into fiction featuring
the intrepid heroine Elnora Comstock, a widow's daughter who lives on
the edge of haunty lowlands. Elnora's mother refuses to so much as enter
the miasma, avowing to her daughter in *A Girl of the Limberlost*, "Folks
hereabout are none too fond of the swamp. I hate it like death. I've never
stayed here a night in my life without . . . [a] revolver, clean and loaded,
under my pillow, and the shotgun, same condition, by the bed." Porter,
who for a time lived along the creeping wetlands that inspired her fiction,
parlayed the Great Black Swamp into sales of more than ten million copies
by the time of her death in 1924. By then the Limberlost had itself died
its own untimely death, its thirteen thousand murky acres drained for

the less frightening domesticities of agriculture. Still the loss didn't deter Hollywood, who made the first of several films based on Porter's most popular novel in 1934, changing the title from *A Girl of the Limberlost* to the decidedly more Gothic *Romance of the Limberlost*.

In between its Regionalist heyday in the Great Depression and its modern-day revival in the form of Keillor's Dark Lutheranism and the Coen Brothers' Prairie Gothic aesthetic, the Middle American Gothic bubbles up frequently as theme, meme, motif, and trope, creating a wellspring of dark undercurrents as culturally influential as the Southern Gothic. Examples abound. Ray Bradbury's 1962 fantasy *Something Wicked This Way Comes* offers readers a nightmare version of the author's hometown of Waukegan, Illinois, just as Jane Smiley's *A Thousand Acres* renders the depravity and tragedy of Iowa farm life in her recasting of the Shakespearean tragedy *King Lear*. Toni Morrison's Pulitzer Prize–winning novel of 1987, *Beloved*, diversifies the genre further, merging the Southern and Midwestern Gothic traditions in a portrayal of a shuttered, spirit-possessed home in Cincinnati, Ohio, and an African-American family haunted by their former lives as slaves in a place ironically called Sweet Home, Kentucky.

In nonfiction the neo-Gothic finds expression in 1973's *Wisconsin Death Trip*, a book in which journalist-historian Michael Lesy resurrects the disturbing photographs of late nineteenth-century photographer Charles Van Schaick, who documents the endemic disease and mental illness in an Upper Midwest yet to heal from a heartrending agricultural depression. Osha Gray Davidson's *Broken Heartland*, written from the depths of the 1980s farm crisis, documents the hunger, social isolation, and economic despair and degradation of the "rural ghettos" dotting the nation's midlands, including my own hometown. A similarly ambivalent depiction of Middle America and the haunt of home pervades J. D. Vance's best-selling autobiography of 2016, *Hillbilly Elegy: A Memoir of a Family and a Region in Crisis*, which tells the story of the author's hardscrabble upbringing in small-town Ohio and Kentucky.

In 2010 the journal *Midwest Gothic* launched to feature the black sounds played by native artists in an "often-overlooked region of the United States ripe with its own mythologies and tall tales that include realistic aspects of Gothic fiction." "Not every piece," the editors remind their readers, "needs to be dark or twisted or full of despair" but may instead be characterized by "real life, inspired by the region, good, bad, or ugly." For the new generation of websites, blogs, webzines, and digital journals, the appellation Middle American Gothic intends no slight, but instead offers an objective descriptor of a time-honored world view with deep roots. Today's regionalists and localists—champions of all things homegrown—reclaim the Gothic, reapplying it in ever-widening cultural circles to describe settings in which death, fear, and romance mingle in landscapes marked by thwarted desires, subliminal repressions, and difficult secrets. Ancestral homes, fields, forests, farms, and ghosted or gritty factory towns and industrial cities—all at times manifest the telltale brooding or ominous atmosphere. Even the quintessentially Midwestern film *Field of Dreams* is steeped in the Gothic (the "Ghost Players," the field as phantasm, the liminality of life and afterlife, youth and age comingling in such figures as Moonlight Graham and Shoeless Joe Jackson).

Film portrayals of the region over the last sixty years also frequently invoke the Gothic to represent the Heartland both as alluring and exceptional terra incognita and as cautionary tale of social isolation and cultural depravity. In 1959 Wisconsin writer Robert Bloch published *Psycho*, a novel that encapsulates a notion similar to Sherwood Anderson's grotesques, namely the idea "that the man next door may be a monster unsuspected even in the gossip-ridden microcosm of small-town life." While Hitchcock later moved the Bates Motel to California in his film adaptation of the same name, the horror of Norman Bates and his infamous motel was originally of Midwestern vintage, as Bloch concocted the plot while living in Weyauwega, Wisconsin, coincident with a series of grisly murders in nearby Plainfield.

Hitchcock's treatment of Middle America as both unsettling and uncanny blossomed in 1959's *North by Northwest*, a film set almost entirely in flyover country. The action takes us to Chicago, where protagonist Roger Thornhill meets femme fatale Eve Kendall, before moving to rural Indiana, site of the famous crop-duster scene. The stifling grid of geometric cropland seen from above, the withering corn and desolate landscape with the ominous crop-duster circling overhead connote the eerie silence of open places. The iconic line "That plane's dustin' crops where there ain't no crops!" conveys the psychological unease of Roger Thornhill, a city slicker tragically out of place and vulnerable to predation.

The 1980s ushered in a more gruesome brand of Midwestern film coincident with the real-life violence of the farm crisis, a period of near-record debt, foreclosure, and farmer suicides. Growing up, many Midwesterners learned from their screens just how frightening the rest of the nation found their rural and small-town lives to be. A number of the era's filmmakers detected in the prairies and plains an underlying, brooding violence, from 1984's film *Children of the Corn*, to the 2009 made-for-TV remake filmed in the swampy bottomlands just a half mile from my Midwestern home. *Husk* from 2011 updates the long-standing cinematic association between horror and the region, locating terror in abandoned farms and endless stands of almost preternatural corn. The Coen Brothers' 1996 black comedy *Fargo* joins "Minnesota nice" with downbeat Prairie Gothic. In the film farcically rounded Midwestern vowels mingle chillingly with cold-blooded murder. Like novelist Robert Bloch before them, the Coen Brothers based their murder mystery in part on a real-life cold case, demonstrating once again how a region's darker disposition can transcend mere fiction.

A Gothic lifeblood runs in us, pervading nearly every aspect of Heartland life and culture from politics to policy making. Like Grant Wood's rendering of the pitchfork-wielding man and his companion in *American Gothic*, writers of the neo-Gothic look circumspectly and sometimes satirically at the region's most emblematic repressions, assigning value to characters who choose to hang their hat or grind their axe in the nation's overlooked midlands, characters who are often poked fun of elsewhere for their Chicken Little world views, their fusty, fuddy-duddyisms. That the nation's rural Heartland should be home to a confederation of the old should come as no surprise to those living on the coasts, who often equate the flyover states with the passé, with yesterday's news, with funerals—a great gaping kingdom somewhere on the horizon; like death itself, felt but largely unseen. While the rest of the nation sometimes begrudges the Heartland its homegrown cult-of-the-dead, its native necromancy, many of the region's most important writers and artists argue that an instant-gratification, death-denying nation should pay closer attention to a people and a place moved by, and sometimes infatuated with, pasts and passings.

And though we may seem world-weary to some—perhaps it's fairer to say *world-wary*—we are not passionless, visionless, or otherwise resigned to live our lives without all due courage. The poetic lives we summon in response to our own ever-present mortality resemble the death-aware, life-affirming energies with which the boys in "That Could Have Been You" respond to their elder's grave warnings: "Of course it could have been them. [They] knew that. They also knew that it was impossible to explain that they still lived without fear, lived as if every day held the promise of adventure in the sunlight, even if the sky was dark, even if icicles hanging from the eves … could drop at any moment like dazzling swords and impale them."

In *The Haunt of Home* I embrace the duende, considering the ways fatalism both intrinsically enriches and inherently limits regional culture, shaping an ethos of a land and its people. I endeavor to explore, examine, and reanimate our fatalist esprit de corps, analyzing a regional psycho-inheritance while simultaneously seeking to manifest and enact Gothic tropes. Together the creative nonfictions that follow inscribe the many ways death as animating force mingles with geography, producing a kind of geofatalism or geomortality that quite literally puts Middle America on the map. In them one finds death as leaving and loss, death as rebirth and return and reunion, death as celebration and commemoration, natural and supernatural.

In Part I, "Legacies," I consider the sudden death of my father at age sixty-one, and the bittersweetness with which death comes to farm country. In Part II, "Visitations," I travel across the Heartland to commune with others experiencing death and rebirth in their home communities. While my journey takes me to the region's thriving technoburbs and booming cities, in keeping with the Gothic I cast my vote in the episodic chapters that follow for the far-flung, letting the spirit dwell in the sort of remote places that so often nurture a haunt. Part III, "Resurrections," brings the narrative full circle, as it considers ways that the seemingly lost return to us in a new shape or form, lighting our path and spiriting us on our journey.

Here is death in its myriad variations and visitations as I experienced it firsthand in journeys across the region begun in 2011—the death of loved ones, the death and life of our small towns, the death of habits of mind and the birth of new ones, the death and cyclical rebirth of our crops and seasons. Grief, sadness, loss, fear; all these are markers of the Middle American Gothic, to be sure, along with the mystery, life, love, longing, and romance that lend to this heartbeat region the enduring haunt of home.

Part I

Legacies

1

LIFE IN SUNNIER CLIMES

The first of two auctions of our Midwest family farm occurred on March 3, 1987, one day before my mom's thirty-seventh birthday. "Mike has rented the farm and will pursue other interests," the oversized advertisement in the *Cedar Rapids Gazette* read. "He is a perfectionist, and has been an innovator in ridge till and soil conservation for many years. His equipment is highly specialized, and not for everyone. However, if you're fussy about the equipment you own, you can buy with confidence at this sale. All the equipment is immaculately clean and well maintained. Feel free to stop by the farm prior to the sale and view this fine line!"

By the time of the second auction, twenty-two years later, my father was downsizing further after the loss of both parents to cancer and his own failing health. This time the auction ad was smaller, belying the cataclysmic events happening in our long-grounded family. "The Jack trust along with Michael Jack have selected Wear's Auctioneering to conduct a public auction." The top item on the list, our immaculate John Deere 4720 tractor with loader had 440 hours on it but looked, the auctioneer avowed, "like new."

Later that same fall I had an inkling that my father, who had auctioned many of his personal effects along with the farm equipment and had purchased a trailer to pull behind the pickup truck he'd inherited from my grandfather, was bringing his own story, and ours, to what he always called its "inevitable denouement." He had begun to divest himself of little things—even the hand tools that our ancestors had used to wrest a living since before the Civil War.

Now he e-mails to say he will be leaving for the South before a predicted record cold snap insinuates itself into the uninsulated camper-trailer he's purchased with the auction proceeds. He won't say exactly where he is going, only that he'll be making a beeline for the Mason-Dixon before the heavy snows set in. I have my bets on Florida, the place my grandparents took the family nearly every February from the time my father was old enough to ride a bicycle. Growing up I had heard countless stories of these dramatic overland treks—how magically lush Florida had been for a boy arriving from the frozen Midwest, how it felt like life after death. At times my father's early enchantments, relayed to me vicariously a generation later, had grown so large in my mind as to become my own.

I realize as soon as I read his missive that Dad's hastily planned trip in my grandfather's pickup truck represents his attempt to close up circles, to touch again the thing that had enthralled him as a child. Who among us wouldn't reach for such a peace if it were within our grasp? More than that I am convinced that this is to be his farewell tour—his swan song. A year earlier, deep in his cups, he had confessed that he was sick, that the same thing that "got Grampy"—cancer—was likewise getting him. I mustn't tell anyone, he warned me, if I wanted to keep his trust. There would be no hospital trips, no treatment plans. Did I understand?

What was I to make of this, the latest in a series of my father's grave admissions; my mother had always insisted that my father was a hypochondriac, that he had claimed to be ill even in his twenties, in the early days of their marriage. Maybe it was his way of making other people care about him, she had theorized, or a behavior learned from his own fatalistic father, who famously declared each autumn that he would not live to see another harvest with the same morbid fascination cowboys contemplated their last roundup.

The future my father sketched out wasn't the conventional narrative farmers' sons like me had been taught to expect since the time we were old enough to drive a tractor. The standard narrative went something more like this: Farm Father grows old gradually and cantankerously, doted on by loving family members despite his prideful protestations. To avoid becoming housebound in his old age Farm Father develops hobbies—small engine repair or furniture refinishing in his workshop maybe—and gradually turns the farm operation over to his son or daughter. Eventually and inevitably, a dread disease strikes him in his eighties—cancer if the pattern holds—and he fights it gamely, Farm Son taking Farm Father in for radiation and chemo appointments in a long-overdue gesture of tenderness and care. Farm Father is buoyed at first by this familial show of support, by the powerful cocktail of drugs he receives at the hospital in the nearest high-tech metropolis, and by the passel of beautiful and healthy grandchildren arrived at his bedside to tell him how loved and needed he is. He fights the malignancy for months or for years, fights it tooth and nail until one day in December or January—the kind of day Farm Father hated in his previous life as a husband to the land—he succumbs, his tenure on earth a robust four-score years or more in sum.

For us the narrative never applied. The key characters in what Dad always called our rural "passion play" had never assumed their prescribed positions. The dramatis personae needed to perform first the healing, followed by the rite of passage, had gone missing—the brothers-in-law had died, divorced, or else taken jobs in town. The son-in-law too, had been a casualty of divorce, and the farmer's son, me, had been an inconstant and ill-prepared understudy. Still, I had stayed close—set up shop on my own small farm a handful of miles away, just across the county line—close enough to step in when our already compromised narrative reached that inevitable denouement.

My father's sudden flight from the farm that has been ours for seven generations had been precipitated by an unthinkable series of events—first an OWI in which he'd plowed my grandfather's old Buick sedan into a ditch in a snowstorm on the way to check for frozen pipes at a neighboring property, followed by a swift and punitive intervention against my and my sister's wishes. This, in turn, was followed by court-ordered outpatient treatment. Next came a brief redemption, followed by a relapse that precipitated a second intervention, this time to an in-patient facility in the nearest university town.

A well-trod path extends from the hinterlands into the nearest university hospital city. Any aging or ailing Farm Father can expect to follow it eventually, like an unwilling horse, pulling against the reigns. The irony turns the stomach; Farm Father has spent a life assiduously avoiding this distant Oz and Gomorrah, with its confederacy of specialists and technocrats. Often he has resented the city for its many enticements—the way it took his grandchildren, changed them, and never gave them back—and still he knows he will end up there at its flagship hospital someday at his weakest, warehoused and wearing a paper-thin gown while the talented specialists charged with taking care of him bustle in and out. The uninsured Farm Father knows the ugly bottom-line best—even paying for the smallest out-of-pocket procedure, or meeting the largest deductible, can cost him and his would-be heirs the equivalent of many acres. If he is uninsured, and not indigent, it will cost him the better part of the farm for which he has cared his entire life.

A few days after his intake, my uninsured father, summoning his characteristic agrarian stubbornness, simply walks out of the treatment facility, daring the staff to stop him. The story, of course, is more complicated than this—isn't it always—but the upshot is that my father, aged sixty, confides in phone calls and e-mails to my sister and me that he now intends to slip away into the early dawn before the first snowstorm sweeps across the Heartland—a time when Mom will be in town and most of the rest of the family will be away or else hunkered down in advance of the coming blizzard. Like me, the only way Dad knows to overcome the gravity of seven generations is by flinging himself into oblivion without route or plan in an ill-fated attempt to achieve escape velocity. In his bon-voyage note he warns me not to wake up early for his departure, and for the first time in my adult life I quietly resolve to ignore him.

The next morning I arrive to his leave-taking in what half-blind Homer calls the rosy-fingered dawn, worried sick that I have already missed him, that once again I have played the role of the too-late-to-rise, too-late-to-help son. The door to the machine shop is locked tight, but a bank of fluorescent lights flickers when I peer inside. I knock and call, knock and call. A minute or two later, a dark shadow stirs. A lock clicks open, and I am in. We stand for a moment, boot-to-boot, neither of us completely ourselves. Dad looks older and younger all at once, his mane of raven-black hair buzzed as if shorn for a prison sentence or made sleek for a long flight.

A few short hours after he lets me inside I'm following his rig down the gravel road leading to the blacktop that leads to the highway that leads to the interstate that leads to ultimate freedom from his past, from the prying eyes of judgmental family members who have lately begun to see in his every move the dangerous unpredictability of a suffering and wounded animal. I have offered to escort him, citing the pretext that I can confirm that his brake lights are working on the pull-behind camper-trailer. In truth I need to be near him, his right-hand man. It's a splitting of the atom, Dad's abdication, like those that sometimes happen in families like ours when a patriarch or matriarch, measuring up their remaining days, up and does something strange, like taking up with a younger lover or buying a condo to overwinter in Maui.

Up ahead now he attempts to wave me back at the first left turn leading to the blacktop. I ignore him, strangely mesmerized in pursuit, his trailer kicking up an epic plume of gravel dust that chokes my little car. I need him to see me, flesh of his flesh, in his rearview mirror for a little while longer, determined that he experience the sweet feeling of someone you love following you on a difficult journey. When he reaches the highway I angle my car to watch him go as he banks south, solo, around the big bend in the county road famous for ditching drunks and snow-blind travelers. He rides into the rising sun in my grandfather's cherry-red Chevy Silverado truck dulled with dust, the back of the pickup dipping precariously under the trailer's weight. The whole rig looks impossible— a traveling circus—and to think that my father, who hasn't driven more than two hundred miles from home in nearly a decade, is at the helm of it, slowed from too much vodka and wine the night before, his body laboring as hard as any engine bearing an impossible load. The sight fills me with equal parts joy and dread.

He is light again, and I am light again with him, for a single sunrise. The impossible has happened—my ailing father, the man who always said he'd draw his last breath on our home ground and who set out a decade ago to inexorably make it so, has literally sold the farm, saddled up his own father's dusty mount, and set off into the dawn, a dark angel on a fatally wounded wing. He leaves me, his middling only son, idling behind, contemplating the strange fissures that sometimes open up in winters so coldly beautiful they bring a lover's tears to the eye.

What am I? The inheritor of his mantle? The prodigal? Or am I the unrequited lover fishtailing the gravel roads in an ill-fated attempt to call him back, make him reconsider, wondering what, if anything, I might have done to make him stay.

My grandmother Julia, a farm daughter whose dislike for car travel was trumped only by her absolute loathing for airplanes, was reluctant at the prospect of the family's maiden Florida voyage scheduled for February 1955; my preschool-aged father, by contrast, was ecstatic. In the weeks leading up to departure, he ignored his homework in order to painstakingly construct his list of "Things I Am Taking to Florida." Exactly four of eleven items listed were trucks. He would be sure to bring his dump truck, cement truck, and of course his moving truck on the roughly 1,300-mile journey. His fourth truck was the famous Marvelous Mike, a robot space tractor/bulldozer popular in the fifties with whom he shared a name.

In the winter of 1955 all roads south from the frozen Midwest led to the world-famous resort at Silver Springs, Florida. Among its endless stream of tourist brochures, the water attraction put out a map showing a great cascade of America's north–south roads all funneling into the Great Dixie Highway on the way to the sister cities of Ocala and Silver Springs. Silver Springs promised otherworldly attractions, including scantily clad underwater mermaids, springs with legendary names like Bridal Chambers, and a reptile institute where a boy could see Ross Allen milk a viper with his bare hands.

Even within Florida, Silver Springs and Ocala were widely acknowledged as exceptional. The earliest promotional materials for the city marketed it as "a truly different Florida," a land of "lakes and hills, forest and farmlands and thriving communities"—Florida's "Region of Great Wonders," its "Kingdom of the Sun." Middle American snowbirds accustomed to the pure water drawn from deep aquifers of home could be assured that the waters of Marion County weren't the hard, sulfurous kind found in much of the rest of the state, but "very pure and healthful"—so healthful, in fact, that tourists flocked to the mineral waters reputed to have "special health qualities." The average annual mean high temperature, claimed the vital stats, was a perfect 70.2 degrees with average highs in winter nearing 60 degrees.

Like many other Northern snowbirds on the wing toward inviting and exotic lands my grandfather carried guidebooks with him as the family traveled—guidebooks like *Norman Ford's Florida: A Complete Guide to Finding What You Seek in Florida*. For a mere $2, travelers in 1956 could purchase the comprehensive 140,000-word compendium. Ford, the honorary vice president of the Globe Trotters Club, headlined his popular travel book with a chapter entitled "Climate—the Key to Florida," which began, "There is good reason why climate is the first subject discussed in this book. For in one way or another climate is responsible for every phase of the Florida scene." In the pages that followed the author left no stone unturned in his argument for the state's climatological supremacy, citing arguments ranging from the "percentage of possible sunshine" (the highest in the East during the winter months) to the unusually high degree of the sun itself (12 degrees higher than New York and 20 degrees higher than Seattle). A more direct hit from the sun's life-giving rays meant less refraction, Ford claimed, and this, in turn, partly explained the state's healthful "wine-clear" air.

Like much of the rest of Florida it was a heaven then fifty years in the making, cultivated for the simultaneous comfort and allurement of migrating Midwesterners like Michigan automobile magnate Henry Ford on whose tastes its economic fortunes depended. As early as 1908 the state created something it called the Florida Internal Improvement Fund to drain the low-lying malarial state to preference, contracting Ohioan James B. Hill and his patented Buckeye Traction Ditcher to dig, dredge, and tile the Everglades until they were livable for settled farmers. Hill had already used his enormous steam machine to drain much of the 1,500 square miles of Midwestern marshland where he had been born and raised, the Great Black and Limberlost Swamps his world-famous ditcher had been invented to wipe off the map.

What they didn't understand about the magical southland Midwestern boys would attempt to fix with a combination of internal combustion, horsepower, and heavy machinery. Naturally, my boy-father filled the family's Edsel station wagon with his dump trucks and bulldozers and tractors, playing farmer until the family arrived at Silver Springs on the morning of the fourth day and my father burst forth into the parking lot like the Tasmanian devil. This moment of annunciation, of arrival in the promised land, would linger with him the rest of his life, drawing him back and in, as if by gravity, assuming the power of only the best kind of haunts.

In 1930 Florida's entire population numbered less than 1.5 million, on par with sparsely populated Nebraska far-off on the Great Plains and a full million less than agrarian Iowa. For a Middle American in the 1950s traveling to the Sunshine State meant traveling to a sort of terra incognita. In fact, my grandfather's Conoco map showed that south of Tampa, only West Palm Beach and Miami topped the threshold of ten thousand or more inhabitants. Every traveler needs an Ultima Thule, a place beyond his or her reckoning, a place of myth and magic both sincerely feared and fervently sought after, a Hades and Elysian Fields in one. Medieval cartographers spoke of Ultima Thule as a place beyond the borders of the known world and rendered it in their maps as a distant island guarded by sea monsters. The notion goes all the way back to Virgil, for whom Ultima Thule was a metaphor for something far-off or dreamy, a place forever beckoning.

Florida was my father's Ultima Thule, and his father's before him.

Nearly sixty years later, the days that follow my father's escape from the farm are the loneliest I have known—the first time I have been without the comforting thought of him, our paterfamilias. Winter, too, has conspired against us. The epic snow and ice storm that hastened his departure now has us in its crosshairs. It's the mean kind that could easily knock out power for days if not weeks—the Big One my father had rightly anticipated.

I pack only nonperishables, a card table, an electric blanket, clothes and toiletries, and my laptop, leaving my own farm home for the home place, where a generator has been readied for years, anticipating just such a calamitous occasion. Of all the things in which a dad could train his son, my fatalist father always chose triage—beginning with preparations for the worst that might befall us, and working backwards to what he deemed more prosaic knowledge, like how to plow a straight row or repair a combine. This means that while I have received from him very little instruction on the day-to-day operations of a farm impossible to imagine under anyone's care but his own, I have, ironically, received a thorough training in the hulking immensity that is the back-up generator he purchased for just such a superstorm as this—the one he warned me of in nights of anxiety-fueled diatribes.

On the first night I am surrounded by his spirit, the knotty pine still speaking his name along with every blotted wine stain and cigarette burn on the carpet. A few remaining boxes of his memorabilia, thrown hastily into Rubbermaid containers, occupy nondescript corners. When I e-mail to tell him I am holed up in the house to outlast the coming storm, he writes from Louisiana to assure me that his spirit still protects me and this place. Much as I would like, I cannot quite believe him. Ironically, it's not a lover who's left me here, alone in an empty house, but my father, a demon lover of a different sort. Hadn't the strength of our bond promised that we would be fighting this and other storms together, forever? Weren't we supposed to be, in keeping with the classic regional narrative, helpmates to the end, Odysseus and Telemachus, brothers in arms and to the death?

Instead I find myself hunkered down with the remnants left behind in the small apartment he built onto the back of our machine shed, a place intended to house both himself and a fleet of John Deere tractors in the years after he and Mom separated and before they reunited. On the rare occasions that my reclusive father would be asked by some stranger where he lived, he would reply, "We live in a pole building" and leave it at that. It was true, of course, but by the look on the face of the poor soul who had broached the question, I could tell they were thinking dirt-floored machine shed instead of the drywalled annex where I have come to outlast the storm.

"The den," my father called the apartment home we furnished together at the back of the pole building, fancying himself, as ever, the lone wolf. From that point forward he began signing his notes to my mom, my sister, and me "W," for Wolf. And as he aged he grew further into his animal persona, always on the outside looking in. In leaving for his Ultima Thule he must have known he would be at the mercy of the very people his totem animal had taught him would be predisposed to misunderstand him.

Arriving on December 8, my father's first dispatch on his journey southward from our farm reads:

Briefly for now . . .

    With god as my fickle copilot, I have finally made it down south to just north of New Orleans. I am weathered in here due to extremely heavy rains (5 to 7 inches) and resulting flooding. Seems that you only trade one sort of bad weather for another—Mother Nature never gives you a pass.

My heart and thoughts are always with you, and I am well aware of the hellish weather you are facing. Please be safe! Down here at the current moment, it is about 70 but with heavy, incessant rain. I haven't even been able to venture outside, and they are talking about evacuating the campground!

When reasonable to travel again I plan to gradually head southeast into northwestern Florida, but as some wise person once said, "God laughs at all plans!"

He has reached Louisiana, the place my grandfather first dipped his feet in the Gulf as a young man, the place from whence he had written love letters to my grandmother while serving as a chauffeur and travel companion for his own aging mother and father on their first trip to the Deep South. My grandfather's pining letters had arrived in my grandmother's mailbox on elaborate letterhead from the Hotel Frederic, run by the Patout Brothers, in New Iberia, Louisiana. Still, the road that had promised my grandfather romance had instead brought him loneliness. Late on a Sunday night in November 1939, just a few short days after Thanksgiving, he had written my grandmother, the woman he would marry almost one year to the day later, to tell her he would go mad if he didn't see her soon. "I am not having the fun on a trip like this that I should have, all because you are not here. I would much rather be with you right now than travel around the world. What good does it do a person to travel if he is unhappy?"

My father's next note from Louisiana delves more deeply into the subterranean currents propelling him forward:

People have constantly inquired why I am out here with a 1990 vehicle, and I respond that it was my dad's pride and joy, and that I'm merely carrying on his will. He would love to have his old truck make the journey of a lifetime! I feel Grampy and you with me all the time, and I am not embarrassed—not for the most part . . .

The sentence trails off there, ending with ellipses followed by the words:

Evacuation eminent . . .

By design my father has not set up the voicemail on the new cell phone he purchased to aid and abet his escape, so that any and all calls—like those I am attempting to make to him now—would go unanswered. It is a lone wolf's ploy, a way of insuring against the unscripted moment when the phone rings late in some wine-dark night.

The following morning Dad's next missive arrives as, home in the Heartland, the blizzard strikes with a vengeance:

> I've been actively watching weather reports from the Midwest, and it sounds absolutely horrendous! Please be safe! I can't fathom how you managed to get weathered-in on the farm, and of course you know that it is about the worst place north of hell to be in a blizzard. There is still some of my personal power residing there, though, and I hope you will draw from it to protect yourself.
>
> I hate to rub you in the face with this, but it is a gorgeous day down here! Rain stopped last night (we didn't have to evacuate), and it is a sunny 73 here today. As I write I am sitting at my picnic table in the most balmy weather imaginable, although it is forecast to turn sharply colder tomorrow. You'll laugh, but I am at the Yogi Bear RV Park in Robert, LA. The ironic aspect is that I haven't seen one single child here!
>
> Tomorrow, I plan to pick up stakes and head southeast toward Biloxi. I have a vague desire to be further south and closer to the Gulf, although I can't complain about this place—$33.50 a day all-inclusive and very quiet, a few miles north of Interstate 10. The traffic is heavy beyond belief down here!
>
> I am beginning to love the RV community; mainly older couples who are helpful and friendly. But "couples" is the operative term; they tend to be suspicious of a man traveling alone.
>
> I'll just say goodbye for now, and best wishes from the core of my heart . . .

Snowed in with only a card table, a desk, and my father's old record and memorabilia collections, I find myself strangely and vicariously exhilarated by his e-mails, by the daring of his last-second Houdini-like escape from the farm, from the scrutiny of family members, from the bills and taxes and paperwork. Part of me revels in his newfound freedom, cheers this unlikely caper. I read the uncharacteristic exclamation points in his letters and marvel at the flush of freedom he must feel after decades of superintending a dying farm.

By the time his next e-mail arrives he has managed another one hundred miles of interstate travel at roughly fifty miles per hour. My father had always been a speed demon, the daredevil of the family. But one hundred miles a day is not the kind of mileage logged by a younger man hell-bent on reaching his destination, not the "rode hard and put away wet" kind of travel that, once past the magical age of fifty, my father so strenuously decried. One hundred miles a day is the modest allotment of a man almost old enough to collect Social Security, traveling on his own, a fatalist pulling an impossibly heavy load, addled by fog and slowed by alcohol. And yet from the lucidity and ebullient tone of his e-mails I can tell the demands of the trip have temporarily sobered him, a man simultaneously humbled and awoken by the vagaries of the open road.

> I am currently at an RV park in Biloxi, MS about a 1/4 mile from the Gulf. It was in the low 70s yesterday, but only mid 50s today, but still very comfortable for a northern boy. It has been stressful and lonely on the road, but I have found that most fellow RVers to be friendly folk. I plan to gradually work my way towards northeastern Florida, but I really don't have any definitive agenda beyond that.
>
> It is much too congested here for my liking but, oh well, any port in a storm will do. I think about your horrible weather, and I worry for your safety. Please take care!

Whether it had been rain, biblical floods, or fate that had caused him to linger in Louisiana and Mississippi, now, as the snows piles up outside the window, a thousand miles south he points the nose of his father's Chevy truck southeastward toward Ultima Thule. New Orleans and Biloxi have detoured him, detained him for forty-eight hours, his time there a prelude of sorts to the main attraction. These early stops amount only to a kind of foreplay, a heightening of suspense leading up to the ultimate romantic encounter. He is now on his way to Florida, the haunt of his happiest moments as a boy, with the vague wish that its present measures up to his memories.

In his escape my father has defied logic. He is leaving home rather than coming back to tie up loose ends, as do the archetypal heroes of old. But if it's possible for a person to be born out of time, an *old soul*, then surely it must be possible to be born out of place, a *displaced soul*. Maybe in fleeing the farm for Florida, my father is returning to the home that might have been had his parents chosen to settle permanently in the Sunshine State rather than perennially snowbird their brood from the frozen Midwest.

A thousand miles north I am housebound, listening to Dad's old records to pass the time as the snow flies outside, remembering how intensely he hated what he dismissed as the "bubble-gum pop" of his adolescence. He was a Beatles man, a member of the Lonely Hearts Club not a Pet Sounds or Neil Sadaka kind of guy. He was one for minor chords, for the darker notes that signified that an artist had truly touched bottom, achieved duende and lived to tell about it.

My father taught me to listen to music in absolute silence, in near darkness, reclined with my eyes closed. As a boy I would sometimes sneak a peek at him, his tumbler balanced on abs turned washboard from farm work, his eyes shut tight, and for a fleeting instant I would be terrified that he had died. A minute or two later he would groan, whether at the ecstasy of the music or the silver tongue of the Cutty Sark in his system, and I would close my eyes again, relieved to find him among the living in time to hear the whiskey-smooth voice of Sam Cooke bewail another Saturday night ("and I ain't got nobody"), the first chords of which took Dad straight back to his days courting Mom in 1965, and to the love songs that led first to my sister and, three years later, to me.

From him I learned to take the Level-B backroads whenever possible, to shut my eyes tight when listening to music, letting the vibe wash over me like a good deep kiss. I learned from him to let backtracks and B-sides like those I am listening to now tickle the earholes into trance. I learned to let the music take me, like it always did for him as I looked on, watching as his dark eyebrows knit in the inexplicable combination of pain and pleasure the soundtrack of first love brings.

A Boomer, my father was born into a world advocating travel away from the nation's colder, homelier places to its warmer, more exotic ones. Nary a page could be turned in the glossy magazines that sat on the end tables in my grandmother's living room without running into an advertisement for happy, Eisenhower-era families on vacation. Open the cover of the *Life* magazine that arrived at the farmhouse in my father's birth month of July 1950 and one would see a full-page ad featuring golfer Sam Snead hawking B. F. Goodrich "Rhythm Ride" tires for "safety, comfort, miles." Mercury, a division of the Ford Motor Company, ran an image of an enormous, mint-green Mercury sedan with the caption "Just What the U.S.A. Ordered," encouraging Middle Americans to "go for a ride" and see the forty-eight states. A few more pages in, another full-page ad waited, this one trumpeting the virtues of Seven-Up, urging families like my grandfather's to "be a fresh-up family" like the one shown in the illustration of a beautiful young wife handing her husband a Seven-Up as he returned to the dock with his two joyous boys and a line heavy with freshly caught fish. Chevy jumped on the travel bandwagon, too, hawking its Powerglide transmission and the Styleline Deluxe convertible that would take young couples to the beach in style. The adverts, like the lines on the cars being unveiled that summer of 1950, were big and bold, sexy and on the move, like the culture itself that had fallen hard for the romance of the open road.

By the age of five my father was already in the fields driving a tractor. For Middle American boys growing up on farms and ranches a tractor functioned as a gateway to greater mobility, a rehearsal of the power and freedom their father had harnessed and that would one day become theirs. With Eisenhower championing a great interstate system, an American Autobahn of sorts, and a booming postwar economy, it was growing harder for kids like my father to justify staying put. Dad's earliest report cards reveal a boy who couldn't sit still long enough to please the fifties schoolteachers who still wholly subscribed to the notion that rambunctious man-cubs should be civilized if not fully domesticated. That had been the point of public education in Middle America for generations, to teach the boys and girls who raised the nation's crops and herded its livestock to be settled ladies and gentlemen. Leading up to the family's first Florida vacation in 1955, my father was unusually restless. In total he missed twenty days that first semester, with seventeen of those coming in the six weeks before Christmas vacation. During the first semester his kindergarten teacher, the aptly named Mrs. Sauer, marked his name with a series of checks noting his lack of "self-control" and his inability to "rest quietly." Mostly, however, his long-suffering teacher lamented that he did not seem able to focus on his tasks. "Mike has been a better worker since vacation," Mrs. Sauer wrote when the family returned from Florida in February of that year. "He can stay with a job longer and works quietly." Maybe he had, as the saying goes, "gotten it out of his system," whatever the "it" was our authority-minded school system had hoped to cure him of. No doubt Florida had rejuvenated my father. The timing of his "reformation"—coming as it did on the heels of the family's sojourn in the sunny southland—was surely something beyond coincidence.

By fourth grade my father's restlessness continued to give his teachers fits. Report cards came home crowded with concerned comments. Under "Teacher's Remarks" for the fourth quarter, Mrs. Klouda concluded, "Mike is quite a problem. He cannot seem to be quiet and therefore disturbs the whole class. His being nervous seems to create a slight stutter in his speech. I feel Mike can improve a great deal when he settles down to actually working." My grandfather dutifully signed his son's progress reports three times a year, doubtless wondering what kind of son he had raised. Only when a vacation was in the offing did his boy-child seem to amend his behavior. "Mike did much better in his conduct before Christmas vacation. He seems to have reverted back to some of his old problems once he returned to school," Mrs. Klouda bemoaned at the end of the second quarter.

Each and every year through middle school, the pattern would be the same. My father's worst terms would come in the fall and winter, then would improve dramatically once the family returned from their Florida respite in mid-February and a late winter thaw began. By the end of the year my father had shown just enough progress, and just enough ability to wear down or otherwise charm his teachers, to earn promotion to the next highest grade. Even Mrs. Klouda observed in her fourth quarter remarks, "Mike seems to have, at last, settled down. His grades have improved and his class conduct has also been better. Have a nice summer vacation!"

Dad limps into Florida now in a biblical rain, his Jayco pull-behind trailer already damaged from an unholy line of Southern storms that have dogged him without cessation on his route. He finds the state less benign than he remembers it from childhood. Still the thought of dipping his feet in the Gulf, that baptism for a boy from the Heartland, buoys him, filling his sails. He reports:

> I finally made it to "The Sunshine State." Problem is, there is no sunshine here. In fact, it has been incessantly raining since my second day on the road! Spent three days in Biloxi, and only got to venture outside for a couple of brief walks. I'm telling you, it is literally FLOODED down here! I'm currently staying at a campground in the Navarre area (southeast of Pensacola)

that is right on the Gulf. It is a nice, friendly place, but rather expensive for my blood; I'm trying to pinch every penny. Last night a thunderstorm damaged my awning and, of course, the insurance didn't cover it because it was "an act of God." I'm hard-pressed to understand how any insurance company could truly understand the will of God, but that is their catch-all, fallback position. Bastards . . .

Then, not long after, this:

It gets damn lonely out here on the road, as I'm sure you know from your travels. On the positive side the vast majority of folks RVing are friendly and helpful. Now, if it weren't for the goddamned dogs . . .

As I mentioned my current site here in Carrabelle, Florida, is reserved, so I'm breaking camp and headed south tomorrow. No problem, as I intended to do that eventually anyway. My next destination is inland on the Suwannee River. . . . I love isolation, but the further south you go in Florida, the more congested and expensive it becomes. My health isn't good, though.

Total love, Wolf

On the fourth day after seeking refuge from the winter storm I emerge into a world I scarcely know, covered as it is in fresh white snowpack and waist-high drifts simultaneously beautiful and grotesque. Today or tomorrow the snow will need to be moved, cleared in the name of progress. In the Heartland we do not abide impediments long. We are straight-ahead and hard-driven, God's frozen people.

For the first time in nearly forty years I am left to clean up after a serious storm without my father, the ultimate cleaner-upper, the man who, at the very moment that I am sizing up the immensity of the task he has left me, readies himself to plunge further into Florida, pushing deeper into the dream of his long-ago. I read the thrill of the journey between his lines now; read his senses reawakened in his writing, the beast temporarily soothed by road noise. Hurling toward death, he is paradoxically becoming young again, seeing the world through the eyes of a child.

So too am I. I trudge out to the car through snow up to my boot tops, following the lane until I'm leaning face-first into a wind whose bite a mild autumn had caused me to forget. When I reach the car, the temperature reads a big fat zero. Even the hand-sanitizer has frozen, its bubbles suspended as if in freeze-frame.

Every year about this time an elderly person somewhere in Middle America inexplicably clambers into their car and disappears, driving into what they know not for reasons that escape them. Concerned family members stop by to find their houses unlocked and the car gone, the garage left open; they notify the authorities. My father would sometimes be called out by the county sheriff to assist in the search.

Hours or days later he might spot the missing vehicle from the air on some little-traveled country road, the nose of the sedan buried in a snowdrift. On happier occasions the wanderers would be found, ice-cold but still alive, to answer the rapid-fire questions of EMTs and county sheriffs with dazed incredulity, as if they had just woken up from some Rip Van Winkle sleep.

Love calls in the middle of the night and at bright noon, in the midst of winter, each day and once in a blue moon, and we answer, as if in trance. We slip the car into gear, moving forward, toward. We seek something to awaken us from our lethargy, a voice or a song or a spot from some sunnier realm we knew long ago. Cabin fever? Temporary insanity? Whispered prophecy? We don't always know why we went, only that we felt a powerful need to go.

My fatalist of a father forever warned not to romanticize nature, that winter's cold could kill, that happiness was an illusion, but that moments of happiness were not. Somewhere, 1,200 miles away, a bright spot flickers now on an otherwise gray horizon, and a bright-eyed restless boy who is also a dying man pulling an impossibly heavy load sits down at a park bench, feels the warmth on the back of his neck, and writes:

> I love watching the birds, which are copious here. The pelicans and sandpipers are my favorites, and there are several other species that I know by sight but can't put a name to. The seagulls are ubiquitous, and quite tame.
>
> Being on the Gulf is inspiring . . . the endless horizon reminds me of home.

When the nineteenth-century Scottish explorer Basil Hall surveyed America's midlands in summer he chanced upon a mystical natural feature he heard called looking-glass prairies. Geophysically, the phenomenon could be easily enough explained—shallow glacial basins slickened with rainwater and rooted with blue-green sedges reflected the bluest of skies.

The tall-grass basins provided an almost magical topography of reflexivity for travelers then pioneering America's latest Ultima Thule—its Middle West. In the prairies they found their dreams and desires, their appetites and anxieties, reflected in a new and peculiar emptiness.

"The resemblance to the sea, which some of the prairies exhibited," Hall wrote in *Travels in North America in the Years 1827 and 1828*, on first encounter with the Heartland's virgin prairies, "was really most singular. I had heard of this before, but always supposed the account exaggerated. There is one spot in particular, near the middle of the Grand Prairie, if I recollect rightly, where the ground happened to be of the rolling character above alluded to, and where, excepting in the article of color—and that was not widely different from the tinge of some seas—the similarity was so very striking, that I almost forgot where I was." Hall, a captain in the Royal British Navy who had sailed the globe from Java to Japan, knew the oceanic. Here to him was a chimera, a land-locked, almost lunar maria that like the sea itself, caused its wayfarers to look powerfully inward.

As a child my father's uninsulated bedroom—a tiny shoebox of an annex built onto the back of the garage to house the surprise baby boy—looked south and east onto an endless sea of cornfields, rising and falling gently in the gentle swells and ebbs that defined the landscape of his memory, and that prefigured the pattern of his future migrations.

Ashes to ashes, dust to dust, crest to trough, we imprint on our native landscapes as we do on mother, father, or lover. Wittingly or not, we spend the rest of our lives looking, most of us do, realizing too late that the thing for which we have been searching is the same heart song, the same gut string, we knew in the beginning.

2

PLAYING BALL FOR THE
TEAM OF THE DEAD

After long days of making hay and burning falling limbs on the farm, I want nothing more than a late dinner, a cold drink, and a dimly lit computer screen. Late summer and already the days have slipped away from me.

I spend the waning hours of the season maintaining the physical legacy of a family farm, and my nights, of late, securing a digital space for my kin. I say "of late" and yet many months have passed. Time stops when a life partner is lost, the bereaved falling into a timeless sleep while the living move busily about their chores. Incredibly, my father—my farm partner and ideological soulmate—is gone.

And yet reminders of him arrive daily. Letters to my dearly departed fill the mailbox from financial gurus predicting the next big market collapse and urging him to "Act now!" Notes are dispatched to thank my deceased father, cruel irony, for his continued listenership of Public Radio and to ask that he kindly make his tax-deductible contribution now, before it is too late. Recently arrived is a letter inviting my paterfamilias and me to a night out on the town—an April in Paris Taste of Jazz party. The notice promises "French music, French food, wine, cocktails and heavy hors d'oeuvres" beginning at 6:00 p.m. with "charcuterie, fromage and desserts starting at 7," RSVP requested. With regrets, I and my long-gone partner will not be attending the jazzy soiree with its cardboard cut-out facsimile of the Left Bank and Eifel Tower. My partner has already crossed a timeless river, but it is not the Seine. His heavy hors d'oeuvres are earthworms.

Fifteen miles down the county road, Jackie burns the midnight oil working on the family's genealogy. Both of us have lost our on-the-farm partners: she, her husband—my second cousin—Phil of lymphoma, me, my father, Michael, age sixty-one, of what he diagnosed as late-stage cancer. Like me Jackie remained on her rural acres after losing her beloved, despite the advice of friends recommending that she move back to town. A generation younger, and male, I've heard the same well-meaning counsel from those who care about me, and, like Jackie, I politely decline, hunkering down instead, lost in history and its bittersweet grievances, contemplating the vicissitudes of fate and circumstance.

Tonight I think of Jackie sitting at her computer in the old farmhouse where my maternal great-grandfather—her grandfather-in-law—once held court in his overstuffed easy chair. I imagine her with her fleece blanket pulled tightly over her lap, lost in her Ancestry.com. I stop my Internet surfing long enough to pity her—poor thing, languishing in that old four-square. She should be in town, living it up! Others would have her play the role of Gothic heroine for us—shut up, sequestered away in her castle, prisoner to her grief and pining for her long-gone lover while the hounds bay in the moonlight and the candle burns to tallow. But Jackie does not need the comfort of literature on the nightstand or hot-dish casserole, heavy on pity, brought to her door. She keeps her powder dry and her rifle warm.

Jackie is a widow, a familiar trope in culture and literature, but what is the word for a farmer's son who has lost his business partner and ideological soulmate? Where are the fruitcakes and soups baked by concerned neighbors? Where the handmade quilts and hands reaching out for us, where we stew, steeped and mellowing in our grief? Has the loss of my grandfather, grandmother, and father in such close succession provoked in me the burning need I now feel to cultivate our family history, the way losing Phil much too young spurred Jackie to complete her long-delayed genealogies? And I, who have never desired to create a Facebook page, why am I up these late summer nights traveling the endless digital super-highway, lonesome traveler, wounded and wary?

In grief, the Internet is a terrific tease, a proxy thing that allows Jackie and me to endure a series of deathly quiet evenings on the farm and still maintain our sanity—the way others treat their loneliness with meds or too much TV. The life we see on screen furthers the illusion of nearness to peers who have made far different choices—gone to town—while we root down stubbornly, pursuing our own peculiar eulogies.

Tonight I point my browser in the direction of Wikipedia, eager to know what others in the crowd-sourcing crowd have to say about our hometown and township, these two places nearest and dearest to us. Have any of the Internet Robin Hoods constructing our hometown's page bothered to include mention of my great-grandfather, a farmer-writer who wrote a well-known book in 1946, or my second cousin Doug, a decorated broadcaster taken too soon by stomach cancer and Parkinson's in his sixties?

I locate this bare-bones entry: "Mechanicsville is a city in Cedar County, Iowa, United States. The population was 1,146 at the 2010 census." The geography section likewise consists of two lines. Under the heading "History" the entry reads only: "Mechanicsville was platted in 1855 by Daniel A. Comstock. It was so named from the fact several of its first settlers were mechanics. A fire in 1883 destroyed the south side of the business district." The entry includes no timelines of events or important people who arrived on the scene after 1883. Indeed, I'm reading an entire history reduced, burned and boiled down to our village's platting followed by its most infamous conflagration and calamity. As far as the rest of the world knows, nothing good or newsworthy has happened in Mcville, as we call it, since the eminently forgettable Chester A. Arthur occupied the White House.

Wikipedia is a crowd-sourced encyclopedia, but where is the crowd jockeying to update our mothballed history? At first blush I'm shocked by the paucity of information, a conspicuous deficit all of us born of this once prosperous place must surely be complicit in. Is it that we, secret nihilists, don't want to be remembered beyond our most basic demographic data? Do we welcome the oblivion of the grave as a reprieve from life's petty trials and tribulations, the kind of persistent and perennial slights and sorrows we'd just as soon drown, burn, or bury? Perhaps we learned our lesson in the 1990s, when Osha Gray Davidson's book called us out as a "rural ghetto," our little town on the edge of the prairie now quite literally become exhibit A, chapter 1, in a book entitled *Broken Heartland.*

Maybe it's the vigilante in me who creates an account on the world's most popular encyclopedia, the one working late into the night in the far-off farmhouse, the one who desperately wants to rewind and reanimate history, to raise his father from the dead. I feel a rush of adrenaline mixed with trepidation as I proceed to my first-ever Wikipedia edit. I change the heading "History" in the Mechanicsville entry to read "History and Literature," adding, for good measure, the name of my great-grandfather, the farmer-writer who passed away in 1965. If nothing else, I console myself, it's an update from the fire of 1883.

Still aflame with my newfound power to shape history I introduce the same small change in the stub entry for our township, Pioneer, a place whose entire history in the world's most popular encyclopedia reads only:

> Pioneer Township is one of seventeen townships in Cedar County, Iowa, USA. At the 2000 census, its population was 1,810.
>
> History: Pioneer Township was established in 1848.
>
> Geography: Pioneer Township covers an area of 36.53 square miles (94.6 km^2) and contains one incorporated settlement, Mechanicsville. According to the USGS, it contains four cemeteries: Andre, Pioneer, Rose Hill and Union.

We are known mostly by our formalities: our government data and geographic coordinates, our common legal status as an incorporated city, our cemeteries. Our most important cities are cities of the dead, apparently—the names of our famed deceased are not noted here, but rather the names of the necropolis in which they take their eternal rest.

Morning: I wonder why I've come to this ruined rural cemetery again to pay my respects, a "young man" still in the eyes of my elderly neighbors. Though the first flecks of gray now grace my temples I'm still somehow the rambunctious kid underfoot, *Gail's boy, Michael's son, the last of the Jack clan, the one who liked to write.* At other times I'm no one, the oldest of the old-timers routinely mistaking me for my dead father when he was raven-haired and famous among the barns. They amble up to my table at the last remaining restaurant in town, where I'm bent over my Western omelet, in communion. Conjuring my father's name in greeting, they have forgotten that I am me, and that he is no longer among the living. Sometimes I bother to correct them, knowing I will see them again here over eggs and coffee, wanting to spare them the public shame of names forgotten or misremembered. Other times I decide to let sleeping dogs lie, and we chat amiably for a while until they depart my table all smiles, with the swagger of the socialized, pleased to have been neighborly even if the neighbor they believe they have spoken to is a ghost. In their wake, I feel for them, their late middle ages lost to the wages of dementia and the blessed myopia of farm and family. They have snoozed away twenty years, rural Rip Van Winkles, and now struggle to remember the names of their great-grandkids, content to keep money in the bank and the old ticker going for another season. They are our well-fed, well-socialized survivors, but not our sweet and suffering martyrs.

There is something fastidious and fussbudgety in the act of grave tending that this morning threatens to unman me. Being here sans shovel, spade, or garden rake makes me feel impotent, weak, and weepy—the opposite of the rural male archetype. The "young" are expected to be out doing "more important things," "living their life"—blanket alibis given by the old for the indifference and negligence of the young.

In pioneer cemeteries like ours, women have done much of the spirit work of Memorial Day since its origins in Decoration Day during and immediately after the Civil War. War served as a predictable widowmaker, especially in the rural South, where roughly one in five soldiers mustered for the Confederate army died in service. Fathers, sons, uncles, male cousins—all gone before their time.

Across those war-torn years mortality rates approached 15 percent for males born in the South aged ten to forty-four. The war's grim math suggested what experience bore out—that more often than not the duty of memorialization fell to the bereaved mother and daughter. If the father was among the dead or captured, in many cases so too was the son. Tragedy made war widows expert commemorators. The Daughters of the Confederacy, the Women's Relief Core, and the Women's Auxiliary of the Grand Army of the Republic—they existed to memorialize.

Our pioneer cemetery hews to its original thesis. All the most recent burials in our family plot, save one, are men who left women behind to decorate their graves. The women in the family bring the decorations—the fixin's, the trimmings, the spread. I coax the bluegrass to grow over the graves, fill the sunken holes, transplant the encroaching trees that threaten to reclaim hallowed ground; my aunts bring the flowers and signs, ornamental rocks, cheerful placards. Our stultifying division of duties registers even in death. Once, when I thought my trespasses into their world might go unnoticed, I slipped a dozen or so amaryllis bulbs beneath the soil underneath my grandparents' memorial arch.

What is wrong with me that I would rather be picked to play ball for the team of the dead, eager as I am to go to bat for them? Sometimes it must seem to others that I love the dead more than living. My uncles in town see a perfectly good waste of youth in my choice to memorialize over the more serious work of money-making and property-getting. I should be building equity, incubating a nice little nest egg. Maybe my choice is better called out as existential cowardice: after all, the deceased aren't needy. They've ceased to be the complicated, stubborn, willfully belligerent people we knew them to be in real life.

The dead don't talk back.

So I'm the young man at the graveside, wasting his youth and his good mornings. But in being here I hope to put my world right. I want to dream the dream of the living and the dead in perfect equanimity, walking between them—life and death—as between old friends too polite to ask that I choose between them, or that I trade my leisure or my labor for their civility.

Another day come and gone and the chores of late summer, this final haymaker, are not yet done. The days bring the sort of Sisyphean barnyard tasks that sometimes feel like an afterlife, ad nauseam. When dusk comes I eagerly shimmy out of my straw-covered blue jeans, socks, and white work shirt before heading into the house, stripped clean to my underwear in a place where, blissfully, no one can see the quiet intimacies taking place in the little house behind the privacy screen of field corn.

Tonight Jackie is on my mind. Settling in at the computer, I type the name of her long-gone partner Phil into my search engine, not knowing exactly what I'll find, if anything. And just as suddenly here it is, a life whose full history was known to the world only after he left it, a life published posthumously and in boilerplate: date and place of birth, names of next of kin and immediate family, cause of death, location of memorial services.

How had I never been told Phil's middle name, or that his given name was actually Phillip, not "Phil," as we had called him, without exception? Here, toward the bottom of Phil's obituary is the date of his and Jackie's wedding: they had celebrated their forty-fourth anniversary just a day before his passing. Beyond the basics, his biography is confined to three lines buried at the end: that he reaped and sowed a Middle American farm in continuous family ownership for more than 150 years; that he enjoyed hunting, shooting, and fishing with his sons and family. The obituary concludes with a URL for "online condolences."

Obits are still free to run in the newspaper headquartered in our county seat town, population 3,500, though the newspaper promises to edit for length and often does. How many years will pass, one wonders, before hard-copy obituaries die the same unceremonious death as the socials? In the nearest big city, a cereal town with a population just north of 130,000, prepayment is required. Cost is twenty-five dollars for online placement plus fifty cents per word and additional photo charges. Name of funeral home or crematory and phone number is required in order to verify death. The newspaper reserves the right to edit content for taste, libel, and grammar. Fill out the online entry blanks, many of which allow a maximum of 150 characters to memorialize your loved one, and the obituary writes itself. Hover over the requisite online data fields and you will be prompted for "birth, marriage, occupation, military service, etc." In uploading your photos and selecting "submit," you agree to assume any and all relevant charges for your remembrance. A standard size photo and a short three-hundred-word obituary will set you back roughly $175, tax included.

Question: How much is our loved one's legacy worth?
Answer: We keep our obituaries short and our secrets to ourselves.

Look closely at newspaper obituaries published in small towns like mine and you'll see a shocking number of fatalities of men and women in their forties, fifties, and sixties. The week's crop of premature male deaths listed in our paper of record includes two rural men ages forty-six and forty-one respectively. One, though our editor mercifully omits the fact, is widely understood to be a suicide.

The week my father's obituary ran in our local newspaper the average age of the male deceased barely topped the age of Social Security eligibility. My father, a farmer, passed away just a few months shy of his sixty-first birthday, and like any rural son I spent more time feeling guilty for whatever lifestyle and risk factors might have taken my dad from us too soon than engaged in the harder problem of solving for demographic x. I remember my father saying, "You can't save people from themselves," and so I sat there, obit in hand, thinking that somehow his untimely passing must have been inevitable or else just punishment for failing to live up to some standard of how good and healthy people live elsewhere—whoever and wherever they were. "No rest for the wicked and the good don't need it," my long-lived grandfather, likewise a farmer, always said, and for decades the plowman's corollary was that if you worked hard, stayed active, and "kept your nose clean and your breath sweet," as Grampy used to say, you would be a good bet to dance a jig at your eightieth birthday.

Such sweet and enduring euphemisms. Such false catechisms as keep us believing. They may have held true when Ike was president, but no longer. In today's chemically endowed Middle America, Baby Boomer sons who work the land are too often outlived by their own fathers.

Tonight I find only blank space where before my edits have been.

I search the Wikipedia page devoted to Phil's and Jackie's hometown and mine, intending to review the sentence (or was it sentences?) I'd added the night before—the name of the great-grandfather, the second cousin, the grandson, all of them instrumental people in this place.

Surely some mistake has been made, I tell myself, navigating to the entry for our township, where I find the same redaction has been made. A bell icon, colored red, illuminates the topmost corner of my screen. Here already is a message from Wikipedia ("We're glad you're here!), and a second note thanking me for my debut contribution ("You just made your first edit; thank you and keep going!").

The next notification in my inbox, now more than twenty-four hours old, has arrived from an anonymous content editor, advising me against what he calls "promotion" of my family and community history.

I click on the editor's screen name, let's call him BgTex, whose public profile reads:

> I'm just this guy, you know. (apologies to DNA) I've been knocking around
> Wikipedia for a long time now, but my edits have been sporadic through the

years. I patrol recent changes, help out at articles for creation, and I do my best to guide new users in the right direction when I can. As far as content, I have some specialized knowledge in linguistics and law, but I like learning about people and subjects while I write about them. I live in the greatest city in the world and am on Central Time.

BgTex's public talk-back page suggests he has succeeded in pissing off more than just me, full of his own power, apparently, at playing self-appointed Wikipedia sheriff. One of his many detractors complains, "My being included in this seems rather unfair. I stopped once I received a notice, while the IP user continued to edit." Another talk-back message consists of a string of angry fricatives elicited by BgTex's heavy hand.

I write BgTex asking that my edits—introducing the connection of the family to the history of the place, the very thing Romans worshiped and called the family *genius*—be allowed to stand, and receive a terse reply: "Just because a statement happens to be true doesn't mean that it belongs on Wikipedia."

I counter that my additions are verifiably true. My great-grandfather really was a well-known soil conservationist and sustainable agriculture writer from our woebegone hamlet; my second cousin Douglas, who likewise grew up in our whistle-stop, really was a Public Radio broadcaster whose passing was covered by newspapers across the region. Doug won the Most Outstanding Media Person from a national sports organization, received the Governor's Award for the Best Arts Radio Program in our state, and earned two honorary doctorates for his lifetime achievements from colleges and universities. And yet prior to my proposed edits, there had been no mention of him—no mention, in fact, of any of our town's VIPs other than the long-buried pioneer who had platted the place so long ago.

Is advocating one's hometown and its human resource crop promotional, and if so, isn't it the kind of advocacy a proud native son or daughter from a forgotten corn town should be engaged in? Shouldn't we, its citizens, offer the world a recitation of the good and true things we've achieved since the fire of 1883 apparently scrubbed our town's history clean? Is the local historian honoring the established genius of their place, its genius loci, and its homegrown people doomed to fail by any "objectivity" standard created and codified elsewhere?

Genius loci, defined in Wikipedia as:

A genius loci is an intelligent spirit or magical power that resides in a place. Very few genius loci of this form are able to move from their native area, either because they are "part of the land" or because they are bound to it.

When I'd first read BgTex's message I'd felt a hint of shame. Had I done something silly or stubborn or otherwise selfish? Now I find myself growing indignant. What is his censorship, after all, but the Digital Age equivalent of the ugly concept I struggled to wrap my tongue around back in college—*hegemony*: histories recorded and maintained not by the denizens of the towns and places in which that history is made year after year, but by overwatching, overzealous, often anonymous editors ensconced elsewhere. They with their "specialized knowledge of the law," with their class-mandate for erasure, for manipulation and revision of what they have never lived and therefore cannot possibly fully understand. In other words, histories recorded at their pleasure as an extension of class privilege, by fiat and majority rule.

Emboldened, I write to BgTex:

I understand your position, though I'm beginning to feel as if Wikipedia and its editors don't have much appreciation or respect for local knowledge or fame. I list my great-grandfather as a well-known person from the home township because he wrote a nationally known book. To an anonymous content editor sitting somewhere in Texas or New York, this may seem like only so much promoting of a family or a family name. But what if your family is one of a handful of pioneering families, and deserving of mention in their little corner of the world and beyond? And who will promote our own forgotten history here if not we, its citizens? When I enter my grandfather's name as a literary figure from our township, with citation, it hurts to see his name removed by an anonymous editor. Don't grandparents who achieved great things deserve mention, if accompanied by proper documentation?

Lately Jackie's genealogies have moved from our people to the places where our people have lived, each one blessing us with its genius loci. When she e-mails her latest discovery relating to our hometown—a little known "centennial" history she's turned up—I feel strangely elated, as if a guardian angel has gifted me a runestone.

Runestone, defined by Wikipedia as:

> The main purpose of a runestone was to mark territory, to explain inheritance, to boast about constructions, to bring glory to dead kinsmen and to tell of important events. . . . Virtually all the runestones from the late Viking Age make use of the same formula. The text tells in memory of whom the runestone is raised, who raised it, and often how the deceased and the one who raised the runestone are related to each other.

I'm eager to share news of Jackie's discovery with my good friend Alyssa, but first I must explain to her who and what this widow guardian angel, this self-appointed keeper of family and community history, is to me. "Phil, Jackie's husband, was my father's first cousin on the maternal side," I tell her, and she translates: "that makes Phil your second cousin." I ask Alyssa to tell me what Jackie would be to me, and without hesitation she replies, "The wife of your second cousin is . . . well, she's nothing to you," and an awkward silence falls between us. Phil, a generation older than me, had always felt more like an uncle, and Jackie like an aunt, especially since her children were both my cousins and my childhood playmates.

And yet this "nothing" has come up with something indeed, word of a "Rip Van Winkle centennial" celebrated by my hometown not one hundred years after its platting, as custom would dictate, but by an oddly belated marking of its 120th birthday, its twenty-year oversleep explaining the Rip Van Winkle theme. Jackie has found a small booklet prepared by town burghers to commemorate the unorthodox occasion. The volume offers no explanation for the peculiar fete beyond a poem by Lillian Nie entitled "Why 'Rip Van Winkle'?" whose last two stanzas read:

> Today Mechanicsville is close to poor Rip's side.
> Mind you, we weren't sleeping, we were preoccupied
> With bringing our city up to par,
> Our eyes intent on that distant star.

> So engrossed with our labor of love were we,
> "Centennial Year" slipped past surreptitiously.
> Now you know why we are twenty years late—
> At least our city is "up to date!"

In our "centennial" history, beneath a picture of a mucky, unpaved Main circa the late nineteenth century, runs this tribute to the genius of the village's original clans: "It has rightly been said we 'grow on the back of giants.' The men and women who chose our land to people, were pioneers, giant types . . . on the occasion of our hundred and twenty years . . . we salute some of those pioneers." Included in the list are my paternal grandmother's people, the Puffers, and a complicated, almost biblical family tree whose last paragraph ended in me: "Julia was married to Ed Jack, parents of: Patricia, married to Charles Coon, parents of Arminda, Timothy and Jason; Susan married to Robert Sullivan, parents of Rodney, Sara, and Andrew; Barbara; Michael, married to Gail . . . parents of Tasha and Zachary."

Is this the sort of bibliographic artifact BgTex had wanted of my hometown's founding families, its *genius*? And yet there's no way to link to this locally printed limited edition via Wikipedia, no address to which I might post my proof to my anonymous, placeless overlord and arbiter. Besides, how many copies of this rare Rip Van Winkle history remain intact? Ten, maybe twenty? How many have succumbed, instead, to the overstuffed pyres and unsentimental burn barrels of Middle America, by which we return dust to dust, reducing our pasts to ashes, much as we set ablaze the dried husks of last year's green grasses until we've achieved a pleasing scorched earth tabula rasa, purged and purified, so that we might start each spring with a clean slate. Isn't this humble homespun booklet, produced and printed on-site and born of the place whose history it means to share, the truer history in many ways, written and edited by the townspeople themselves, who know best? Isn't it more accurate and objective in its up-close details and discernments than a displaced Wikipedia sheriff could ever be?

In BgTex's Chicago, armies of well-endowed, well-fed nonprofits fight to preserve and protect urban and suburban histories. Deep benches of salaried employees and leisure-endowed retirees mobilize to enact the necessary preservation. Meanwhile we nonmetros living on Middle America's minor moons, miles beyond metropolitan orbit, accept it as a fait accompli that if we should fail to protect and preserve our histories, no one else will. Much as it falls to us to repair and right the gravestones of our friends and neighbors, and to mow and maintain our rural rights-of-way and roadsides, we sustain our local lore. No president of the board or cheery ombudsman is going to show up at our door begging to restore and renovate our old barn. We know that our spaces and places are viewed as more ubiquitous and unremarkably utilitarian than their metropolitan counterparts, and therefore less worthy of preservation.

In the view of many historians our provincial histories are industrial and agricultural, and not prettily so. Our monoculture, they insist, is drably monolithic. Why preserve another decrepit barn or four-square farmhouse when their kind might be found in every section and township? In the eyes of the overwhelming majority living in the nation's cities and suburbs, preserving a sagging barn or a fallen corn crib, no matter how architecturally remarkable, is merely dressing up a pig. Why spend good money to make a shrine to a dying industry that has long since outlived its utility? And yet in BgTex's Chicago, they've made historic monuments of stockyard gates and museums of packing houses.

From his Windy City roost BgTex is up to his usual mischief, removing with missionary zeal mentions of my family from the town and township histories. And I am still trying to help him see that the names of our pioneers belong in the encyclopedia entry for the tiny hamlet they founded in the 1850s, since all of us who come after are only building "on the back of giants," as our Rip Van Winkle centennial booklet puts it.

I am almost pleading with him now: "We stand side by side in our successes and our failures in this part of the world," I write. "I understand your position, but I would hope you would reconsider the removal, at least, of our names from our town and our township history." How different, I want to ask him, is a supposedly egalitarian encyclopedia entry maintained by and for the people, from an obituary written by the family and published in the local or regional newspaper of record? In each we shape our histories while striving for both factual accuracy and greater truth—the letter and the spirit.

Among the genealogical keepsakes Jackie sends me is a copy of my grandfather's obituary. I recall my aunts and my father wordsmithing it around the kidney-shaped kitchen table in my grandparents' farm home. Faced in their collective grief with the task of summing up the life of a man who had meant so much to a family and to a community, they finally agreed to describe him as an "inventor," in addition to his chosen profession: farmer. And though he had never once filed a patent for his many barnyard inventions and frequent and well-publicized pioneering of agricultural methods, *inventor* is perhaps closest to what he truly was.

Is his obituary—the sole published history of this national runner-up champion corn picker and agricultural innovator—therefore subjective beyond redemption? Shouldn't the obituary written by his family and friends, who knew him best and most completely, be considered a viable source, one worth citing by historians and genealogists? By analogy, isn't Wikipedia itself a sort of collection of obituaries posted and edited by a wider "family" of advocates and enthusiasts—those with a particular stake in preserving and perpetuating a person, place, or thing?

What do we do then with our ancestors' legacies? And if we opt to post or to publish, are we prepared for the inevitable loss of control of those memories, for the specter of anonymous hands laid on the runestones, on the genius loci, until such time as our sacred reliquaries and histories belong not just to a family and a community but to everyone—even Internet trolls and Wikipedia sheriffs? Seeking to soothe our sense of historical injustice, do we painstakingly make a forever place for our ancestors' spirits to dwell, housing their memories digitally, in 1s and 0s, only to see the edifice we built razed overnight by overzealous editors willing to wield the ultimate power of erasure? Nurturing that which is fragile and fleeting—caring for it in spite of the fickle vanities of overlords and the vicissitudes of tastes in the metropolis, in the capital city with its great chambers of commerce and boards of trade—turns out to be the yeoman's life exactly. We bend our shoulder to difficult tasks; we do our best; in the end we call it good and lay down to rest.

On nights like these I'm tempted to retire once and for all from the lost cause of advancing the histories of people and places history's arbiters and masters long ago deemed second class, like the roads we travel deep in the Heartland. Our rural routes are "secondary" by definition, roads of lesser importance in what Wikipedia names a "Hierarchy of Roads." Decades ago, the fair legislators assembled in our distant capital made no distinction in levels of maintenance and service needed by our byways. Shortly thereafter these same clever lawmakers codified a hierarchy of caregiving, and "Level B" signs sprung up at the crossroads of many of our rural routes to warn us of sanctioned neglect: "Enter at Your Own Risk." Then the lawmakers saw fit to amend their own jurisprudence again, this time creating a third class:

"Level C" to signify the sort of backroads and byways our headstrong farmers have refused to vacate, and that, simultaneously, our officials refuse to maintain even to Level-B, secondary road standards.

Yellow caution signs rear up like strange daisies in our ditches, warning us against trespass under penalty on the abdicated routes that lay beyond the posted disclaimers. Our Level Cs devolve to waist-high weeds. The newer tertiary classification means gates and restricted access, means "maintenance ends." Officials have now all but abandoned their authority over Level C roads to our rural property-owners, who have become the "local authority" whether they want the responsibility or not. Of the arteries nearest my farm home, two are marked Level C. With their specialized knowledge of the law, our overlords have hereby granted us the dubious honor of maintaining the unmaintainable.

Letter, and spirit.

I would do well to remember the widow's fortitude—toiling late into the night in honor of her late husband—and steel myself. Like the field-work for which this place is known, preservation promises no return on investment or guarantee of yield. And rail as we might against the powerbrokers trading our futures and our fortunes, we do not control the perceived value of our crop, be it literary, historical, or human. We cannot raise Lazarus from the dead, only do our part to maintain his grave when no one else will.

Down the road, sepulchral with moonglow, is the small meadow housing the Civil War–era gravestones where we have wept and picnicked as well as cursed and laughed, finding sadness and solace not for a single day, but for many days. As teens my cousins held the contract to keep our pioneer cemetery mowed and looking its Sunday best. Trimming around our ancestors' tombstones earned them extra income and brought them face to face with their long-gone kin, as well as to their knees in a posture ideal for both weeding and penitence.

My grandfather and father worked here for free—cutting back brush in the dog days of July and otherwise grooming the place within an inch of its life. As a boy—*Gail's boy, Michael's son, the one who liked to write*—I could sometimes be convinced to join them at the genius loci, rubbing sleep from my eyes as I chiseled a deeper chip on my shoulder, thinking about how unfair it was that we donated our labor for free, risking life and limb with balky chainsaws for a cemetery where fully half of the graves had been abandoned a half century before I took my first breath. At the time it seemed a shameful waste—evidence of my kin's predilection for devoting its time and treasure to lost causes and sinking ships. Now I see things differently. I see our local boneyard as a life-giving third place to gather. It's a community annex, a neighborhood living room, a marbled house of memory into which no distant overlord dares trespass. It is ours to have and to hold, for better and for worse.

I buried my grandfather here two days before my twenty-ninth birthday and laid my uncle to rest after a sudden heart attack stopped him dead in middle age. I planted my grandmother in her chosen spot beneath the good Midwestern loam as I listened to my father's own forebodings of death, our mutual sweat and tears mingling in the dirt. If I didn't see to it that he was planted here beside his mother and father in a simple pine box, in a country burial, he would personally haunt me, he pledged. And he meant it.

3

SPRINGTIME ON THE PRAIRIE

A Middle American Gothic

Regular as clockwork it happens. Canadian geese ply flyways, check ancestral routes against hard memories, against ribbons of rivers. Vs point northward, blazing contrails. They're here to herald the season, to trumpet the first push of Gulf air come to redeem us.

Our red fox stops in the chill, cocks his ear to the rising trill of blackbirds in the air, bravest among the early-returning prodigals. They ride the snow-bent cattails, early-season cowboys, mount the rough husks of head-high horseweeds and hang tight. A week later the robins join them, full-throated in their presumptions, worming earnestly in the side yard as if winter were mere commercial interruption.

They too spent their lives probing the dirt, did our fathers, awakened by this Lazarus-like season to original callings, to repeating in reverse the make-ready and button-up of autumn. Now they who have made it through winter open up again, play dirt-farmer. They are hauling things—any and many things—for reasons they cannot fully explain. Just now they are struck dumb by the crux of it—that to carry something is to be alive. So they load their truck beds to the brim with lime to overspread the sodden earth, ride the newly graveled roads in their pickups dreaming of full leaf and tassel. They pull anhydrous tanks roughly across overwintered corn stubble. They turn the grocery shopping and errand-running back to the wives; they are through with domestic trifling.

And the red-wings ride the fenceposts, mocking their ambition.

Spring, and we are old, the oldest in the Union by some accounts. Many of our elders have taken their last breath in the winter now ended, reached for death's icy hands not never-come, no-account Spring's. How painful would it be to pass in May instead, a song on the edge of the lips. Kisses and tulips. We stomach death best in frozen times.

Those who do not live to see first thaw keep our funeral parlors busy. Booking face time with the undertaker proves trickier than the taxman. When I reach the mortician he answers grimly, "I answer my phone all the time . . . except when I'm in the shower," and still his phone rings endlessly in this season so unkind to Caesar. I am adding my calls to his voicemail, to his death-a-thon. After all, Dad deserves the dignified rest the undertaker holds in monopoly. Dad is one-of-a-kind, our scion and patriarch, the last of a noble line, but to the funeral man he is a type.

The mortician watches the old farmers ease up in the field each fall, watches them slow with a new hitch in their giddy-up, a strangely musical catch in their ticker. Something in his hawk-eye glints like a surgical instrument. Winter is good for business.

The estimate arrives itemized, void of bells and whistles. There will be a pine box not a velvet-lined casket. There is something called a "graveside celebrant fee" we can live without. We are God's thrifty people, and why should Death come dressed in this year's frock and gown? For the cost of a low-mileage pickup truck our father will be returned to the good dirt that is his heritage and birthright. We will pay dearly for the right to redeposit him.

The cemetery still wears winter's brown when the farmer's son and his sweetie drive up, great-grandfather's sharpened spade in hand. They park the car on the dormant grass, looking suspicious with their instruments held high, hazy noon, the temperatures briefly touching 60, the shovel spurred to action by an exhortation of phoebe-song: *do-it . . . do-it . . . do-it . . . go-on . . . go-on . . . go-on . . .*

Scientifically the instigator is a tyrant flycatcher, of the family *Tyrannidae*, but that's just splitting hairs. You don't need to know his pedigree to know he says *fee-bee*, that he is an in-betweener, neither wren nor warbler but a mover between worlds. He's your middle manager of gnatcatchers. A vireo, in stereo.

A man with a shovel is up to something. A man and a woman with shovels are up-to-somethinger still.

The cemetery is the only place in the man's memory that grows larger with the passing years. There are ancestors buried here whose names even he, who fancies himself an expert on the family tree, cannot quite recall. Winter renders us amnesiac, slips us a mickey.

The season's obituaries read descriptively, read: *reaper*, read: *sower*; read: *farmer*, *schoolteacher*, or *caregiver*. We are remembered not by our given name nor by the notes of our given song but by the job done. You shall know us by our work.

For my yoke is good, and the weight I take up is not hard.

There's a scale for endangeredness, you know—a Red List ranging from Extinct and Extinct-in-the-wild to Least Concern. FYI, the eastern phoebe is LC; he's a model of mass-production, a topper of the pop charts. No wonder he is chipper. The world is his oyster-catcher.

We save our roadside staves and our benefit dinners for the tragically dead, for the martyred young on their crosses who will never have a road named after them nor steal a kiss beneath the blankets in frozen times. For them we will don our coveralls and our overboots and eat soup, our elbows resting heavily on the fold-out tables in the afterlife of some school gymnasium or church basement where we die trying. Our coming together to eat and bow our heads is our prayer for your safe passage, for your eternal soul.

Mostly our dead slip away quietly, though. There's no riot of lilac bloom to be immortalized in song.

The annual listing of endangered species is published to coincide with the seasonal sharpening of plowshares and the application of the necessary poisons. Thus begins our growing season. This year's laundry list of the doomed or damned includes the Indiana bat, least tern, piping plover, whooping crane, eastern massasauga, pallid sturgeon, Topeka shiner, and a bevy of clams with names like Higgins eye pearly mussel, sheepnose, and who could forget the Pleistocene snail. Of our particular flora, the eastern prairie fringed orchid, Mead's milkweed, northern wild monkshood, prairie bush-clover, and the western prairie fringed orchid are all going the way of the dinosaur.

We wouldn't recognize a western prairie fringed orchid if we met it on the street, if it bit us on the ass. We ask death to end our ignorance.

At the small-town grocery the farmer's wife was asked once about her husband's sudden absence. Considering Bismarcks, there in the bakery aisle, she does her best to explain, her words a mere dusting covering something much deeper, sweeter: *sickness, heartbreak, die in peace*. You mean like an animal? the clerk asks.

We are the human endangered. We are biding our time, living off our savings or our Social Security, holding out for better things. We emerge to retrieve a few windblown shingles, collect the mail with our hair wilding, half-expecting hailstones. We wait for the UPS or the Schwann man to deliver us, barreling down our lifeless roads, spraying rock like manna.

We keep our hopes hung in the closet like a wedding gown.

The burdens carried by the farmer's son and his paramour make them shy before their neighbors, suggesting grave robbers not do-gooders. They are relieved to stow the spades in the trunk when the job is done, away from public viewing, all too glad to turn back toward the noisy highway, where the traffic belongs to a different world than the pioneer cemetery where the old farmers and their long-abiding wives intertwine phalanges and metacarpals, breathe black dirt deep beneath frost lines. They pledge allegiance to the republic of old ghosts and accordioned earthworms, of marbled flames and badly listing tombstones lapsed to illegibility. They listen to the oldies, ad mortem.

One day I will be lowered in a pine box to the requisite depth. My bones will molder beside my mother's and my father's. I do not know whether such proximity matters or whether to consider such nearness cosmic crutch or human failing. It is fitting, though, to lie down next to those who made us in ecstasy, riding atop a warm bed with all the good give and bounce of loam in Spring.

Yes, like an animal.

At his father's deathbed, his mother revealed to him that his sister had been conceived on Independence Day. Can you really pinpoint it exactly, he had asked her, the moment of conception? Yes, she had said, serious as a heart attack.

We have religion and we have dirt. We have metatarsals and old relics. We have a few good Bonemen who'll spade it all up for a song.

The lovers' trip back to town is brief, and they startle when the well-preserved cars of the myopic old roll to the end of their long country lanes without stopping, without looking first left then right. It is custom here to assume unimpeded passage.

Bullfrog, *Lithobates catesbeinaus*, deep throat, sex addict, Lenten barker and bawler, priapic amplexer. A watched frog never croaks, never emotes, yet vernal equinox finds him singing lusty shanties in boggy corners. Somehow he knows we are nigh, on tiptoe, wondering at his whereabouts. He stops his sex, trepidatious at the sound of footfalls, wary at any rumble or sigh that does not come from deep inside the lover.

Why don't you take a picture? It'll last longer.

Lent is upon us, just like that. *But when you fast, anoint your head and wash your face, so that you may not appear to be fasting, except to your Father who is hidden. And your Father who sees what is hidden will repay you.*

They call this path the Grant Wood Trail, for gravitas, but it's little more than an abandoned railroad bed picketed by unstrung electrical poles, the sum grim as a crucifixion. Along the side of the ghost-trail, wild carrot, the first verdant green of the season, shocks us with its chlorophyll. Otherwise the ides of the month are drab, corn-husk browns with the odd dollop of snow dotting the ditches, the woodlands. Like us it is a strange survivor, a hanger-on.

The air at the factory farm like the one up the road from where the farmer's son plays house is dirtier than it is in America's most polluted cities, studies have shown. "No other major industry in the U.S. would be permitted to pollute at these levels without EPA oversight," the study's author, an attorney, said, only to have a naysayer fire back, "Another tempest in the TreeHuggers' teapot: the sensors for these studies were placed at some specified level a few feet above the feed lots, or inside chicken coops, etc. Had they placed them directly at the bovine anal verge, they would have recorded 100% CH4, H2 & H2S—OMG! We're all gunna die! There's no oxygen at all!"

A decade ago the U.S. Geological Survey informed Grant Wood country its rivers were among the nation's most polluted. They warned us we would have a harder and harder time catching "naturally reproducing fish." Still the neighbor boys pull six-pound catfish from waters roiling with the season's toxic run-off. They seem to wear their smiles naturally.

I do not know whether we will reproduce without assist. But hell, we'll give it the old catfish try, won't we?

The season's clouds are mammarian, inversions of cobalt and gray laden with rain, driven by winds aloft while below we idle in wait-for-the-hammer-to-fall stillness. Mammatus, a.k.a. mammatocumulus ("mammary cloud" or "breast cloud") is the term applied to a cellular pattern of pouches hanging from underneath a cloud. In Latin *mammatus*, derived from *mamma*, means "udder." Around here, Caesar, you might as well just call it a tit.

Our houses emerge from another merciless season looking shabby—sullied and shaken. Shutters hang askew like limbs akimbo; a scattering of windblown shingles decorates yards. Our cars, by comparison, are relatively cherry: someone's new fire-engine-red Prius parked at the roadhouse; an equally sweet Equinox accessorizing the broken-down modular on the county road. These days it is the sound of our wheels our neighbors know us by.

What we remember of Latin we save for dreamy rides and high horses; Germanic we reserve for bodily functions, curses, and kin. Weeds we cut and cast aside with biblical zeal, naming them for the genius of their devilry—*horseweed*, *pigweed*, *smartweed*. We call our God *God*, capital G, small d, for sturdy consonance, the way we barn-raise, the way we name our sons John and James. We call a spade a spade and the dead a doornail. Soft vowels we don't much truck with. They're for Yahweh, some say, for Allah, for babies.

You know, he's not a parking meter, she shot back, when someone at the funeral parlor uttered the word *expired*.

Driven outside by cabin fever, the lover quits the house to unearth artifacts of last season's bonfire—a defunct flashlight and lighter accidentally left to overwinter beside the harvest fire.

He remembers the night but not the flame. He remembers the combustion but not the spark. He suspicions the necessary heat was achieved through the communion of cheap wine labeled something like Pheasant Ridge or Park Hills. Have you ever wondered why the names of housing developments sound like cemeteries, he recalls asking as the night comes back to him now, night of conflagration and crooked sticks held to a fire come to ambiguous end.

We make wine here now, you know. It's a cottage industry, for the gentri-
fied. Meanwhile the farmers wouldn't be caught dread drinking the stuff.
Ditto the Boneman. They're beer-men, both of them.

The neighbor's pyre sits overdue for a burn, overreaching the ditch, a mat-
tress thrown atop for good measure, for giggles. Burn while the snowmelt
drips through the ditches like an IV or else risk the threat of the thing getting away from you, turning bedsprings to blazing effigy. Burn when the
wind blusters from the north, and there's the neighbor place to consider;
wait for the breeze to swing around from the south, and it's your own
home liable to get lit.

The funeral director's eyes are bright as a boy's. You take him for the sort
whose first kiss turned him red as the blood of our savior, who considered the ministry, who refused to dissect the sanguine pig in biology class
on grounds of good conscience. He would have left for New York City or
San Francisco long ago, but he settled instead for the messy business of
burying our dead.

"Providing services," he calls it.

We will take the pine box for $1,000 and the gratis in-casket pillow. He
will check the forecast and get back to us if shelter will be needed. He will
have a template eulogy prepared for our use; all we have to do is fill in
the blanks. Sometimes all mourners need, he says, is a push in the right
direction.

The undertaker contracts for his gravedigger, his Boneman. He farms the
spadework out. They all do now, he says, sounding wistful. Our mortician
lives in town. There is no dirt beneath his fingernails. If you squint hard
enough you might mistake him for a man of the cloth.

Consider, if you will, the curious case of the missing Boneman. It's harder
than hell to find yourself a good shovel-man when the crop's going in, unless you're willing to let him leave tracks in the boneyard with the backhoe
or the Bobcat to get the job done quick. They double as farmers, remember. Their dance cards are full.

Beneath an ebony headstone, all alone on the left-hand side of the cemetery, rests a recent suicide we're told, scooped into the bucket of a front
loader tractor and dumped unceremoniously into the earth as if the dis-
graced were mere feed or fodder. The farmer ensures the feet of the man
who took his own life do not point east to meet his maker, as prescribed
by rite, but west, toward the eyesore trailer with the half-blind pit bull. He
was lucky to have had a burial at all.

We have monks now, émigrés come from out of state to tend the monas-
tery's hardwood groves, eager to trade their need for peace for our need for
boxes to place our loved ones in before they're lowered into the ground.
The monks have become naturalized citizens of a state that specializes in
death and dying. It's what you call a boom business. Who wouldn't want a
handmade casket made at a monastic pace? "We view our casket business
as a ministry—a corporal work of mercy. We hope to impart a sense of
sanctity into all that we make," reads the literature. For a price the monks
of the Order of Cistercians of the Strict Observance are pleased to offer
us an exclusive line of custom-designed caskets and urns for University of
Notre Dame alumni and their families.

When you find him, the Boneman will tell you we're not the custom colle-
giate type. We park our cars in concrete college lots the size of cornfields
when we get the itch to educate ourselves. We buy our degrees like our
groceries, out of necessity, before the snow flies.

Slice deep enough into soil and the Boneman's singing shovel hits
drainage tile, not dirt, from days when men saw boon farmland here
in the meadow, not boneyard. Someone was here before us. Someone
always is.

For right around a grand, the monks are pleased to offer your premium
rectangular casket, your premium shaped casket, your simple shaped casket, your simple rectangular casket, or, Heaven forbid, your children's casket. We feel most holy when we are properly fit. "We tenderly craft caskets
specifically in children sizes: infant, toddler, child, or youth. Each casket
receives the same attention to detail that our premium adult caskets do,"
says the website.

Heard on a dying signal from a Czech cereal town where Lawrence Welk still walks on water: *You always hurt the one you love, the one you shouldn't hurt at all.*

Play the cynic if you must, but I for one thank God for the monastics. Would you rather buy your simple rectangular caskets from China?

The job of sodding over the newly filled grave is done in an hour, the farmer's son and his sweetie hunched over the black slabs of dormant bluegrass while the flycatcher auto-tunes on the fencepost. The earth is heavy. They cut a section seven-foot long by thirty inches wide—big enough for a grown man to lay in—lever lovingly underneath, heft the good earth onto an unfurled roll of garbage bags, and drag it over to cover the grave. They do not look up when the vaguely familiar car rockets past in its glory of road dust. The pioneer cemetery is theirs to do with as they please.

In the cities they pay thousands for a bare-bones plot like this, languishing on waiting lists for dibs to lay their heads and rest. Here our vacancy sign buzzes all night. We are not always sure whether we should be gladdened or saddened by our lack of popularity, our dearth of subscription. Mostly we are the kind of folk who prefer our own company, but then sometimes, when the kerosene runs low and the candle burns down to wick, we would give anything for a knock on the door, for a big man with black boots and hooded eyes to sit with us for a spell, maybe hold our hand in his until we are ready for bed.

You can bury your father here with confidence thanks in part to James B. Hill, inventor of something called the Buckeye Traction Ditcher. The average depth to water table in the alluvial soils of his home state is roughly eleven feet and falling. Rest assured your dearly departed will not float to the surface for last rites as he might in the lowlands of the Delta, where even above-ground tombs yield their cryptic contents to the rising floodwaters, sending the bones of the old South spinning down the Bayou St. John where they resurface as rot-gut Blues and other Lost Cause anthems floated in a minor chord.

Surely you've heard the old advice: Molder where you're planted.

With a little coaxing our snow fences finally come down, reassuming the form they once memorized on the shelf, like the soul. We celebrate their removal, joyful at the casting aside of seasonal crutches. The neighbor strolls her new baby down the gravel lane in jubilation, dreaming of paved roads and windows thrown open to lilac song. Who knew she delivered in the dead of winter in that forlorn four-square while the rest of us survived on hope and propane alone. That little beating heart warm in that cavernous house . . . why, it's amazing.

It's all benediction in the end, Mr. Boneman, the baby bundled up and rolling down the road on moon-buggy tires, swaddled up in vestments. And somewhere over the hills the monks at their matins. Give me eulogy, and I'll give you litany:

The blush of spring like blood rushing to the cheeks, the swell of earth rising before them, the mother's burden, the shy red fox, colored auburn, bouncing buggy, little boy, sky blue like a robin's egg, little heart with room to grow, little blackbird with flames for wings.

Part II

Visitations

4

THE PROMISE OF NEW BLOOD

I seek not gaiety nor mirth, not the bright voluptuousness of much
sunshine and sparkling waters which please the young and gay. I am
no longer young; and my heart, through weary years of mourning
over the dead, is not attuned to mirth.

—COUNT DRACULA

State Senator Bill Weber stands at the front of the high-ceiled fluorescent-lit room at the University of Minnesota Southwest Research and Outreach Center (SWROC) outside Lamberton, Minnesota, a town of approximately eight hundred 110 miles southwest of Minneapolis. He's come to address the afternoon's gathering of regional development–vested folks—mayors, city managers, extension agents, educators, tourist board representatives, and chamber-of-commerce types all laser-focused on a single Herculean challenge: how to bring economic development to the hinterlands.

It's an almost vampiric conceit—these burghers and boosters and community developers gathered together under one roof for the afternoon, united in their thirst for new blood to ensure their very survival. As in Bram Stoker's *Dracula*, blood is currency here, 75 miles from the western border of the Lower 48's northernmost state, more than 1,200 land-locked miles from New York City and Washington DC—a far-off realm not unlike the Transylvania of Bram Stoker's *Dracula*, the ur-Gothic novel published in the same era in which Lamberton was platted by railroad official Henry Wilson Lamberton.

In any case the topic suits the setting: a large university-owned experimental farm that meticulously documents every aspect of the dirt beneath our feet to optimize growing conditions. It's a place devoted to historical data, current trends, and practical solutions for those hoping to grow and sustain crops, whether those crops are human or vegetable. The fertile soils underneath the campus of steel-sided farm buildings where we've gathered is of the Clarion-Nicollet-Webster variety—the type endemic to the region. Scientists point out that soil and landforms develop together, coining the term *geomorphology* to, as soil experts Randall Schaetzel and Sharon Anderson put it, "elucidate the nature of that genetic dance." In short, the pasts of a soil and a land, and by extension a people, are inseparably bound to one another—metaphorically speaking, the reason Dracula must sleep atop a bed of his native soil to reanimate himself each night.

It's not by accident that an experimental station designed to enhance production and increase crop yields set up shop here in 1959, the year that marked the beginning of Lamberton's decades-long struggle to grow and to thrive. At the moment Senator Weber is warming us up with a Lutheran anecdote he hopes will help illustrate the systematic nature of the grim demographic challenges facing the southwestern corner of the state. "In our denomination last year we had twenty thousand births. You go back a number of years and we had thirty thousand births. . . . Our synodical president had visited with the men's club in one of our congregations. . . . He looked out at the fellas sitting there and said, 'Guys, with this problem we're having in terms of the birthrate you gentlemen might have to step up to the plate once more.'"

The crowd chuckles ruefully at the Lake Woebegone-esque predicament—late middle-aged folks required to procreate on demand. Mustachioed, clean cut, and dressed down, the senator is a hard guy not to like, even in spite of the off-color joke whose punchline he is nevertheless determined to deliver. "And the president said they were actually quite willing, though they said he was responsible for clearing it first with the Ladies Aid." Weber laughs briefly before turning deadly serious again. "It's really important that we get a handle on this, and that we make Minnesota more amenable to job creators."

Only the day before Weber paid a visit to Education Minnesota, a union of professional educators and students with seventeen statewide offices and a headquarters in Saint Paul. The organization's leadership wanted to know the best way to pump more money into education. Weber's answer: produce more kids to populate the state's classrooms. "We aren't probably going to reverse the trends in terms of family size and that sort of thing," he admits now to a roomful of experts eager for creative solutions to systemic challenges. Weber himself is living proof of the depopulation demon with which many of the state's prairie counties grapple. Not long ago Senate District 22 encompassed six complete counties; now, due to declining population and reapportioning, it covers those original six complete counties and large parts of three others.

Weber brings a business lens to the conundrum of youth out-migration in southwest Minnesota and eastern South Dakota, and he's predisposed to see the problem as originating in economic opportunity. As an example he points to two long-lived businesses founded in his hometown of Luverne: Luverne Fire Apparatus and Luverne Trucking Equipment. Though they retain Luverne in their titles, both relocated across the border to Brandon, South Dakota, a suburb of Sioux Falls, decades ago, taking several hundred jobs with them. Weber says he looks forward to "taking the battle to the halls of St. Paul," and we believe him, though his concerns, and ours, boil down to a seemingly unerring equation: fewer jobs = fewer young parents = fewer students = fewer opportunities for revitalization in towns like Luverne and Lamberton. It's not that an educated thirty-something is inherently more desirable than the senior citizen or retiree; it's that the penny-pinching retiree, lacking children in the school system and often holding property purchased and assessed at yesteryear's prices, doesn't prime the economic pump in quite the same way, nor offer the same degree of stimulus.

In closing the senator tells us, with sincere regrets, that he won't be staying for the evening's 6:00 p.m. feed; his elderly mother back in Luverne needs his help. "Yesterday I got another item added to my list when I got a call from Lifeline. . . . My mother, who is going to be eighty-nine, had fallen in her house. She didn't break anything, but she needs a little extra attention these next few days. So I gotta go back and take care of things."

In Lamberton Weber's mother would be in good company. In fact, more than a third of the town's residents are sixty years or over—making up a greater percentage of the burg's dwindling population than the fifteen- to forty-four-year-olds on whose backs towns are most often built. In 2009 more than half of Lamberton's residents were over sixty, and a population that easily topped 1,000 in the 1980s now struggles to break 800.

If Weber notices the irony in concluding what was to have been a hopeful address with a story about his octogenarian mother taking a tumble, he doesn't let on. He's presumably selected this hard-luck story as the culminating anecdote on which he hopes to solidify a connection between himself as a community leader and a roomful of his constituents. The fact that he's played a downbeat, minor chord for our would-be communion is telling. The topic for the afternoon was supposed to have been "Rewriting the Rural Narrative," but Weber sounds more like he's reinforcing it.

The haunt of past prosperity is still felt in Lamberton, a one-time railroad boomtown that enjoyed its halcyon days when Queen Victoria held the throne. Named after pioneer H. W. Lamberton, the city gloried in a population bounce of more than 200 percent from 1890 to 1900. Back when the Chicago and North Western Railway brought science, industry, and settlers to this prairie outpost, the moralizing novels of the era portrayed not just the seeming conflict between science and humanity but the idealized lives of a working class whose hard work and pluck brought just rewards in the end.

As the residents of the youthful city in Redwood County gathered to dedicate their first new school building in 1897, half a world away in London literary reviewers weighed in on a sensational new Gothic novel, *Dracula*, taking the English-speaking world by storm. The *St. James's Gazette* in London observed that it could think of "no tale among those of recent date in which the possibilities of horror are more ingeniously drawn out. . . . There are a hundred nightmares in *Dracula* and each is more uncanny than the last." The lonesome Count Dracula, with his undying devotion to his provincial Transylvanian home, was a sort of "prince among Vampires." Meanwhile, *The Argus* in Melbourne, Australia, insisted that Stoker had almost singlehandedly begotten what it called "the romance of vampiredom" then overtaking even the most far-flung corners of the globe. Apparently, the British Empire, with its strict Victorian mores, craved a good scare.

The popular novel opens with visiting English lawyer Jonathan Harker earning an audience with the mysterious count, who reminds his highly educated visitor, "We are in Transylvania; and Transylvania is not England. Our ways are not your ways, and there shall be to you many strange things." The count relays a brief history of a contested land, exclaiming, "Why, there is hardly a foot of soil in all this region that has not been enriched by the blood of men, patriots or invaders. In old days there were stirring times, when the Austrian and the Hungarian came up in hordes, and the patriots went out to meet them—men and women, the aged and the children too. . . . When the invader was triumphant he found but little, for whatever there was had been sheltered in the friendly soil." The pride of "peasants," Dracula says, has kept his little developed region backward and haunted, secreted away from outsiders.

By way of self-introduction Dracula tells the young solicitor, "I am no longer young; and my heart, through weary years of mourning over the dead, is not attuned to mirth. Moreover, the walls of my castle are broken; the shadows are many, and the wind breathes cold through the broken battlements and casements. I love the shade and the shadow, and would be alone with my thoughts when I may." Dracula, Harker learns, possesses a special affinity for regional histories, and relays them with the circumspection of a very old man, despite his outward vitality and strength. "In his speaking of things and people," Harker notes, "and especially of battles, he spoke as if he had been present at them all. This he afterwards explained by saying that . . . the pride of his house and name is his own pride, that their glory is his glory, that their fate is his fate."

Dracula is the ultimate fatalist: as the fates of Transylvania go, so go the fates of the count, who attributes the ability of his hard-pressed region to fight off outside influences to something he calls "Dracula Blood." With "Dracula as their heart's blood, their brains, and their swords," the nobleman proclaims, his forgotten region could boast a record of prideful resistance to outsiders that even the Hapsburgs and the Romanoffs could never hope to match. Ironically, Harker has come to Transylvania to help Dracula achieve escape velocity by arranging for the count's purchase of a sizable estate outside London, where Dracula is soon scheduled to travel. The castle, the weight of history and ancestry, and the declining glory of his people have become too much for the aging nobleman to bear, and he now craves new vistas and new blood. Allegiance to the soil of his melancholic homeland and the allures of a new more prosperous land do war within the count's divided psyche until

Harker learns of Dracula's strange compromise: he must take with him aboard the ship fifty boxes of his native Transylvania soil, by which, via literal contact with his homeland, he will be able to retain his strength. The nobleman's search for new life and new blood in London can only happen if he transports with him "earth-boxes" filled with samples of the land from whence he came. In short, Dracula depends on the known, the familiar, for the longevity he has achieved in his remote region. Too much change, or change without the compensatory sustenance offered by his home ground, means death.

University of Minnesota research fellow Ben Winchester makes an ironic choice to follow the senator on the day's docket of speakers in part because he's a glass-half-full kind of guy. A self-described "data geek" with bright blue eyes, and a hint of a *Fargo* accent, he's a generation younger than Weber. Instead of telling us what we want to hear or choose to believe, Winchester has come to tell us the truth about new blood in rural Minnesota and in Middle America more generally. In a nutshell, he's here to tell those interested in rural development that they've got it all wrong, starting with their appetite for attracting "young blood"—college students and twenty-somethings—at the expense of others. His data demonstrates an unlikely trend he calls "Brain Gain"—a counter narrative, backed up by decades of data, showing a net gain of thirty- to forty-nine-year-olds in many rural communities experts had assumed were dying.

"As I started to look into the rural data all I heard were these things," Winchester recounts from the lectern, offering a recitation of the doom-and-gloom stuff he hears emanating from the small towns he visits: "We're closing our hospitals . . . our Main Street is shuttering our businesses . . . we're seeing a decline in our manufacturing." Winchester recalls hearing the word "Brain Drain" cited over and over again as a catch-all bogeyman for a threat so chilling even the mere evocation of its name—like *Dracula* for the Transylvanians—begets irrational fear. In fact, the small-town burghers and businesspeople Winchester encountered used the words "dying" or "bleeding" so frequently to describe their losses he began to worry that he had chosen an "industry that was overly negative in how we describe where we live, what we do, and what our towns struggle with."

By the late 1910s Lamberton's population topped 850 people. Now, more than one hundred years later, the town does well to reach 800. And since the 1950s, when its population briefly topped 1,200, outside experts have been deployed here and throughout southwestern Minnesota to solve the riddle of a population that has shrunk in every census but one since, with declines of over 15 percent in the 1970s alone. The Gothic formula endures here: outsiders drawn to a ghosted city or region to solve what seems to many an increasingly urgent demographic whodunit.

Today Lamberton offers an enviable range of services and amenities for a small rural town with a population under 1000, ranging from curbside recycling, to composting, to an eco-industrial park. There's a hotel here, a newspaper, a law office, a bowling alley, real estate offices, and at least five churches, only two of which are Lutheran. And yet as much as the city has to offer would-be twenty-first-century pioneers, gazetteers from the 1880s listed a far more impressive array of local businesses extant back then, including a butcher, a lumberyard, a hardware store, and as many as four general stores, all serving a provincial place of less than two hundred people. Published in 1916, *The History of Redwood County Minnesota* describes it as a community of great "prosperity," and "the metropolis of southern Redwood County."

Fast forward a full century, and the city's website pulls the curtain back on the statistics contemporary demographers find most alarming. As of 2011 the median age of Lamberton's residents was over fifty with less than 13 percent of the population holding a bachelor's degree or higher while just 2.5 percent held a graduate or professional degree. Median household income in 2009 was approximately $38,000 compared to more than $55,000 in the state as a whole; estimated median house values here, under $50,000, are dwarfed by the median home values in the state overall, which topped $200,000.

Only when Winchester moved from the prosperous small city of Winona to Hancock to work for the University of Minnesota's Center for Small Towns located in nearby Morris, Minnesota, did he begin to fully understand the deficit mentality operant in prairie towns like Lamberton. Within two weeks of moving into Hancock, population approximately 750, Winchester stopped for groceries only to learn the store would soon be closing its doors. Staring at the two expired loaves of bread remaining on the store's barren shelves, the research fellow and his family of four briefly succumbed to exactly the woe-is-us, the-sky-is-falling narrative he now rails against.

The self-professed data geek had made a rookie mistake where Hancock's hard-luck grocery store was concerned, conflating emotions with the unsentimental truth of numbers. After he left the store, he returned to his desk to crunch the data and found, among other things, that rural America had experienced a net gain of residents like himself for three of the last four decades. He found that 2.2 million more people moved from the city to the country in the 1990s than vice versa, and that was especially true in the thirty- to forty-nine-year-old age bracket—not young perhaps, but young enough. Their numbers weren't always sufficient to reverse declining populations overall, but they did meaningfully reduce them.

"Thirty- to forty-nine-year-olds are moving into rural areas like never before," Winchester tells us now, working his way through the finely honed "Rewriting the Rural Narrative" PowerPoint he's delivered in hundreds of Middle American communities like Lamberton. "Again, this has been happening for thirty of the last forty years . . . right under our noses, without us even noticing."

The slides tell the tale. In Minnesota's rural prairie counties numbers in the thirty to thirty-four age bracket jumped over 30 percent from 2000 to 2010, while in its rural recreational counties—those with an abundance of public land, parks, lakes, and other outdoor opportunities that tend to draw those in early middle-age—the increase totaled nearly 40 percent. Contrast that with the percent cohort change, negative 17.5 percent, in core metropolitan areas in the state over the same time period, and it's easy to see Winchester's theory born out in the numbers. Rural areas tend to suffer dramatic losses in the twenty to twenty-four and twenty-five to twenty-nine cohorts, only to experience less heralded gains in the thirty to thirty-four and thirty-five to thirty-nine cohorts. And it's true across the region.

Winchester argues that the thirty- to forty-nine-year-old "Brain Gain" demographic is far more valuable than the eighteen- to twenty-five-year-old "Brain Drain" cohort so often associated with leaving their small rural communities for life in the city. Thirty- to forty-nine-year-olds are more likely to come as family units, offering host communities a population bump of not just one individual but often three or more. Winchester's graduate degree in sociology taught him to follow the cohort more than the individual, leading to a career's worth of discoveries about the movement of people into, and out of, communities. One of many epiphanies arrived when he was asked to conduct a study for a coalition of eighteen school districts in west central Minnesota. Combined, their starting school enrollments had plummeted from about two thousand students to one thousand over a number of years. The obvious culprit, teachers and administrators felt certain, was Brain Drain. However, a closer look revealed that while starting Kindergarten enrollments and K–12 sum enrollment had indeed gone down, year-to-year enrollments in the coalition schools were growing 10 to 30 percent in every age cohort from fourth to eighth grade and as much as 7.5 percent in grades 2–6. In fact, the beleaguered school districts suffering losses in their Kindergartener numbers were gaining ten- to fourteen-year-olds due to the corresponding influx of thirty- to forty-nine-year-olds returning with preteen and early teen children in tow. The gains in the ten- to fourteen-year-old age cohort were so pronounced that Winchester advised the districts to plan for increased seats in those particular classrooms even though K–12 sum enrollments in the coalition schools had declined overall. Therein, Winchester claims, lies the difference between low fertility rates—the declining number of children born to parents living in southwestern Minnesota and elsewhere across agrarian Middle America—versus the increasing number of children moving into such districts at a later date. A similar paradox can be found in the 2000 to 2010 population change map as a whole; the statistics show an overall population decline in many of the region's rural counties, while the number of thirty- to thirty-four-year-olds living in many of those same depopulating areas showed steady growth.

Randy Cantrell, a community development specialist with the University of Nebraska extension service, confirmed similar trends in his home state. Cantrell found in his study "Rural Depopulation: A Closer Look at Nebraska's Counties and Communities" that smaller communities in the Cornhusker State significantly outperformed larger cities in their ability to attract émigrés in their prime earning years from 1990 to 2000. On average Nebraska communities with populations of fewer than 2,500 experienced an increase of nearly 25 percent in the population aged thirty to thirty-nine. More striking still—more than half of Nebraska's 531 unincorporated communities saw increases in their college-degree-holding population from 1990 to 2000.

In 2008 Cantrell and his research team drilled down on the identity of the region's migrants in a groundbreaking study of the eleven rural counties that make up Nebraska's Panhandle region. Instead of finding a stagnant older population of rooted ruralites, Cantrell and his team found that one in every eight residents living in Nebraska's eleven western counties had arrived there from another state or country during the previous five years, with a total in-migration of 10,500 individuals into the Panhandle alone. As a percentage, profoundly rural western Nebraska had seen more recent in-migrants than any other part of the state, and two in three of the newcomers had not previously resided in the Panhandle county into which they moved, meaning that a majority had moved not because of a prior affiliation or obligation, but by self-selection—part of the 51 percent of Americans Winchester claims, citing Pew polls, who prefer small-town living for its slower pace and lower cost of living. These newcomers to Nebraska's Panhandle were not Great Plains dregs or dropouts, but a highly intentional well-educated group free to make a lifestyle choice—not aging vampires but mobile and educated gentrifiers of a sort. Cantrell and his team found that 61 percent of newcomers to Nebraska's Panhandle had come from metro counties seeking, in more than half the cases, a simpler pace of life in a less congested place.

Forty-one percent of the newcomers were between twenty and forty years old, compared to 23 percent in the wider region. With 48 percent having incomes greater than $50,000, they were also considerably higher earning than the population in the region overall, where only 28 percent exceeded the $50,000 mark. Forty percent of the in-migrants reported at least a bachelor's degree versus 18 percent in the wider region; on average the newcomers were almost twice as likely to be trained in professional and related occupations than they were in agriculture (23 percent). Sixty-seven percent moved in with a partner or spouse, and 37 percent brought children with them.

That's the good news Winchester insists he and Cantrell are determined to share in a policy climate wherein rural developers are too often incentivized to pen horror stories concerning rural Middle American demographics in order to earn grants and beget systemic interventions. "We don't always look for the good things all the time because the good things don't get help," he reminds us. "You get help when things are going bad, so you want to frame things in a poor way to help with grant applications;

you want to find out about out-migration trends because it may help you get a group of people together or to pay some staff to help to stem that tide, though ultimately it may be a solution to a problem that is never going to be solved." Put another way, many in the rural development industry have a vested interest in telling a fear-based narrative.

Today's presenter exhorts us to use anything other than a decline narrative relayed using a "deficit language" when talking about our hometowns. "We're doing a major disservice to our thirty- to forty-nine-year-olds who choose to move back if we can't quit calling our towns Brain Drain communities," Winchester says, adding, "Let the kids go. If you want to do something, bring the thirty- to forty-nine-year-olds back." Winchester puts his well-rehearsed presentation on pause to issue his audience a challenge. "Raise your hand if you've been recruiting thirty- to forty-nine-year-olds in the last thirty years." In a room of perhaps 150 attendees only one man speaks up, and it turns out the thirty- to forty-nine-year old he's been actively lobbying to return is his daughter.

"My whole life has been during a time period of rural rebound," Winchester declares from the front of the room. "I know nothing about the [rural decline] a lot of you went through in the 1950s and the '60s. But if we don't change the language that we use to describe what's going on in our small towns, you're not going to be able to get people to move back, including our own kids." The trouble is, the rural developers in the room are focused on the wrong number—the digits on the population sign at the edge of town. Winchester knows from experience that when that number goes up, town burghers and boosters will crow and eventually get complacent. Then, when inevitably the tally goes down, they're hand-wringing, practically holding prayer vigils when instead they could be cheering the growth in a key demographic that's likely growing right under their nose—thirty- to forty-nine-year-olds.

Rather than ride the community morale rollercoaster, towns across Middle America should understand that population is forever in flux. In any given five-year period nearly half of everyone in Minnesota choses to move. If previous patterns hold, many will relocate to prosperous suburbs or to towns along the Interstate 35, 90, or 94 corridors, facilitating an easier commute to the Twin Cities or Rochester or Duluth. Still, some pioneers may choose to join Senator Bill Weber in Luverne, a county seat town of approximately five thousand in the far southwestern corner of the state that has been growing slowly but surely for the last fifteen years; still fewer may opt to try Lamberton, whose population, by contrast, has been in steady decline since the 1980s. Or relocators might choose Walnut Grove, Minnesota, ten miles due west from Lamberton on Highway 13, where the population grew nearly 50 percent to nearly nine hundred between the census years of 2000 and 2010 in large part due to an influx of Hmong immigrants who constitute the majority of a 30 percent Asian population in the childhood town of iconic prairie girl Laura Ingalls Wilder.

"Losing your kids [to Brain Drain] is the rule not the exception," Winchester declares, moving toward conclusion. "Don't beat yourself up over the fact that 40 to 60 percent of your kids leave your town after high school. Migration studies will tell you that the local health of your community will stagnate if you don't encourage the migration in and out." New blood, rather than exclusively young blood, keeps a community's heart pumping, ensuring vigorous circulation and exchange. As in a body, stagnation in a community often gives way to disease, ensuring the sort of anemic blood not even a vampire would want.

And yet for all the vitality and entrepreneurship brought by the influx of Asian immigrants to nearby Walnut Grove (the town's population grew by nearly 50 percent between 2000 and 2010 while Lamberton's dropped 11.6 percent from 1990 to 2000 and 4.1 percent from 2000 to 2010), the growth in Walnut Grove has not created greater wealth within the community when compared to Lamberton, which still easily outpaces its more rapidly growing neighbor by tens of thousands of dollars in median household income and median house or condo value.

In other words, population gain is not quite the cure-all some would make it out to be.

I meet Winchester one-on-one in a nondescript side room of the SWROC. Away from the dais I find him more relaxed but no less on-message. I've asked for the bonus meeting because I'm eager to compare notes, both of us currently living in towns with populations of less than 750, and both of us eager, each in our own way, to rewrite the region's narrative.

Though I'm sympathetic to his advocacies and grateful for his optimism, I'm not buying everything today's keynote speaker has been selling. The fact that his résumé features time at think-tanks with names like the Center for Small Towns tells me he's paid to spread the good news in much the same way a board member of the American Farm Bureau is expected to advocate for Big Ag. And I'm still not sure why, given the Brain Gain the research fellow claims is happening across the rural Midwest, Lamberton, just thirty miles from Southwest Minnesota State University in Marshall and located on a well-traveled state highway, logs just one permit for a new single-family home every few years on average. If the thirty- to forty-nine-year-olds are indeed coming here in their prime earning and fertility years, shouldn't the new permit numbers show them to be building new nests, especially in an era of low interest rates?

Sipping casually on a glass of ice water on this, a warm June day, Winchester reminds me of a telling statistic: since 1970 rural population has increased by 11 percent, though he's willing to concede that rural America's share in the overall U.S. population has steadily declined. In 1970 for example, rural Americans accounted for roughly 26 percent, a number that diminished to less than 20 percent in 2000. By contrast, over 80 percent of Americans lived in urban areas in 2010, with the growth in urban population over that same decade several percentage points above the population growth in the country as a whole.

At 80 percent urban, Minnesota, a land of almost legendary open prairies and well-forested lakes, is now as urban as the rest of an urbanizing nation. Winchester argues that such high rates of urbanity have been affected by Census Bureau reclassifications of once rural communities into micropolitan areas orbiting larger metros. "Rural areas look like they're having problems because we graduate certain counties to urban status," he explains. Since 1972 many once-rural counties in Minnesota have left the rural rolls, including Winchester's home county of Winona in the far southeastern corner of the state. The Office of Management and Budget reclassified Winona County several years ago as a "Micropolitan Statistical Area." Meanwhile, the Census Bureau now ranks the Winona Core-Based Statistical Area as the 582nd most populous in the United States. In other words, when counties like Winona or Carleton "graduate" from rural to urban they take with them their difference-making statistics. And when high-achieving counties tip from rural to urban they leave rural places looking poorer and more depleted than ever. Winchester chalks up the bloodletting in nonmetro America mainly to such statistical sleights of hand, but I argue that the declining number of rural counties in America represents a vampiric tendency—annexation by transfusion of the life-blood of the countryside into the heart of the city. While the shift cityward may bring the benefits of shorter commutes, greater cultural diversity, and greater economic opportunity, it also results in diminished influence and collective bargaining power for voters self-identifying as rural or for those living in ag-dominated communities with a dwindling share of the population.

Winchester interrupts to quibble with the terms themselves—*rural* and *ag-dominated*. "There is no rural," he argues. And as for ag-dominated places, statistically there are very few, if any, even in rural Minnesota, where education and social services now employ a far greater percentage of the population than farming. Here in Lamberton, a town whose residents City-Data lists as 100 percent rural, farming fails to make even the top seven most common occupations, with construction (at 20 percent) leading the list. Winchester makes no bones about his indifference to agriculture as an economic engine. He insists that during his five years as a master's student at the University of Missouri he was the only rural sociology graduate student who "wanted nothing to do with agriculture." And the intervening years of canvassing the region have made him even more determined to see things from the perspective of the rural nonfarm worker.

"I don't care about ag," he confesses to me. "I don't know how to grow *anything*. But I do know the statistic that tells me that 95 percent of rural people don't have anything to do with agriculture. Who's here to speak about that 95? . . . I'm called an ag-hater all the time. . . . I'm glad they help farm our rural communities, but it [agriculture] is not going to drive where we go anymore."

Winchester offers this tagline for his research: "rural America ain't what it used to be," though many Baby Boomers refuse to see the changes, preferring to offer eulogies for the death of small-town USA rather than see the diverse, surprising ways in which it's being reborn. Instead of casting aspersions on Middle Americans who don't bowl together anymore, sociologists like *Bowling Alone* author Robert Putnam need to wake up and see what sorts of leagues younger Americans do join in their scant free time—disc golf, for example. Too many older ruralites, Winchester feels, are stuck in a fifties and sixties mindset, even when "things never looked like they think they did."

Winchester likes to use the analogy of first and second shift to explain why he finds numbers more revealing than observational evidence. Social circles don't overlap as much as they once did, he claims. By analogy, a town's first and second shifters eat at different times, shop at different times, and play at different times, thereby ensuring their invisibility to one another. Those working the graveyard shift might as well be denizens of an alternate nocturnal world, so brief is their exposure to the retirees who run their errands and attend their social functions and church services in the broad light of day. "You might have one hundred new people work second shift in your town, but you don't even know they're there because you don't see them every day," he points out. The same goes for houses of worship. Empty seats in pews since the 1970s have meant bitter lamentations on the demise of the rural church, but the truth is that younger people are worshipping in less traditional ways and at less traditional times, as America secularizes across the board.

In Winchester's view the boom-bust cycle of rural America—the same that has left so many Middle American places, like Count Dracula's Transylvania, ghosted by a grandeur that now lies firmly in the past— was a haunt largely created by invaders, in this case the wrong-headed professors, pedants, hustlers, and hucksters who have been encouraging small towns to grow beyond their means since the Gilded Age. He sees a similar mentality at work in a Digital Age where many in the rural development industry he describes as a "netherworld between private and public sector" hope to make a quick buck from beleaguered towns determined to rekindle lost prosperity at any cost. He notices communities all across the region making dubious investments in brick-and-mortar storefronts on Main Street in a desperate attempt to thwart the specter of empty storefronts and for-sale signs, even when those same businesses (grocery stores, cafés, pharmacies, etc.) have been in decline in many small towns for more than thirty years. As he travels across the state and the region, hand-wringers bemoan the death of their local grocery store, assuming Winchester will be sympathetic to their plight. Instead, he often finds himself issuing a tough-love reply: "Well, maybe [the grocery store] shouldn't have been opened in the first place." In other words, the one-stop-shop idea of the 1920s—a self-reliant market town complete with its own grocery store, café, hardware store, and post office all conveniently located on Main—isn't necessary for the highly mobile American worker who spends, on average, close to sixty minutes in the car on their daily commute, spreading their retail spending across several communities and the World Wide Web.

"Yeah you probably need a hair stylist in every town, and a gas station is awful good to have," Winchester concedes, but other than that, not every whistle-stop needs to have a full set of services to qualify as having a pulse. As an illustration he recalls the grocery store that closed in Hancock, a shuttering that to some old-timers there, might as well have signaled end times. Instead, my interviewee points out the local gas station, By-Lo Gas and Groceries, quickly filled the vacuum, serving as the town's fuel stop, bakery, lunch buffet, barber, and used auto lot all in one.

Winchester believes that many communities, in a mistaken drive to earn the coveted mantle of "regional center," take for granted what they do well in favor of trying to be something they are not, in much the same way that an individual, seeking popularity, often loses what is best in themselves. In his eyes even the pejorative label "bedroom community" should be redeemed or reclaimed; at the very least it offers a town an economic calling card, a purpose it can take to the bank rather than treat as a mark of shame or scarlet letter. The misguided rural developers trying to teach Lamberton or Luverne how to be Minneapolis or Saint Paul are like self-interested technocrats trying to turn provincial Transylvania into cosmopolitan London. In Winchester's view, for-profit developers charging $15,000 and more to help struggling rural towns feel less scary to educated twenty-somethings are in many cases taking the money and running without first determining whether it's feasible for a town to accomplish a true makeover.

In so many words Winchester claims we can't all be the cool kids in class, and that, in so wishing, we're only setting ourselves and our communities up for disappointment. But what troubles me is the pecking order implicit in such a world view. If functionalists argue that every town needs to understand and enact its economic function to survive, what of the places tasked with doing inglorious work or engaged, against their will, in a tacit kind of servitude to other, more desirable communities nearby. For example, if Morris, Minnesota, well endowed with its county seat, its five thousand-plus population, its branch of the University of Minnesota, and its Center for Small Towns, effectively brands itself as the brain of Stevens County, Minnesota, what functions remain for a town like Hancock to play? Using the human body as analogy, if one place is the heart and one place is the brain, then, to avoid duplication and harmful competition, another has to be the stomach or worse.

"Yeah, who's going to be the gut bacteria?" Winchester says as he piggybacks on the point, though the implications for struggling rural areas cut up and compartmentalized like cadavers are far from comedic. If American small towns yield their autonomy to perform a service role, they become analogous to a single organ in the body—uniquely ripe in their specialization for exploitation and predation, and all but eliminated from the prospect of self-sufficiency. I prefer a more holistic view of economic development to the every state's got to have a brain and an armpit functionalist approach.

"But it *is* the economic perspective," Winchester replies. "So it's what I continually have to respond to as I work every day in the industry. We've had the economic perspective invade every discipline. Heck, it's why we have the term *social capital*. Because *capital* makes sense to an economist! They're like 'Oh, I can understand social relationships now because you put the term *capital* in it!'"

At times the twenty-first-century rural development industry can feel more like Hanna-Barbera's *Scooby Doo* than Bram Stoker's *Dracula*. The setup is essentially this: A group of bright-eyed young people arrive in a corporate vehicle—their very own Mystery Machine—eager to solve whatever haunt has been plaguing the out-of-the-way community in need. Their fact-finding mission consists of cursory interviews with townspeople reluctant to share information with precocious and presumptuous outsiders who, they well know, will leave town just as soon as a culprit is unmasked and the mystery supposedly solved. Usually the perpetrator is older and determined to carry out some self-serving scheme that depends on scaring away unwanted visitors and newcomers. The super sleuth interlopers are "meddling kids" hoping to free the afflicted community from the forces conspiring to hold it back.

The number one predictor for success for any community isn't the ability to afford $20,000 consulting fees or five-step programs, but the caliber and quality of interaction experienced by its residents. It's a matter, Winchester maintains, of getting people working together to build things real or virtual.

"I don't care if they're doing it online. . . . We just have to paint with a new brush," he tells me. It's an intriguing metaphor, and one that lends agency—the community as an artist with a full palette of choices—to rural citizens who seem almost congenitally predisposed to paint in tones reminiscent of Rembrandt or Vermeer, the darkness of their canvasses more impressionistic than photo-realistic or documentary. If Winchester's explanation is accurate—that concerned citizens often make their towns' plights out to be more desperate than it really is in order to warrant scholarly attention and justify state and federal grants—why would ruralites regionwide, the vast majority of whom are neither academics nor politicians nor policy wonks, choose to paint with such dark palettes?

And there's a larger paradox to consider, one so uncanny as to suggest deeply entrenched conspiracy theory: for all their Eeyore-like complaints, the residents of America's rural places consistently report greater levels of satisfaction and happiness with their lives than their suburban and urban counterparts, and they've been doing so for thirty years. Scholars Brian Berry and Adam Okulicz-Kozaryn have long contended that statistical data show what they call an "urban–rural happiness gradient"—in other words, as they move from city to suburb to small town, Americans report a gradual increase in subjective well-being.

By mapping responses to the General Social Survey question on happiness with data on place of residence, the researchers found that between 1972 and 2008, "happiness has been lowest in the nation's largest cities and has consistently been at its highest levels in small towns and rural areas." Their findings, consistent across any number of surveys, intimate that rural Americans may in fact be painting trompe l'oeil—"trick of the eye—suggesting one way of life (blighted, declining, struggling for life) while living another (inwardly happy, quietly contented). Count Dracula embodies a similar paradox; though he speaks in gloomy terms of the broken walls of his crumbling castle and the disquieting shadows that darken his mood, he does so with a tone not entirely convincing—or, as Harker puts it: "Somehow his words and his look did not seem to accord, or else it was that his cast of face made his smile look malignant and saturnine."

Such stoicism can serve as a barrier to potential newcomers—one reason why residents of demographically challenged small towns who are nonetheless statistically happy with their lot sometimes make their home places out to be less attractive when speaking to potential relocators, applying a sort of reverse psychology wherein community shortcomings are highlighted rather than withheld. Consider the difference in a long-time Lamberton citizen telling a prospective resident to prepare for January temps in the negative 30s (in 1970 Lamberton once recorded an air temperature of -34 degrees Fahrenheit) while omitting the fact that *average* January highs, in the low to mid-20s, are consistent with the very livable Madison, Wisconsin. The "go away" sentiment of closed communities is part and parcel of the classic haunt, wherein the haunt is often made up of two seemingly contradictory impulses—the desire to be left alone, and the desire to be discovered, ergo Dracula telling the young Mr. Harker, "You may go anywhere you wish in the castle, except where the doors are locked, where of course you will not wish to go. There is reason that all things are as they are, and did you see with my eyes and know with my knowledge, you would perhaps better understand." The warning to stay away, and its inevitable disavowal by the curious interloper-trespasser, is a distinctly Gothic trope.

As the dinner hour approaches, I say goodbye and thanks to my Lamberton hosts, opting not to stay for the 6:00 p.m. feed. I've enjoyed my day among the region's rural developers, grateful both for the afternoon of isolation-lifting commiseration and for the hopeful gospel of the day's keynote speaker. However, like a good whodunit, I'm unsure who to believe as I pull out of the lot and make the long drive home—those who insist the glass is half full or those who claim the sky is falling. Still, speeding through the twilight, I'm fully engaged in the plot and plight of small towns and eager for the next chapter, though as with any good horror story, I'm both excited and afraid to turn the page.

Many months after returning from Lamberton I get back in touch with Ben Winchester. In the interim he has won an excellence in research award from the Minnesota Association of Community and Leadership Education Professionals and published an article on his Brain Gain research in *Rural Minnesota Journal*. I call him in January and find him up to his ears in end-of-year reporting. He has continued to deliver his well-received "Rewriting the Rural Narrative" PowerPoint from Minnesota, to Texas, to Iowa, generating newspaper copy in small and midsized cities across Middle America interested in airing positive stories that push back on the Brain Drain narrative.

We chat for a while about family, about research, about our respective rural counties—the usual conversational fodder for professional acquaintances catching up. When, in a lull in the conversation, he casually mentions that he and his family have moved from Hancock, population 750, to St. Cloud, the tenth largest city in the state, I feel oddly betrayed. Or am I simply envious, having stayed rooted outside my own struggling rural town despite what may be good for me? Why should I begrudge him a move to a more prosperous city, with better and closer medical care, more options for his school-aged children, and enviable professional opportunities for both Ben and his wife? I can tell he is no less passionate in his support of rural communities, and he is still working for the extension service, albeit out of the St. Cloud office. Still I find his happy news jarring, something akin to hearing that the Roberson family of *Duck Dynasty* fame has left West Monroe, Louisiana, for Midtown Manhattan.

I have fallen victim to exactly the regional vice Winchester calls out: the desire to keep things the same rather than inviting and celebrating change—migrations in, migrations out, life and death, yin and yang. Ben and his family have only joined the crowd, acting in concert with the nearly one in two Minnesotans, Nebraskans, Wisconsinites, and South Dakotans who moved from 1995 to 1999, joining the new wagon train procession bravely doing what Americans do to ensure greater prosperity for themselves and their families: moving on to greener pastures.

PITCHFORKS AND PIES

"Do you want apple, blueberry crumble, or Shaker lemon?"

It's the sort of question asked in small-town kitchens all across Middle America on a hot summer day, but this isn't just any old kitchen: this is the American Gothic House, home to Beth Howard, aka the pie lady, aka Ms. American Pie. Howard moved to Eldon, Iowa, population just shy of one thousand, from Malibu, California, where she baked pies for Barbra Streisand, Steven Spielberg, Mel Gibson, and Robert Downey Jr. Not long before my arrival a *CBS This Morning* camera crew visited from New York City as the pie lady and her small staff attempted to bake one hundred pies in the location Grant Wood made famous—the house Howard now rents for an almost unbelievable $250 a month.

I first heard Howard describing the grief that had brought her two thousand miles from the Golden State to the American Gothic House while listening to an NPR account of her memoir *Making Piece: A Memoir of Love, Loss, and Pie.* Her story, headlined "Grieving Widow Turns to Making Pie as Therapy" caused me to turn up the volume. Its basic outline—prodigal son or daughter moves away, makes it big, and returns in middle age on whim, or whimsy, to buy a restaurant, café, winery, or bed and breakfast somewhere in Middle America—was sufficiently cliché that I had been tempted at first to turn back to the farm reports. But this story felt different for the obvious reason that Howard had come back in pain rather than chock full of bravado. Life had served her a taste of humble pie, and in a region that honors modesty, that particular flavor matters.

Asked by NPR host Viviano Hurtado what she remembered of the day in 2009 when Howard learned her young husband, Marcus, had died of a ruptured aorta at just forty-three-years-old, the pie lady answered with one word, "pain," before elaborating: "I remember laying on my cement floor and sobbing so hard, I wanted to throw up. It was torturous and unfathomable, and I'd never known any pain like that, ever." It wasn't so much the baking-as-therapy that drew me to Howard's story but the bravery in telling a nation exactly how badly she was hurting. Howard's book followed to a T the recipe of best-selling author Elizabeth Gilbert, whose 2010 memoir *Eat, Pray, Love* had been an Oprah Book Club selection. Like Gilbert, Howard had had a difficult relationship with her husband prior to their estrangement; at the time of his passing the two were living 1,200 miles apart and planning a divorce. Like Gilbert, Howard's route to recovery involved the sensuousness of food, friendship, and fellowship en route to exotic places. But while Gilbert's healing destinations included Italy, India, and Indonesia—locales known for transcendent food and life-altering gurus—the pie lady made pilgrimage to a less heralded "I" place, Iowa, where she had grown up before moving West after high school. In the three decades since, she had lived in a series of metropolitan meccas—Seattle, Los Angeles, Chicago, finally Portland—where her jet-setting husband had been living when his heart stopped.

Devastated, Howard returned to her adult home—Los Angeles—looking for comfort in the familiar. Baking had helped her overcome previous life traumas, so when her good friend Janice asked her to make a pie documentary by traveling across southern California in the RV Howard had inherited, the pie lady enthusiastically agreed. That decision, in turn, led her to road-trip back to her Midwest roots in the motor home she affectionately dubbed "The Beast," where she volunteered as a pie judge at the state fair and, thereafter, returned to her hometown of Ottumwa, Iowa, where a serendipitous detour off Highway 34 took her to the town Grant Wood made famous. What was one more change in itinerary for a woman who had been thrown life's ultimate curveball?

Within minutes she had fallen in love with the famed American Gothic House with its crisp board and batten siding and white lace curtains. Poking around a bit further she learned that the home, now owned by the Iowa State Historical Society, had been sitting empty and was in urgent need of a tenant. What's more, Howard's high school friend Meg, now living in Des Moines, had served on a board with the director of the Iowa State Historical Society. Rent was next to nothing compared to LA; if nothing else, the pie lady reasoned, she could empty out the Beast and use the historic home as glorified storage. Shortly thereafter she filled out the rental application and waited for fate to extend its warm hand.

Days later she signed a lease that required her, among other unorthodox provisions, to keep the original lace curtains in place and to "always treat the public in a friendly manner." She now found herself faced with the difficult task of telling her coastal friends and family that she would not be not be moving back to Los Angeles, where her parents and two of her four siblings lived, or to Portland, where a support group awaited her, but relocating to a small town Howard described as a "struggling, threadbare village" that was "dying a slow death" due to "decline and decay." The pie lady's inner circle thought the idea was nuts—a youthful widow still deep in mourning confining herself not to a tower or dungeon, but to a Gothic house.

The litany of their concerns proved almost comical. How would she survive the harsh winters? How could she risk living alone in a town where she knew no one? One friend took the liberty of sending the pie lady pepper spray with a note that read, "Because I know you would never buy this for yourself." Another pal gifted her with a four-pound bottle of Snake Stopper snake repellent. Where Howard saw peace, open space, and a chance to compose her fraying thoughts in writing, friends and family on the coasts saw the potential for violent intrusion, cultural isolation, and abject despair—a Middle American version of *Deliverance*. It was one thing for an individual to move across the country solo to a tiny farm town deep in flyover country, but quite another to move into a house known worldwide for its spooky, sideways-glancing spinster and her pitchfork-wielding companion. Each year as many as fifteen thousand strangers peered through the home's famous windows, inevitably asking whether it was haunted, while trying hard to see what Wood saw in the famous facade behind the unsmiling pair immortalized on canvas.

That's how, and when, Howard began to turn sour grapes into sweet homemade pies at exactly the time when a Grant Wood renaissance had begun with the 2010 publication of R. Tripp Evans's eye-opening biography *Grant Wood: A Life*. Wood's personal life had been much darker and more fraught than art historians had previously supposed. The Grant Wood brought to light in Evans's exposé lived in a world "magnified and distorted through the lens of memory, dread, and desire." Biographer Steven Biel, meanwhile, described in Wood's paintings the "gloom, terror, haunting, possession, decay, seduction, incest, and hidden perversions of the nineteenth-century Gothic novel." Wood, Evans asserted, lived a kind of Jekyll-and-Hyde double life that "disguised the personal content of his work" by wrapping it in the American flag or cloaking it in homespun humor. When he returned from Germany to his native Hawkeye State, Wood "had no choice but to face the ghosts of his past."

In discovering what he described as the "queer Gothic window," Wood found an evocative suggestion of the ornate cathedrals he had painted in Europe anomalously superimposed on a provincial American house built by local craftsmen in the Carpenter Gothic style. The home, a contradiction in terms, positively haunted the artist, and when, in 1930, he returned from Eldon to his studio located in the carriage house of Turner Funeral Home in Cedar Rapids, Iowa, he immediately set to creating what would become the most recognizable painting by an American artist. It's an image more famous than any of the treasures held by the New York Museum of Modern Art according to the MoMA's former director Thomas Hoving, who writes: "*American Gothic* has been lavishly praised, brutally condemned, waved aloft as a symbol of the greatest good of our land . . . viciously attacked . . . vilified, psychoanalyzed, mocked, accused of being the Devil's work . . . snickered at, called a corpse, caricatured, used for myriad parodies, and held hostage for any number of advertisements and Halloween costumes. Since it's been in the public eye, its significance has been puzzled over more than any other painting in American history."

Adventuresome visitors have been coming to Eldon ever since, and more so with the addition of the visitor center in 2007, which, in addition to telling the story of the painting and the place that inspired it, provides visitors from across the country with the period clothing to dress as the dour man and woman the canvas portrays. In an era of highly produced theme-park attractions and high-dollar historical exhibits with all the bells and whistles, a two-hour roundtrip detour from Interstate 80 can be a tough sell for the average tourist blazing a comet's trail across Middle America. Those willing to undertake the pilgrimage are often a bit "touched" to begin with, obsessed with historical oddities and haunts, out-of-the-way places, and historical footnotes, perhaps explaining why Howard has witnessed eccentric visitors posing in front of her home with everything from cars and motorcycles to sheep, horses, goats, and llamas. Reviews of the attraction on popular travel apps range from enthusiastic thumbs up from history-loving families to comments typified by those of screenname Hollywoodhorror, who writes "Nothing really wrong with this place, but all it is the house from the . . . painting. It's neat to see, but there is no museum or anything and you cannot go inside." And therein lies the rub: the pie lady's presence can be pointed to as both a big factor in the increasing number of yearly visitors and, simultaneously, as an obstacle to scores of disappointed travelers who believe they should have the right to tour the house at will.

I have driven six hours on a late summer Sunday not just to witness first-hand the window that inspired Wood's famous painting but to achieve a wider appreciation for Howard's uncanny life recipe, suspended as it is somewhere between the Romantic, Gothic, and erotic. I've come to wonder aloud at how life can resemble literature, and vice versa. She's offered me a slice of Shaker lemon, and I've volunteered to take the apple, since it has already been cut. Still the pie lady hands me the lemon instead, suggesting I live a little. She claims the filling's as good as lemonade.

"Nice choice," echoes her friend Kevin, who, like me, is visiting for the day, hoping, I presume, to rub shoulders with the California culinary dynamo that's turning this small Middle American town upside down. After a day selling from-scratch desserts from her Pitchfork Pie Stand, Howard's sharing one of eighteen unsold pies that currently await an uncertain fate. Some can be frozen and brought back to life the following weekend. Others urgently need to be consumed or thrown away. Several are burned around the edges, making tangible Howard's mantra that pie, like life, is about more than perfection.

Two lemons gave their lives for the piece Kevin and I devour. The Shaker lemon makes my lips purse into a shape similar to the sour pucker of the pitchfork wielder in Wood's iconic painting, though the bitterness quickly gives way to pleasure. Still, even with the added sugar I struggle to name its exact flavor profile until I settle on "zesty"—a word that applies to the pie lady herself, with her sunny blonde hair, double French braids, and dark wit. The pie lady will turn fifty this summer—Wood's exact age when he passed away of pancreatic cancer—though she attacks her work with an ageless spirit. When visitors tell her how good she looks she demurs, reminding them that making one hundred pies a weekend in a stifling ten-by-twenty-foot kitchen is as good as any weight loss program. Returning customers swear her pies have changed their lives, though the pie lady maintains that her real experiential credential is as much in survival as in baking. "I became an expert at grief," she tells me of the tragic events that led her here to her own private Woebegone. "I did the grief counseling. I did the crying. I read the books. I even wrote my own book about it."

Taking lemons and making lemon pie: that's what Beth Howard is all about.

Consider: our heroine receives the news of her husband's tragic death deep in the south Texas desert, where she moves to initiate the divorce she is sure killed her husband's spirit before it stopped his heart. She is wracked by guilt and grief and living alone in a miner's cabin near the Mexican border. "Everything I had loved about the place before—the isolation, the vastness and emptiness of the desert wilderness—now threatened to consume me, and draw me further into a new world of quiet madness," she writes of the pining that ultimately leads her back to Portland, where she occupies the same guest house where her husband stayed at the time of his heart attack. She makes a shrine of his belongings and steeps herself in all that remains of him. She is, she vows, waiting "for his ghost to materialize." When the apparition does not appear she grows anxious and even paranoid, thinking how, if death could take a man in the prime of his life, it could surely come for her, too. In that moment she longs for the reaper to come to her doorstep. For weeks her sobs can be heard throughout the guest house, "late-night cries echoing off the hardwood floors." She realizes for her sake, and for others', she must find a room of her own and, by a series of fortunes and misfortunes, finds lodging in this historic home on the edge of the Plains, where she simultaneously seeks community and attempts to shut it out, barring it at the door, the greedy eyes of eager onlookers forever wanting in, attempting to pry not just into Grant Wood's private life but into her own: "It is behind this window and its last curtain that I sleep, dream, read, cry, snuggle with my two small dogs and escape the peering eyes of the passersby," our heroine writes. But even as they clamor for the beautiful widow to come down from her tower to commune with them and bake for them, they gossip about her, too, both drawn to and made anxious by a difference that both terrifies and titillates them.

My visit occurs just the second weekend after the pie lady's return from a six-week book tour in her "Pie Across the Nation" RV, and the day's disappointing sales haven't been the welcome-back party she had hoped for. "I don't know how to run a retail business, and I don't really want to run a retail business, but here I am," Howard confesses to Kevin and me. Our host is a charismatic, high-energy talker with lots to say and an uncanny ability to magnetize others to lend a hand or an ear to flights of fancy. Where the feel-good cause of pies is concerned she's a pied-piper and proselytizer rolled into a singularly persuasive package.

Pitchfork Pie Stand is really more of a weekend pop-up shop than a business proper, as it's open just Saturdays and Sundays, weather-permitting, from Memorial Day until Labor Day. The pie lady's weekdays are spent preparing for the onslaught of weekends for which she, and a small seasonal staff, sometimes bake a hundred pies. She spends Monday through Friday on a quest for the best fruit at the best price, and what she can't source locally at stores and fruit stands she buys direct from wholesalers. Ordering pie tins and up to six hundred pounds of ingredients at a time, fulfilling T-shirt orders (including one whose message reads "Bake Your Own Damn Pie!"), paying bills, and updating social media occupy the rest of her idle moments. All of which leaves her, she tells me, "desperate for solitude," though something inside resists rest. Despite her must-sleep sentiments she appears genuinely grateful to have Kevin and I here: people to vent to, people to bounce ideas off, people to lend a hand in bringing to fruition long-percolating dreams. An empty house is what she both sincerely longs for and fervently fears. The book tour recently completed is exhibit A in the can't-stop, up-by-the-bootstraps energy that perpetually propels the pie lady into the unknown, trusting that her safety net of friends and fellowship will save her from the free fall felt by all those who grieve endlessly.

Twice on her recent journey she landed in the emergency room nursing a bad case of bronchitis that never had a chance to heal thanks to an exhausting tour schedule. "Don't get down, get busy" had been a Howard family mantra, she tells me, and I understand all too well the nose-to-the-grindstone choices that remain after losing a loved one. My own father was the one who taught me this survival skill—something he called "creative avoidance"—the habit of staying busy enough to keep self-pitying or despairing thoughts at bay. Dad practiced what he preached. A hard-working farmer, he doubled his output when his failing health and growing despair troubled his heart and mind. And me? Today I've driven all the way from the Great Plains without stopping, riding the horse hard and putting it away wet, as he used to say. I should be sitting at home with my feet up watching TV, but instead I've pulled off the highway, one hundred miles from home, seeking the communion of homemade pie, conversation, and a slice of commiseration.

After giving readings and pie-baking tutorials at trendy bookstores from Los Angeles to Austin, Texas, Howard's reentry into tiny Eldon has been fraught. Faced with the decision of whether to treat herself to a $40 restorative massage or a $40 floor-to-ceiling house-cleaning as a homecoming gift, she chose the latter, only to find herself in a profane argument with the housekeeper over whether or not she actually performed the promised domestic makeover. The pie lady claims the not-so-merry maid left a note saying "I done the job. That'll be $40," though the neighbors reported that the woman did little more than sit under a shade tree.

"She screwed me over big-time," a bitter pie lady says now, though she ultimately paid up to spare herself a showdown. "That happened, then someone in town beat up their seventeen-year-old son and to a bloody pulp because he's got an anger management problem and he didn't take his medication. I was like . . . what hellhole have I just returned to? Then I got a little overwhelmed like, 'This place sucks. I don't want to be around this negativity.'" Other neighbors, those Howard openly describes as "nosy" and "mean," welcomed her back with multiple calls to the county sheriff to report her two terriers, Daisy and Jack—collectively "Team Terrier"—roaming the neighborhood off leash. In reply the pie lady parked the Beast between her house and theirs, using it as both a privacy fence and as extra storage for her pie ingredients and pie-related merchandise.

When the pie lady dons her blue denim overalls or red-checked gingham apron for weekend appearances at the Pitchfork Pie Stand she looks more like a Midwest farmers' daughter than a surfer from Malibu. The outspoken transplant admits she's a fish out of water in a region known for the emotional repression and taciturn reserve seen in the faces of the implement-wielding farmer and his buttoned-up female companion in Wood's famous painting. In nearly thirty years living away from home Howard has become more self-aware, more self-directed, and more determined than ever to make her own art rather than simply accept the canvas she's been given. The same ambition that drives her to spend her Thursday nights peeling apples and lemons by the case also sometimes makes it difficult to fully acclimate in a community that believes in simply accepting, with grace, what comes your way.

Some fancy the pie lady's unreal life here as a modern-day fairy tale; if so, it's surely more of the darkly Germanic Brothers Grimm or Brothers Coen. Some have even made Howard out to be the town's savior—the blonde-haired princess riding in on her RV from the Golden State, terriers in tow and Mini Cooper trailered behind—though the pie lady is the first to admit that small-town living in the twenty-first century is something less than Norman Rockwell. "I do not know everyone in Eldon, contrary to what it might seem in such a small town," she confesses. "Some people I don't want to know. . . . Absolutely low-life meth addicts or just very, very uneducated people. You can see the houses with the junk in the yard next to the pristine houses. It's just interesting to me how in this town they're the 'Oh yuck' [houses] or 'That's so nice and so pretty.'" She's unapologetic in announcing that she doesn't drink at either of Eldon's bars because there is no one there she would care to meet and none of the imported beer she's developed a taste for. As an alternative she keeps good wine at the house for visitors and rides her bike to the local bar and grill for the occasional plate-sized tenderloin ordered takeout. Dating within the city limits is absolutely out of the question for her. Not long ago she met an independently wealthy businessman on a popular online dating site. He could work from anywhere in the United States and was willing to give Iowa a try, though the promising relationship soured after just a few months.

The pie lady would have me keep in mind that after a long day, I'm listening to "overtired" Beth, the one who, she admits, sometimes struggles to cope. Still, Ms. American Pie refuses to feel sorry for herself. In the hour we've been talking she hasn't once used the word "widow." When she complains, it's mostly about her own lack of time. When she judges others it's primarily because they have judged her first or otherwise broken her faith. Years of living in densely urban, politically progressive cities have taught the pie lady the necessity of a "you do your thing I'll do mine" philosophy—one that doesn't always square well with Eldon's need-to-know residents.

Howard's recipe for surviving her Gothic circumstance has been one part positive attitude, one part devil-may-care, and one part what she calls her "mercurial nature." With her RV at the ready and a history of dropping everything to go everywhere, she can hit the road anytime the gravity of her famous house begins to make her feel unwilling prisoner to her own, or the town's, sometime melancholy. "I choose not to embrace fear. . . . I choose to see the good in people," she insists as the three of us move the discussion into the living room, where, on weekends, the pie lady sets up tables for her pop-up pie cafe. "I'm not looking for trouble, so trouble doesn't find me. If you want to give it that energy, you're going to attract that energy." And for friends and acquaintances who so badly misconceive her life that they feel the need to send pepper spray, she has a message: "Don't impose your fear on me."

Two years ago, when Howard moved in, the interior of the 1881 home looked more like a haunted house than a building on the National Register of Historic Places. The window shades, pulled down tight, let in the sickly yellow light characteristic of unlived in, unloved homes. Spider webs festooned every corner. Mouse droppings and the carcasses of dead flies and beetles littered the floor. Black mildew blanketed the bathtub. Once she signed her first year-long lease Howard set to scrubbing the place to the bone. Months into her stay she found a six-foot bull snake hiding out in her bathroom; thereafter many of her visiting friends were sufficiently spooked by the snake-in-the-bathroom parable that they refused to use the facilities in the house, no matter how badly nature called. But where friends saw danger Howard saw pure potential in the structure's evocative details: the curvy staircase leading to the lofted second floor that held not just the front-facing Gothic window of

Grant Wood fame, but also a second, secret one facing the park-like setting behind the historic home.

From that point forward the house many found haunting felt fated.
The pie lady scrubbed and painted until the faded paint on the walls
became bed-sheet white again, and the wide wooden floors transformed
from dingy and distressed to ship-shape enamel gray. When, on one of her
first days in town, she went to city hall to set up her utilities, she found
mayor Shirley Stacey waiting for her with a slice of peach pie and a teaser
offer: $1 rental of a downtown storefront if Howard would utilize the
space as a pie café. "Eldon needs you," the mayor pleaded, though the pie
lady said no to the discounted space in favor of baking in her own homey
kitchen, with its red-and-white-checked curtains and fire engine–red cabi-
nets. Still, the generosity of the mayor's offer stunned her into a grateful
kind of silence. Her neighbors welcomed the pie lady's arrival from the
City of Angels, too, glad for a tenant in the town's only real tourist attraction. Still dealing with her grief, and mindful of the fears for her safety
expressed by friends and family, the pie lady welcomed her elderly neighbors' overwatch, finding her newfound allies to be the best security system
she could ever hope for, coupled with the razor-sharp pitchfork she kept
in the corner just in case.

After a few months the pie lady established sustaining relationships
not only with her octogenarian neighbors, who functioned like surrogate
parents and grandparents, but with others inspired by her embrace of life
after death. When another of her neighbors—the mortician's wife—lost
her husband to pancreatic cancer, the pie lady was there to lend support
and ideas to the reluctant heir of the town's only funeral home. "When
your spouse dies it's probably a good thing to change your life up a bit,"
Howard counseled her fellow widow, a long-ago émigré to town who
couldn't wait to leave. She suggested her friend advertise the funeral home
out-of-state, knowing from personal experience how many people on the
coasts were looking to change their lives with one big, bold change in zip
code. She suggested that the handsome building that housed the bodies
could easily be transformed from morgue into campy bed and breakfast,
though her friend rejected Howard's outside-the-box thinking, believing
that it would dishonor her husband's memory. But she did take the pie
lady's advice to advertise the property on Craig's List, eventually selling
to a single woman from out of state who was eager not just to continue

operating it as a funeral home, but to inject color and life into the death experience. Rocking chairs soon adorned the front porch of the mortuary, thanks in part to the pie lady's advice.

Howard felt a new spirit moving in her own life, too. Though she was still getting out of Dodge in her RV as necessary, she was settling down, and settling in, in a village where she felt "protected," "looked after," and "loved." In the past she had always run back to LA whenever life got tough, but now she found solace away from home—ironically in a place less than fifteen miles from the small city, Ottumwa, Iowa, where she had been raised. Now, instead of running for help, she was able to give to others something of the stability she craved, in addition to offering them a slice of Middle America's ultimate comfort food.

Winters spent in the American Gothic House kitchen allowed the pie lady to turn her life back into art, rather than accept the maudlin passivity of a life that felt like it was forever spiraling out of control. At the same table where she rolled out dough and peeled apples with a paring knife to pass the sleepless nights, she fashioned her memoir of grieving and healing, *Making Piece*. When the book hit the shelves in 2012 she worried that locals would turn their noses up at its confessional flavor along with its occasional cursing and unapologetic recounting of one-night stands, but they didn't, at least not completely. "I'm surprised I haven't pissed a lot of people off," the pie lady says now, mentioning that even the folks at the town's senior center tolerated the "racy bits" baked into her autobiography. In particular, the author felt anxious about the book's unflattering portrayal of her childhood home, Ottumwa. "I was like, 'It's gross. I'll never come back here again. It's deserted and who would ever want to live here.' Oh my god, I can't believe they're not sending me death threats but . . . you know, if I had to move after [the book was published] I would have moved. I'm just going to tell my story, and if you don't like it you don't have to read it. . . . I don't need anyone's approval."

Much like the maestro who made her rental home famous, Howard has learned to champion her home state while still critiquing it. "Seven years ago my friends had sincerely pitied me for what they called my 'exile' in Iowa," Wood recalls in his 1936 book *Revolt against the City*. "They then had a vision of my going back to an uninteresting region where I could have no contact with culture and no association with kindred spirits." Rather than lose his critical edge by becoming a "mere eulogist" for the home region he loved sufficiently to return to it, Wood pledged to keep his artist's spirit alive by also being what he called its most "severe critic."

The similarities between the privacy-loving pie lady and the painfully shy Gothic painter—Howard and Wood—are sufficiently uncanny as to suggest parallel lives. First, there are the obvious affinities. Both were born and raised in small river cities in eastern Iowa, communities from which they consistently felt alienated or apart. Both Howard and Wood spent time living in Germany before returning to Iowa (Howard married in Germany to a German husband and buried her husband there). Both set about cultivating larger-than-life personas as artist-intellectuals with a penchant for speaking their mind, while retaining a strong need for privacy. The death of a loved one with whom they had achieved an uneasy peace compelled both the painter and the pie lady to choose professions very different from those their families might have imagined for them. The demise of Wood's father, John, prompted the Wood family to move from the farm life in rural Anamosa to the city of Cedar Rapids, Iowa, where the young maestro benefited from a bigger stage to showcase his art. Howard had been a high-earning mover and shaker in the publicity and marketing worlds on the West Coast, freelancing for Microsoft and other corporations before sixteen-hour days in front of a computer screen caused her to chuck the corporate world to make pies for minimum wage in Malibu. Neither the painter nor the pie lady thrived holding regular jobs but prospered mostly when working by and for themselves. Both predictably floundered when constrained by institutional or corporate mores and mandates. At the Gothic House their biographical synergies blend still further, from their shared need to work with their hands at quintessentially tactile professions, to their penchant for making their respective art wearing denim overalls.

Like Howard, Wood would never have traveled to this neglected town on the banks of the Des Moines River had it not been for friends in high places who sensed artistic promise in what many perceived as a backwater village. In the summer of 1930 Cedar Rapids, Iowa, gallery owner Edward Rowan announced his intention to extend the bustling arts scene of that city one hundred miles south and west to Eldon, home of aspiring young painter and Grant Wood disciple John Sharp. With help from the town's boosters and burghers Rowan rented a five-room house on West Elm Street for exhibition and art classes for a fraction of what it would have cost in Cedar Rapids. Then as now, Eldon's appeal lay not just in its picturesque location, but in its relative isolation. Rowan's aim was both ideological and egalitarian; the mission, as the *Ottumwa Courier* put it, was "to show that the small Midwestern community, entirely isolated from certain contacts, will yet respond most heartily to them when the opportunity for appreciation of the fine arts is given."

By the end of August, Rowan deemed his experiment in arts outreach a success. Despite unusual summer heat he reported that his satellite gallery on Elm Street had attracted more than a thousand visitors, including many locals. Wood studied many homes on his sojourns to Eldon, and actually painted the gallery house on Elm Street. Only after seeing what would become the American Gothic House did he recognize what he had been looking for all along. Rowan later explained to a group of art enthusiasts that "the idea had been revolving in the artist's mind for several years— but he needed the particular impetus which he found in Eldon." Wood found himself mesmerized by the home's incongruous architecture, his eye lingering on the Gothic window in the second-story gable in what was otherwise an unadorned home. He made a sketch of the site, one whose weeds, unkempt grass, and overgrown trees suggested that the house had been poorly cared for. On returning to Cedar Rapids, Wood removed the weeds and trees from the foreground and replaced them with the figures of a stern, upright, unsmiling man (holding a rake at the time rather than a pitchfork) and a similarly unsmiling younger woman. Wood convinced his dentist, Dr. McKeeby, and his sister, Nan, to pose as the man and woman, assuring his models that he would take pains to paint them in such a way as to protect their anonymity.

In depicting the proud pair the painter hoped to make a statement about permanence itself, as it was convention, according to Wood biographer Wanda Corn, for men and women in the pioneer period to pose for photos or portraitures with the tools of their agrarian trades, whether rifle, rake, shotgun, or scythe. Another Wood biographer, Steven Biel, writes that the sternness of the homesteaders' pose, like the permanence of a photograph, served as a poignant counterpoint to the precariousness of a pioneer existence. Wood finished the canvas in less than three months, entering it into the Art Institute of Chicago's Forty-Third Annual Exposition, where he won the bronze medal from the jury and sold the painting back to the Art Institute for $300.

While the canvas's fame grew with each passing year, the house that had been its model suffered, as the tall weeds and grass that greeted the artist in 1930 reclaimed the property by the early 1970s. Meanwhile, *American Gothic* cemented Wood's reputation as a painter of the inwardly dark intermingled with the outwardly domestic. Although the maestro kept his own inner turmoil far from the public eye, his psyche crept into his paintings, not just in self-portraits, but in paintings such as *Death on Ridge Road*, a chilling rendering of a head-on collision of a truck and two hearse-like cars in the split second before death comes.

While Howard had been the juror, rather than the judged, in a state fair pie-making contest, the promise of competition had drawn her out of mourning. One of her first ports of call during her reunion tour with her home state of Iowa was the Canteen, the Ottumwa restaurant where her father once treated young Beth and her siblings to their first tastes of banana cream pie. As coincidence would have it, Beth's father, like Wood's real-life model for the pitchfork-wielding man, worked as a dentist in small-town Iowa. Now, when she makes the fifteen-mile drive there from Eldon to shop for pie ingredients she occasionally runs into people who knew her as a girl. "That's not going to happen for me anywhere else in the world," she tells me. "I didn't grow up anywhere else. I grew up in Ottumwa, Iowa. And that's the only place that could ever happen, where people say . . . I knew your grandparents. Oh, your dad was my dentist? I still have the crown he put in my mouth forty years ago. . . . That little touchstone now and then I still find pretty comforting."

Writing her memoir over the long Heartland winter helped the pie lady view her native region in a more generous light. She realizes that her life, or anyone's life for that matter, is "not about perfection," but about rolling up one's sleeves to shape something sweet into being. As she has learned teaching pie-making classes in the American Gothic House kitchen, pie and the emptiness it satisfies serve as metaphors for all kinds of feelings— pain, loss, grief, remorse, and perhaps especially, guilt, a feeling the pie lady felt intensely in the months following her husband's untimely death. That first winter of pie-making and memoir-writing helped her achieve self-forgiveness, though she insists her story is as much about sadness as it is about redemption. "Mostly it's about my grief over the loss of my husband," she tells me. "Ultimately, it's not about Eldon. It's about how I got through a very dark, dark time in my life. Still getting through it. . . .

I found my way back to my roots as a process. This house just happened to be for rent, and I just happened to see the sign . . . you know, the fork in the road."

Howard finds that grief draws people to her rather than pushes them away. After years of group counseling the pie lady believes that bereavement is a magnet—attracting the legions of the lost and lonely-hearted eager to offer their own stories as soon as they learn that you, too, belong to the fellowship of sufferers. It's what makes the widow and widower such compelling figures in life as in literature. Stripped of their previous life and their "other half," the widow/widower cautiously opens a door by which serendipity enters. Whether they are a widow/er in wanting, or a widow/er in waiting, tragedy places the bereaved on a transformative path. Many who attend Howard's how-to-bake-a-pie classes or public-speaking engagements are seeking exactly the kind of spiritual healing the pie lady felt when she ditched her dot-com job to stick her fingers in the dough. Baking one's way out of personal darkness is no different in spirit than exercising one's way out of despair or meditating to achieve self-repair and renovation. The food and fellowship baked into pie foster a kind of culinary community halfway between the comforts of the quilting bee and the sustenance of the Heartland hot-dish potluck.

All of which, paradoxically, leaves the Midwest's priestess of pie feeling hungry and depleted herself, such that even when one of America's most iconic houses fell into her lap, and even after her furniture fit perfectly and most of her closest neighbors greeted her gratefully and with open arms, the pie lady never really intended to stay in the American Gothic House. She bought a warm coat for that first winter when air temperatures dropped to ten below zero, and kept her own fires stoked by baking and writing until the brighter days of summer introduced her to new friends and customers. And, just as they had for Rowan's gallery in 1930, the citizens of Eldon rose to the occasion, surprising the founder of the Pitchfork Pie Stand by buying not just single slices but whole pies, then staying for coffee.

Now, however, the novelty of living inside one of the region's signature spooky houses has begun to wear off. Some of the locals who bought whole pies and stayed to swap scuttlebutt in the honeymoon period have since been displaced by the rising number of demanding and occasionally boundary-crossing out-of-town visitors. The pie lady has woken up to men on Harleys peering through her lace curtains and to interlopers walking shamelessly past the big sign that screams "Private Residence," demanding to see the inside of the iconic house at all hours. Along the way Howard has earned profits sufficient in a single summer weekend to pay her monthly rent, and at other times, like today, been left with more unsold pies than she can reasonably find a home for. The capriciousness of midcontinental weather has prompted her to bring her patio tables inside, allowing customers to have their piece in her air-conditioned living room. Still, she must take care to arrange the tables in such a way as to block any intrusion into the rest of her off-limits living space. Now, her biggest problem isn't getting the word out about her weekends-only West Coast–style pop-up pie stand, but in helping others understand that she needs a break from donning the overalls and gingham apron to play the role of Ms. American Pie. Howard has hired four people to help on busy weekends—two assisting in the kitchen and two more, local teenagers, working the door, but it's still not enough to beget the head-and-hands-balanced life she longs for. The seasonal pie stand, she claims, has become the "dominant force" in her life and "too much" despite being open only about ten hours a week, twelve weeks per year.

Not long ago Howard's parents visited their daughter in what they promptly declared was her cutest home ever. Assisted by the visitor center they happily dressed the part of the man and the woman in Wood's painting and even took a brief memory-lane trip to the diner where father first introduced daughter to the culinary delight that would one day become her salvation. Still, after the feel-good moments were over, the pie lady's parents were curious to know how much longer their daughter intended to stay, two thousand miles from their oceanside apartment in Redondo Beach. Howard surprised herself with her answer, as she surprises herself now in telling me that she never really liked the West Coast as much as she thought she did. Portland, for example, was the hip city she once though she couldn't do without, though now she feels otherwise. "I can't stand the gray, dark, drizzly, damp bone-chilling weather. It just does nothing for me. . . . There's something about the . . . blue skies and puffy clouds here. The fertility. And green all around you."

For now Howard is happy to take it one year at a time. "I see myself here in another five years," she tells Kevin and me while busying herself about the kitchen. "Life unfolds regardless of what you say you want. . . .

I didn't know my husband was going to die at forty-three. That turned my word upside down. I don't know what else is going to happen, and how it's going to affect me and affect how I feel about being here. . . . What if a parent gets sick? I love it here, but the more my story gets out the less privacy I'm going to have." Still, like taking the first step into a haunted house, she tells us there's "no going back."

With the *CBS This Morning* story getting the word out nationally, Howard's literary coagent is attempting to sell movie rights, a financial windfall the pie lady would welcome if it landed at her doorstep. "I feel like I have a brand here that may be valuable to somebody," she insists, broaching the subject of sponsorships or in-kind donations by corporations such as Maytag, who manufacture the appliances her kitchen requires. She wants to better compartmentalize and monetize, too, leaving the pie-baking and pie-selling to someone else in order to focus more on her baking classes and her TEDx-styled public-speaking gigs showing how others can make peace—and piece—in their lives. And there's a new book brewing, a sequel, for which she hopes to travel around the world sharing her piece-making wisdom while visiting places like Greece and Italy that helped birth the culinary art form. Like the maestro Grant Wood traveling to Europe to learn the techniques of the Old Masters she wants to paint a path back to the roots of her craft.

"People really glommed on to my story," she says, exhaustion creeping back into her voice as, outside, the sun begins to drop beneath the tree line. "I wasn't expecting that. Then they kept glomming on. The story is still very much alive . . . people are still very much interested in it. . . . In some ways it's good and bad. The grief part of it is still there. It's never given me a chance to leave that grief behind."

The pie lady yawns, excusing herself briefly while suggesting that Kevin and I climb the quirky flight of stairs to see the famed Gothic window tucked into the gables. We're forced to duck as we ascend, the old floorboards creaking under our weight until finally we stand up straight in the undersized, sparsely furnished loft that feels as hot and stale as a farmhouse attic. "It's glorious," I hear myself saying when finally I come to stand in front of the famous floor-to-ceiling pane of glass, more to myself than to Kevin, though he agrees. For the moment we stare silently out at the grounds of the visitor center below, as if memorizing the scene to make a painting of our own one day, one made from the inside looking out.

Perspective, as the painter knows, is everything.

Our visit to the inner sanctum is brief, affording us each a moment alone with history, and for the pie lady downstairs, our temporary absence means a rare moment alone with her thoughts in a house she lives in like a modern-day fable or cautionary tale. Clambering back downstairs to the sweet-smelling kitchen I excuse myself for a moment to retrieve the copy of *Making Piece* I've brought with me for the pie lady's autograph. Walking across the sunbaked lawn to the parking lot I'm glad to be free of the house's gravity. After spending a whole afternoon with Ms. American Pie I can feel the curse as well as the blessing. The house doesn't bespeak a bad energy, but like someone else's life, it's palpably different being inside of it, bearing its weight, than to view it from afar. By the time I've returned to the house and Howard has penned her inscription I'm ready to leave, walking past the shuttered visitor center without stopping to don the clothes required to play the part, refusing the temptation to bring Wood's tart, down-in-the-mouth ghosts back to life. I'm glad to be following my own life recipe, and no one else's. The evening, agreeably mild, promises badly needed rain.

Once home, I watch the *CBS This Morning* piece, curious to see what correspondent Michelle Miller made of her time at the American Gothic House. The television crew spent days in town to distill four-and-half minutes of video wherein Eldon itself receives only the most passing attention as "a town that has seen better days." Miller packages it as the story of a woman who, "after a long trip in the fast lane," retreated to small-town Middle America. When the segment finishes playing, the *CBS This Morning* anchors claim their own individual takeaways: one is surprised to learn that the "spinster" woman in Wood's picture is a daughter rather than a wife; another by the fact that "pie can change your life"; and the third by "the notion of tragedy . . . where do you go to seek some relief and some sense of change from grief?"

A little over two years after my visit Howard moved out of the American Gothic House, informing her followers on social media that she would have loved to stay but that the "pressures that came from living in a tourist attraction" wore her down. She had, she said, become a tourist attraction within a tourist attraction. Her hunch about her decreasing amount of space and solitude had been spot-on. She had been right about everything in fact—including her habit of running back to LA whenever life grew dark and the way forward proved uncertain.

Meanwhile the Grant Wood revival continues apace with an exhibit at the Whitney Museum of American Art in New York City entitled *Grant Wood: American Gothic and Other Fables*. Curator Barbara Haskell, the *Wall Street Journal* reports, aims to reveal "the complexities of the Iowa-born Wood" while suggesting that that his most famous portrait held "an undercurrent of 'American Horror Story.'"

"You look at it and you get a smile, but then you look at it a second time and it's very menacing," Haskell says. "The farmer looking straight at you with that pitchfork. . . . It's kind of: 'Don't enter here.' . . . And then the woman is looking sideways in a very nervous, anxious way." Wood's portraits and landscapes, Haskell claims, have "something solitary and alienated about them." Even Wood's unsmiling self-portrait, featuring the artist's sideways glance from behind his trademark round spectacles, signals darker currents roiling underneath.

After moving out of the American Gothic House Howard returned to her old haunts in and around LA, living in Redondo Beach for six months before fulfilling the pie-in-the-sky bucket-list promise she intimated during my visit to Eldon. Leaving her terrier in the care of her good friend Doug, a Midwest farmer and one-time love interest, the pie lady set off on a months-long "World Piece" tour, making pies and teaching others to heal from Auckland, to Sydney, to Bangkok, where, finally forced to rest with a head cold, the voice of her dead husband came to her from beyond the grave to say, "I'm sorry I wasn't a better husband. You should find another man."

In her blog the pie lady describes the exact moment when, returning to Doug's farm to pick up her dog, she realizes she has finally found a place to rest: "With its original wallpaper and crown molding, [it] is every bit as quirky and charming—and old—as the American Gothic House. But it is not a tourist attraction. It sits on 1200 acres surrounded by crops and cows (instead of mean neighbors!), and offers a luxury I had been missing: *privacy*."

Despite her newfound seclusion, death and loss have continued to pursue the pie lady: the gruesome killing of her terrier Daisy at the hands of coyotes in Texas, and the passing of her father—the man who first taught her the joy of pie—in California. But she has found love, too, marrying grief and jubilation just as the Greeks paired their gods Eros and Thanatos, one the life-giving generative force, the other the so-called death drive. And as she walks down the dusty gravel roads of her new farm home— sometimes alone in grief, sometimes companioned in joy, she realizes she is holding hands not with one, but with both. And though she makes more words these days than sweet desserts, the pie lady understands better than ever the truth in the old aphorism Grant Wood's Gothic sensibility wholly embraced: *Life is short. Art is long.*

THE CASKET-MAKER'S SON

"Death has always been around for me," Ross McIntire, the casket-maker's son, tells me over lunch at an upscale sandwich shop in Naperville, Illinois. Happy chatter fills the air around us in a town known for its shiny, happy people—a city recently named the wealthiest in the Midwest with a population over 75,000.

"Rambling Man" plays in the background as we settle into a booth by the window, and yet, contrary to the song du jour, Naperville is an emphatically settled place. The village on the banks of the DuPage River ranks as one of *Money* magazine's and *Kiplinger's* best small cities in the country, boasts the nation's number one public library, and is just an easy train ride away from some of the Heartland's best theaters, Steppenwolf and the Goodman, not to mention iconic sketch comedy at Second City. By all rights it should be perfect digs for an aspiring young actor and playwright like Ross McIntire, and yet here he is, deep in his sandwich, talking about how he doesn't belong here, even after the successful debut of his one-act play about small-town life, *Blight*, at North Central College where he has recently completed a theater major. It was there, several years earlier, that I first met the casket-maker's son.

Up until his recent graduation, Ross wore the cap of college student— a young man who, if you saw him kvetching over a caramel macchiato while reading Kerouac's *Dharma Bums* at the local indie bookstore with his Shaggy from *Scooby Doo* facial hair and his dark-rimmed Buddy Holly glasses, you might mistake for a trust-fund hipster. Truth be told, Ross is a sojourner here, not unlike me. Both of us are here chasing a professional dream; both of us are strangers in the strange land that is this prosperous, exceedingly well-educated suburb on the far western fringes of Chicagoland.

Home for the casket-maker's son is Galva, Illinois, an hour and a half west—a town whose population in 2010, at approximately 2,500, is less than its population in 1900. Conversely, for the last four years home-away-from-home has been a thriving technoburg of approximately 150,000 souls whose recent preternatural growth has turned it into Illinois's fifth largest city. Today we are companionably munching in a municipality ideally located along the Illinois Tollway and the Illinois Research Corridor, a place blessed with a booming population of educated immigrants. Home for Ross, by contrast, is a place roughly 97 percent white with nearly 20 percent of the population over the age of sixty-five. In short, if your family is in the death-services industry, Galva, Illinois, is a capital place to do business.

Given its youthful demographic, it's easy to cast Naperville in the starring role of Life, with a capital L, with just over five percent of the population over sixty-five and nearly 40 percent under the age of twenty-four. Galva, by extension, seems typecast as Death, and yet for Ross the allegory is not so simple. The trouble is, while the casket-maker's son appreciates his four years living in Naperville as a college student, the place is alien to him in many ways. To illustrate the geodemographic differences between here and home, he tells the story of a friend from nearby Lombard, Illinois, nearer still to Chicago, who stood, mouth agape, when she learned that Ross and his family actually dried their clothes on a line growing up—a clothesline he and his father made themselves out of angle iron and U-bolts.

Our conversation is therapeutic for him, I can tell, providing a platform to express the many not-so-little things that have been niggling at his subconscious during his stay here. "There's a lot of things I notice and think about that other people don't." He pauses, looks me straight in the eye, before concluding, "I don't really belong anywhere." From the mouth of any other twenty-something, I would suspect self-dramatizing hyperbole, but from the casket-maker's son I sense genuine befuddlement born of a liminal status coupled with a sincere desire to find his place in the world. He knows he *should* want to be a part of the Life embodied by the parade of happy and healthy people passing outside our window seat—the legions of young and upwardly mobile—but something doesn't feel authentic to him about joining their club. So he resists, mostly. Ross tells me the story of his first trip to Naperville on a long-ago college visit. His brother, six years his senior, had come along and, when the moment was right, pulled his younger brother aside to remind him, "Nobody knows you here. You don't have to be you anymore if you don't want to."

"He said you can be whoever you want to," Ross reiterates to me now, "and I said, 'But I *don't* want to.' Granted, I tried for a little bit, and thought maybe there's something to it. But eventually I realize my knee-jerk answer was right. I shouldn't be someone else."

The casket-maker's son made a few compromises along the way; he earned his theater degree, agreed to get a professional headshot, and conceded to auditions when representatives from Chicago's Goodman and Steppenwolf Theaters visited campus. But in nearly every other way, he has stayed true to the wonderfully odd, eccentric, admittedly strange boy from Galva. Ross still prefers his whiskey out of a jar and never could abide by the conspicuous consumption of the place he called home-away-from-home during his four years of college. He calls the self-conscious teens known for hanging out on Washington Street "little idiots" and captures their je ne sais quoi this way: "One of their parents drives them out in an Escalade and they all get out with their credit cards and cell phones at age fourteen, then go and loiter at the Barnes and Noble." By contrast, fun for the casket-maker's son at the same age back home in Galva consisted of riding with friends and their mom in a minivan to the neighboring town's Pizza Hut.

Ross straddles two very different worlds—one a booming technoburg, the other a corn country town many feel is slowly dying—yet doesn't belong to either one. Like someone in limbo, or purgatory, he feels caught betwixt and between. Given his Gothic bent, it makes sense to compare his predicament to the current zombie meme—how it's possible to be living and dead all at once, doomed to wander without belonging. Ross is damned if he does and damned if he doesn't. If, after spending the time and money to acquire an expensive education, he goes home and stays, he sells himself short, and quite possibly disappoints his parents, who have high hopes for their talented, self-aware son. If he leaves home, he's a traitor and a sell-out to the little whistle-stop that "brung 'im."

A case in point is the casket factory maintenance worker for whom Ross served as an assistant when he was in college, and who derided him as an overeducated big-city boy even though the casket-maker's son had come home to work for the summer. "He just gave me hell to no end," Ross recalls, shaking his head at the irony. "I was down in a pit digging sludge from an old industrial washer for steel parts and he says, 'Gettin' your hands dirty for this one, aren't cha, city boy?' And I said, 'You can't even see out of your left eye.'" Characters like this summer supervisor—who'd had his retina eaten away by a parasite—populate not just Ross's stage dramas, but his real-life existence. Factory work has schooled him in a particular kind of fatalistic lesson—that life can be awfully tough; that supervisors can lose an eye and still somehow keep one on you.

It's been the women on the assembly line that have been the most supportive of Ross's decision to educate himself, and the least likely to tease him for becoming a city boy. Ross tells me that in quiet moments they often express to him the sincere wish that they'd had the opportunity he has had. "Not with a sense of resentment," he adds, "but with a rueful quality of 'Oh, if only I had taken that opportunity. Be glad you did,' they say. But there are people are very hateful that you've done something that they couldn't or just didn't do."

The words the casket-maker's son chooses arrive infused with death and dying. He tells me that a recent research project will be "the death of him"; he declares that Galesburg, a western Illinois railroad and college town where his brother practices law, is experiencing a "forty-year death rattle." Ross's family owns the Dixline Corporation, the world's largest manufacturer and finisher of decorative casket hardware. His uncles actually own the place; his father manages, and his mother, on whose side of the family the casket-making business resides, works in the office. Dixline boasts corporate offices, two manufacturing facilities, a laboratory and waste treatment facility, and a warehouse operation in Galva as well as a warehouse operation in Indiana and sales offices in England and Malaysia. Relocated to Galva in 1924, Dixline Corporation is privately owned by the Thomson family, Ross's mother's people. The casket-maker's son has been working at the family business since he was thirteen, starting with the smaller jobs before graduating to operating the large presses that have several hundred tons of force behind them. At one time or another nearly everyone in the family has worked at the plant, including his older brother and younger sister.

Death, along with parents who were, as he puts it, "adamant that I embrace my individuality and whatever strangeness I possess, and never give in to the status quo," have lent my interviewee a maturity well beyond his years. In a way Ross thinks like an old person; he's deeply circumspect and prone to long bouts of storytelling that sometimes lose track of both time and listener. Spending an afternoon in his company is a bit like whiling away the hours talking with an old soul. Several times during our conversation I have to remind myself that the casket-maker's son is a Millennial, and a full generation younger than I am. In part I'm looking for Ross to tell me how he became the way he is—the most unique, stand-out individual of his age I've ever met, by a long shot—imbued with a quirky kind of fatalism one would expect from someone thirty years his senior. I have my theories: a family that has encouraged his critical thinking and been generous with their words and stories; an exposure to the wide world of workers on the factory floor who assemble the hardware his family ships around the world. All this comes back to death, and his clan's unique relationship to it.

"Growing up it was, 'Of course you're doing to die,'" he explains to me. "We make boxes they put dead people in to make them look pretty. I've never looked at death as something terrifying or something I should feel apprehensive about. I look at it as something that will happen to everyone. It's the only thing you can be certain of. People say death and taxes . . . but you can avoid taxes." Ross's is a wry, morbid sense of humor, but he comes by it honestly. His mother's people were a part of the group of Swedish dissidents who founded the nearby utopian community Bishop Hill under the leadership of Eric Jansson. Jansson's split with the Church of Sweden's brand of Lutheranism in the old country was filled with such animosity that he condemned his motherland to "eternal damnation" when he left for Illinois in 1846, taking approximately 1,200 followers with him. Jansson hoped to set up a pious, God-fearing utopian community, a "New Jerusalem" in the American Midwest, but he himself seemed doomed to bitter conflict, in the Old World as well as the New. Four years after his arrival, "dear leader," as my interviewee facetiously calls him, was shot by one of his disaffected followers, John Root, in the county courthouse in nearby Cambridge, Illinois.

It's a story the casket-maker's son tells with particular zeal, in part because he's fascinated by local lore and family history. The tale also appeals to his sense of the dramatic: it ends with a warm Derringer and a cold body. All told, Ross's family's historical connection to the dissident utopianists suggests the metaphysical machinery by which a certain strain of fatalism can be absorbed almost genetically. When a family or a community evinces a deeply contrarian streak, that streak often endures. Conversely, if a family or community exhibits a certain talent for conformity, such conventionality often gets replicated generation after generation. To Ross's way of thinking, the fact that many of the dissenters and dropouts from Bishop Hill turned off by the utopianists' revolutionary ideas eventually came to settle in nearby Galva accounts for his town's emphasis on conformity, often at the expense of individual expression.

It's not easy being the casket-maker's son, and Ross isn't sure exactly how he turned into a free-thinker growing up in a town where it was difficult to find kindred spirits outside his family. "At first, mine was an ill-defined strangeness in my formative years . . . twelve and thirteen," he recalls, chuckling ruefully. Uncomfortable in his town and among his peers, the middle child of the McIntires turned inward, becoming a voracious reader. His brother, six years older, had left for college, leaving behind a set of 1980s World Books that Ross browsed whenever he was bored. The color plates of poisonous snakes were of particular interest; Buddhism served as another favorite entry. He didn't feel any special calling to practice but found himself fascinated by the faith's views on life and death. In high school the same "ill-defined strangeness" caused the casket-maker's son to stand out in his class of thirty-two in a depopulating town where the middle and high school had a combined enrollment of around 150 students. "It seemed like mostly elderly people in town. There weren't a whole a lot of children," Ross remembers, adding, "a good five or six students every year would stay in the same class. They just kind of ground to a halt around sophomore year and tumbled back over the hamster wheel."

It wasn't that Ross was a stellar student or a teacher's pet, but he never doubted his ability to matriculate and wasn't much drawn toward the interests of his high school peers, which he describes as "experimenting with their first bouts of methamphetamines and drinking stolen Keystone Original." The casket-maker's son, meanwhile, was reading Descartes and Voltaire and trying to supply for himself the kind of education his high school could not provide. "I felt insane," he remembers. "I felt like my entire life was some strange joke and that eventually my joke would be revealed to me because I found very few people I could ever relate to."

Joining Scholastic Bowl introduced him to the first of his influential friends, Adam Rux, the son of an area funeral director. It was Rux, a senior, who introduced the first-year to three compact discs full of music Ross had never been exposed to given his steady diet of Curt Cobain's Nirvana. "It was him opening my mind to music, first . . . and then reading. In Scholastic Bowl I was always impressed by how much he [Adam] knew about books and literature. I wanted to know as much. He was an artist, and he painted a giant mural in one of the English classrooms that had the great white whale, the *Catch-22* figure, Juliet in her balcony, a raven. . . . It drove me to really want to explore the written word and how it was constructed and why."

The tragic characters Ross came to love in literature, coupled with the exposure to mortality he received at the factory, lent the casket-maker's son a pragmatic view of the ultimate end. "A lot of people . . . had a lot of death around them as children, but for me . . . death paid the bills. It was an employer. It was an employee. It was always there to make sure that there was food and clothing and that the heat was on. . . . Death was always something to rely on." Rux could relate; his own family owned three mortuaries in the Galva-Kewanee area. "Death was something very necessary for them [the Ruxes] to live, too," Ross explains, adding, "that was what made me what I really am . . . this tiny group of people. What I jokingly refer to as 'ex-pats,' who read, who were very well versed in the wider world, and who weren't consumed by the problems of small-town life."

Ross and Rux were town kids, the sons of businesspeople, living in an increasingly service- and industry-based small community, albeit one with persistent agricultural roots. It was this slow sapping of vitality from the town's long-standing industries, and particularly from farming, that caused Ross to see the larger lifestyle around him as reaching its inevitable cultural denouement, if not death throes. Ross tells me the story of Kyle, a school board member, "a farmer relic of an older time," who consistently seemed to resist any attempts at progressive curricular reform. He still savors the tragic irony of the moment when Kyle stood up and told his fellow board members, in Ross's words, "I think we need to pare down our curriculum to the four Rs—Readin', Writin', 'Rithmatic, and Ag." Another time, he recollects, they were decreasing the number of spots on the school board allotted to rural townships, and Kyle stood up to ask why a decades-old apportionment was changing. What, he indignantly asked, had happened to all the farms? Ross picks up the parable here: "A man named Keith turned to him and said, 'Well, Kyle, you bought up all the land and tore the farms down.' It was a really telling quip."

In the nearest college town on Interstate 74, the socioeconomic plight wasn't much better. Ross recalls his grandparents describing nearby Galesburg as taking a "nosedive" beginning in the 1960s and 1970s. His older brother, who practices law there now, has shown Ross postcards of grand old buildings in the "town that once was." His good friend Josh Bailey, who grew up in Galesburg, described to Ross a town that, metaphorically at least, "once had a Main Street paved with gold bricks." Ross is still drawn to the place, just fifteen minutes up the interstate from Galva, for its music and art scene, and for its bygone buildings—old train depots and courthouses and other "beautiful, massive, structures" of grand old civic architecture torn down or otherwise left for dead. "It's not a dead place for culture," he clarifies, "but it's a dead place for money. The industry has dried up, not the people." It's almost as if the town needs to be "retooled," Ross claims. Still, he's drawn to Galesburg as an alternative to Galva, and dares imagine a postcollegiate life there working in the arts, perhaps even in regional theater.

Throughout high school Ross continued to work at Dixline. Death was now not just the subject of dinnertime conversation between his mother and father when they came home from the office, but part of his work life, too.

Handles. Hinges. Decorative pieces. That's the sort of thing they make at Dixline, Ross explains, adding that the Midwest is really "the birthplace of the casket mill." The centrality of the region and its proximity to Eastern markets partly explains its preeminence in the coffin industry, as does its historic abundance of hardwood trees (cherry, oak, and walnut especially) as well as a large population of talented woodworker émigrés from the Amish and Mennonite and Quaker communities. These factors, coupled with the development of the steel and metalworking industries that lent the Rust Belt its name, made for a near-perfect coalescence of casket manufacturers in Indiana and Illinois.

Richmond, Indiana, is the boss of loss, the casket capital of the United States. Richmond is home not only to Richmond Casket—Dixline's principal competition—but also to J. M. Hutton, the company said to be the oldest U.S. casket manufacturer operating in its original location under the same name. The Hutton family still runs the operation that manufactures "virtually any type of casket conceivable out of copper, bronze, stainless steel, cold rolled steel, walnut, cherry, oak and willow." The product line includes children's caskets as well as giant oversize units and the "very popular and distinctive" round end units. Hutton employs over 130 Richmond-area people and boasts over 250,000 square feet of warehouse space, making it a formidable competitor for Dixline, which has under a hundred workers on its payrolls, Ross tells me.

Not far from Richmond is Batesville, Indiana, another town that lays claim to the macabre moniker "Casket Capital of the World." Batesville figures prominently in Susan Neville's book *Fabrication: Essays on Making Things and Making Meaning*. Neville writes:

Casket hardware has to look eternal. It has to be carefully made and carefully inspected. A good casket has to have hinges that won't allow the handles to rattle when the casket's being carried in church. It has to have handles that pull up with a solid thud-like sound, like the sound built into the slamming of a car door, to signal the pallbearers that it's time to come forward. Good hardware has to not catch and unravel the clothes of the living.

Now more than ever, a good casket is no casket at all. Recently Batesville has been manufacturing an increased number of cremation urns, a market segment they have entered aggressively, as a matter or survival. In June 2016 the National Funeral Directors Association issued a press release announcing that for the first time in American history the rate of cremation had surpassed that of burial. The trade organization predicts the trend will quicken in coming decades, projecting that over 70 percent of Americans will be cremated by the year 2030. In Canada, where the rate of cremation already tops 65 percent, the rate is expected to grow to 89.4 percent by 2035. Reasons cited for the move away from caskets and burials include increased cost considerations, environmental concerns, fewer religious prohibitions, and changing consumer preferences.

Those opting for cremation cite "environmental concerns" as the most significant drawback to traditional burial. The Philadelphia Cremation Society lists five eco-friendly benefits. Most involve the smaller footprint and the conservation of resources, but number five on the list is the chance to "choose a functional urn." The bereaved can choose to "upcycle" cremated remains by incorporating them into a functional keepsake, for example. "Have cremated remains turned into art pieces, furniture, cement tiles, hourglasses, or a number of other functional objects," the website helpfully suggests. "These keepsakes can be passed down through generations."

Increasingly, the casket-maker's son and I are fossils to believe in the ancient rite of in-ground burial, finding solace in the idea of our bones, and those of our ancestors', moldering beneath good loam, born to places where finding an affordable burial plot is seen as a right as much as a privilege. Still, the move toward cremation intimates a larger zeitgeist shift away from the theology-minded mortuary practices of the Egyptians, to the recycling- and convenience-minded New Ageisms of Californians, for example, where statewide more than 60 percent choose cremation. Already the rate in coastal counties such as Sonoma and San Luis Obispo nears 80 percent.

Rising rates of cremation mean that no casket company is "too big to fail." As a trend it explains why even companies as iconic as Hildebrand, the holding company for Batesville Casket, made national news in the December 2012 *USA Today* headline "Casketmaker Evolves into Major Manufacturer." At that time, according to the report, Batesville held about

40 percent of the $1.5 billion casket industry. In the third business quarter alone that year sales in Batesville/Hildebrand's funeral services division had dropped off nearly five percent. The Indiana-based company was now making most of its sales in areas "far removed from death" such as:

— Machinery regulating the amount of salt in Fritos corn chips.
— Equipment ensuring M&Ms come out the right green, blue, and yellow.
— Instruments that process salt for winter roads and tools that make sand ripe for fracking.

The industry's rapid evolution means that the casket-maker's son may not have an industry to go back to when, and if, he decides to take up the family trade back home in Galva. "I enjoy the idea of it sometimes," Ross confesses, "knowing I perform a valuable service to society. People will always need boxes. One time we tried making urns for cremations, but that didn't work so well. You can't really mass produce urns in the same way you can casket hardware." Instead Dixline's landing page displays a slideshow of elegantly plated faucets, bathroom fixtures, and door handles. Like Batesville, the company is doing its best to take the know-how from casket hardware and apply it to a broader metal coating industry. "Since 1924 Dixline has been a complete one-stop source for coating/finishing," the company's literature explains, adding, without a whiff of irony, "we are uniquely capable to create, finish, and seal your parts."

And yet for all the necessary diversification, powder-coated towel rings don't fire the Romantic imagination in quite the same way as casket hardware. Poetic sensibilities have always romanticized death, so much so that a 2003 study led by James C. Kaufman, then director of the Learning Research Institute at California State University, San Bernardino, found that the prominent American poets in his study of nearly two thousand writers lived on average just over sixty-six years, compared to nearly seventy-three years for nonfiction writers. "The image of the writer as a doomed and sometimes tragic figure, bound to die young, can be backed up by research," Kaufman concludes in "The Cost of the Muse: Poets Die Young," published in the macabre-sounding journal *Death Studies* in November 2003. Roughly one decade earlier Arnold M. Ludwig, a retired professor of psychiatry at the University of Kentucky Medical Center, reported similar mortality rates in his 1995 book, finding that prominent, published poets, in particular, had an average life span of 59.6 years, compared with 73.5 years for social scientists.

The casket-maker's son's passion is playwriting rather than poetry, though as the Bard's own career suggests, the two can be kissing cousins. It's a chicken-and-egg argument really. Did my interviewee become a writer because of the self-awareness elicited by his family's exceptional profession? Or did his sensibilities as a writer make him more prone to see the romance inherent in death, and in his clan's death-services profession? In his last college literature class, Ross wrote a take-home final on the subject of death as manifest in the popular young adult title *The Book Thief*. In it he concluded that his family's chosen vocation had made him unafraid of dying. The only time he felt a creeping sense of mortality was when his parents arranged to have him spend a few days making hardware for the infant caskets the company custom builds. "These are made for people who never see life," he tells me. "Making those really gives you perspective that life is something that . . . for some people never really happens."

His parents made sure that each of Ross's siblings had the same life-altering experience, but otherwise were content to let the casket factory teach their youngest son organically, in time. He was allowed to roam unsupervised, to meet and mingle with the workers on the floor, and to tagalong with management. He remembers one particularly gifted riveter, Val, who put together the arms on casket hinges as if she had been born for the task. She was such a maestro, in fact, that arm-assembly soon became her exclusive practice. "My parents put me in these places because they wanted me to slowly learn that I was not supposed to come back," Ross explains. "I was never supposed to resign myself to thinking that I had to work there, which didn't stop me from wanting to."

Many if not most of Ross's most talented and interesting peers long ago left for Chicago or Peoria, including Adam Rux and another of his good friends on the high school Scholastic Bowl team—this one the class valedictorian and, says Ross, resident dope dealer. A case in point is the McIntires' neighbor back home in Galva. "He's very much Chicago now. He comes back. He brings his green bud and notions of philosophy and new music, and laments having to stay there, in Galva. He lives across the street from me. I can't imagine how someone just severs something. There have been times when I wasn't feeling that great about it. I tried, but I eventually realized that if I wanted to maintain any sense of self I had to continue to remember who I was and how that influences who I continue to be if I'm ever going to try to make some final product of a person later in life."

It seems fitting that the casket-maker's son would think of his life-in-progress as an object of manufacture and assemblage, of making the best of the tools and materials given. At the moment, writing is what Ross enjoys most, but with a big job search and subsequent relocation decisions looming on the horizon, he doesn't feel as if he has the focus for scribbling out dramas beyond those he is currently living. As he considers an uncertain economic and geographic future, he's guided by his parents' reminders that he mustn't ever feel ashamed to come home. Ross has heard it so much he can recite their sentiments to me verbatim: "We don't want you to work in the factory your whole life, but if you need to come home don't feel as if you can't."

It's a mixed message received by many young people raised in agrarian communities in the Midwest. Parents want to empower their high-achieving children to leave in order to achieve their full economic and personal potential. On the other hand, they want to leave the door open for them, and the light on, should they ever opt to return in times of trouble. For his part Ross suspects his parents have empowered him to leave because they see their own decision to return to Galva as a mistake. "My mother never said this to me, but the way I think she looks at it is that they gave up. They took the easy way out and went home to her parents and a job. They moved in next to her parents. . . . They thought it was a great place to raise family, but then they realized it's not a great place to have a life. It's rather isolated." I point out that it's only an hour and a half by train to Chicago from Kewanee, "but it's still Galva," he counters, "and no matter how much I appreciate having grown up there and everything I ever learned from the people around me, I think they wish they would have raised us elsewhere."

To Ross's way of thinking, people who've never lived it tend to romanticize what he calls the "agrarian lifestyle"—in their eyes, a bucolic, unchanging small-town life populated by prosperous farmers and thriving small businesses. Ross sees things differently, describing it as a "harrowing" life full of economic uncertainty, not knowing from day to day if the weather is going to cooperate with bringing in the crop or whether people are going to continue to want to bury their dead in the boxes the family business provides. "That's becoming a problem now," he confides. "It used to be, 'Of course they are [going to be buried].' Now cremation is on the rise." It's not that his family's enterprise is in immediate danger, but that things in the death-services industry are changing rapidly. The casket-maker's son puts it this way: "There's the question of how long it will be viable enterprise for a town of 2,500 to have a specialty shop. There's only one other place in the country that does what we do. . . . And while that's kept us alive for as long as it has, it's unclear how long it's going to continue to do that."

As our lunch nears its inevitable end, Ross gifts me a copy of his script, *Blight*, the one largely based on growing up in Galva. He's convinced the play wouldn't fly back home, or in the nearby college town of Galesburg. "Not that I depict people in my town as rubes necessarily," Ross cautions as I eagerly flip through the pages of his one-act, "but I portray the town in a kind of a negative light. I portray the small town as some relic of the industrialized past of our nation that would be better off just letting it die." He stops to rifle through the manuscript in my hands until he finds exactly the right passage, at the very end of the play, which seems to sum up both his conundrum and blessedness. He reads the swan-song lines spoken by the play's stage manager of sorts, a small-town bartender, aloud:

> Well, fortunately the world doesn't work like that. The earth turns and the sun burns without our consent, and we can watch the moon through its phases but there's nothing we can do about it. If it decided to fall one day, or anything decided to wipe us from this rock, it'd happen. Beyond this place there is naught but dark and cold, an uncaring void. Yet we burn anyway. Isn't that cool?
>
> Places like this town continue to exist. Factories may close, money is lost, lives are changed, but the place and the people remain. They aren't moved. That's what's special, that people continue without the majority of their fellows even noticing. That seems to be the business about smaller towns now.

The casket-maker's son doesn't want to go home to Galva, not now. Galesburg maybe, which despite its postindustrial economy, has served as a reasonably happy home for his older brother. Galesburg boasts a college, a theater, a health food store, and a dearth of drafty, haunty old buildings a life in Galva has well-prepared Ross to see the potential in. Still, the uncertainty of his pending geographic and professional fates sometimes gets this native son down.

As we stand up to leave, I reassure him that I can relate, that I was once there, too, and maybe still am. I tell him what my father, a fatalist himself, once told me when I was Ross's age—"Don't go down a dark path if you don't have to," and to "keep on the sunny side of life."

Ross just chuckles and says, "That's what my Zoloft is for."

It's that dry, wry, whistling-in-the-graveyard sense of humor again, but he's laughing, and after a moment he turns serious again, insisting I have nothing to worry about. "I have stories left to tell," the casket-maker's son tells me. "There's so much more to be said." And I choose to believe him, and believe in him, in part because I know that real artists—those we studied in literature and art and music classes, those we've grown up with and learned to love—keep on singing, even in the face of death.

7

DEATH BY MAIL

When I hear of the potential closing of a post office (PO) less than ten miles from my door, I locate the U.S. Postal Service (USPS) community meeting location nearest me—Buffalo, Iowa—and make plans to be there in person to hear the death knell. I want to pay respects in what I imagine to be a kind of memorial service for what was once a rock-solid fixture of small-town life. The proposed service reductions, part of the vaguely nefarious-sounding Phase 1 of USPS's POStPlan, are slated to impact over thirteen thousand post offices nationwide.

In 2011 the Postal Service shuttered more than 460 mostly rural offices in a series of closings disproportionately impacting Middle American states. With several hundred post offices facing reduced hours or "discontinuance," Iowa's 322 would-be victims placed second only to Pennsylvania's 445. Calculating a post office closure/hours reduction rate per capita reveals a moribund ground zero smack dab in the nation's breadbasket.

Today alone more than twenty small towns will meet with Postal Service representatives to discuss their inevitable downgrading or demise: Boxholm,

Britt, Cincinnati, Mount Auburn Dawson, Hawkeye, Letts, Mystic, Woden, Wesley, Minburn, Williamson, Ottosen, places whose names ring only the most distant bells. Buffalo's 6:00 p.m. meeting is the last of the day, and judging by the number of parked cars lining the city streets, today's wake will be well attended.

An Art Deco–styled gray brick building directly across from the Mississippi River, the Buffalo Post Office commands the corner at the intersection of West Front Street and Washington, equidistant between Casey's General Store and Judy's Barge Inn. Few post offices in Middle America could rival its view, as Mark Twain's Mississippi lazily meanders westward rather than southward here—one of the few prominent calling cards of this consistently overlooked village. The low-lying land atop which Buffalo sits is both bottomland and borderland, the village of Andalusia sitting immediately across the unbridged river on the Illinois side. By no means is Buffalo bereft, as it boasts its own river beach at Buffalo Shores Park, a beach pub, multiple banks, a community center, an elementary school, and a bevy of river-based recreational activities. The business directory lists a few active cement businesses, tool shops, and metal works, and several rehab centers and chiropractic clinics of the kind that thrive in places where people work hard with their bodies.

I park on Washington Street a half block north of well-trafficked Highway 22 and walk into an undersized post office lobby already packed with the denizens of this river town, population just shy of 1,300. By Heartland standards the city's population, coupled with its proximity to the nearby Quad Cities Combined Statistical Area of nearly a half million people, make Buffalo something less than a far-flung rural outpost. In fact, I can drive from the Buffalo Post Office to the western edge of the Quad Cities in less than ten minutes or travel to the international airport in nearby Moline, Illinois, across the Mississippi River, in under twenty.

At precisely 6:00 p.m. an unnamed representative appears in the foyer. She is late middle-aged and clearly senior in the Postal Service, though her voice cracks nervously as she addresses what figures to be a fractious crowd.

"I'm here to tell you the results of your surveys that you received in the mail," she begins. "We sent out 540 surveys and got 347 back. 312 said, 'Keep the Post Office open, realign the hours.' Twelve people said reduce rural delivery. Nobody asked about the village post office option. . . .

Twenty-three people sent responses in and didn't check anything." We chuckle ruefully at this last bit of news, as Postal Rep presses onward. "Being that we had the response of 90 percent saying keep the post office open and realign the hours, that's what we're going to do."

And just like that ten hours of regular Monday through Friday operating hours have been axed. As of January the post office will be open just six hours a day Monday through Friday, with reduced window hours on Saturday. Postal Rep's declaration takes a moment to register, the tone of our collective murmur suspended somewhere between relief at avoiding complete closure to disgruntled harrumphing at an all-too-predictable loss.

"We have to post a notice in the lobby here in the next seven days," she continues. "That's up for a minimum of thirty days. We're not going to change anything yet this year. . . . It would be safe to say sometime next year. I can't give you an exact date. Before the hours change you will be notified." Emboldened by her assurances that Buffalo will not, in fact, completely lose its services, we're trending toward hostile now, the done-deal, tone-deaf feeling of the decree having unleashed a garden variety of grievances ranging from general protests about the unfairness of it all to throw-them-under-the-bus suggestions of nearby post offices whose hours might be reduced to spare Buffalo's.

Playing the part of teacher to our unruly student, the representative continues, "I just want to remind you why we're here tonight, and that's to give you the result of the survey. . . . Anything else we'll be glad to take your questions and get back to you." She raises a preemptive hand to indicate the day's exercise in quasi-democracy is finished.

"I think it was kinda unfair how you did this," a soft-spoken woman in the crowd says, filling the silence. "You would not believe how many people misunderstood the survey. There's a lot of lines on the survey that people didn't understand what it was saying."

"What this meeting is, again, is just to let you know of the survey results of what we received," Postal Rep reiterates, this time more forcefully. She's adhering to script, though our confusion is understandable. Local TV station WQAD had reported that citizens were "encouraged to bring their completed . . . surveys sent out earlier by the USPS" to the meeting, though, as it turns out, that ship has already sailed.

An older woman says, "You don't want to answer any of our questions, do you?"

"Is this just until after the election, or for the year?" a man asks.

"For this whole year."

"Three hundred and sixty-five days?"

"We're not changing anything until next year to start with."

"In other words you could have just posted this on the window and saved the government all the money to have you come down here," the older woman grumbles.

"In a small town like this you knew the turn-out was going to be large," Buffalo's fire marshal pipes up suddenly, identifying himself belatedly and out of the blue. "We're way over the capacity and technically you should have asked to move the event to the fire station."

"Most meetings only last five minutes. . . . That's why I've been giving you the results of the survey. That's it, and we're going to go back in," Postal Rep concludes. And just like that she makes good on her threat, disappearing behind closed doors to calls of "Ma'am?" and "Could we just talk to you?"

"If the building catches fire and people are trampled to death how would you like to have to deal with that too?" the older woman calls after her.

The representative's unceremonious departure can't help but feel a bit insulting, making of us the metaphoric equivalent of a roomful of jilted autograph hounds confronting a door shut in our face by someone much more important than we could ever be. Most of us have come expecting a listening post, or at least a spirited dialogue on the potential down-grading or death of a vital community institution; instead we're being presented with a fait accompli, not a death certificate exactly but notice of life support.

"I don't know who made up the list [of post offices], but I think they ought to rethink it or hire different people," the older woman grumbles. She's the same who earlier accused Postal Rep of willfully ducking our questions. "And also . . . we asked questions here, and she would not answer, so that's going to show that they're afraid to say anything."

"She didn't have the authority to give answers," someone in the crowd says, coming to her defense.

"She just said she was just here to give the results of the survey. She didn't say she wasn't authorized."

We are people who appreciate at least the illusion of democracy. And to make matters worse the Postal Rep had distributed a sign-in sheet prior to pulling an Elvis and leaving the building. It turns out USPS would like our name, postal address, and e-mail address, presumably to keep us advised of reduced hours to come. Still the solicitation of our personal information on the heels of the unhappy news of service hour reductions evokes a veritable chorus of sour grapes.

"They didn't state that we needed to sign it."

"I don't want my name on there."

"I don't even have a computer."

"There are soooo many old people in this city."

I leave the clipboard unsigned, too, exiting the lobby to a much-needed breath of fresh air and a view of the muddy Mississippi slipping by in the twilight. Reality sinks in—I have driven a long way to attend a so-called meeting that lasted fifteen minutes from start to finish and included no opportunity for feedback on a controversial POStPlan that amounts to palliative care for the nation's small-town and rural post offices, in particular.

I replay the evening's encounter as I walk to my car. I'm convinced that we acted like caricatures of ourselves—Enter ANGRY LOCALS—in what is probably the longest-running public drama in Middle America: suspicious citizens confronting government interlopers. And while I personally did not once raise my voice or threaten or malign, I too had come quietly anticipating trouble. And yet what, beyond the promise of conflict or the slim chance our presence might make a difference, had motivated so many of us to crowd into the lobby? Had we "nice" Middle Americans turned out en masse for a government-supplied catharsis—a chance to bemoan and lament—as part of the ritual emotion-letting otherwise denied us? If our social contract prevents us from yelling at our fellow citizens on Main Street, do we instead leap at the chance to raise our barbaric yawps at visiting government reps and politicians—the secret sauce of political caucuses from Iowa, to Minnesota, to Nebraska? Or are we, deep down, simply a passive-aggressive people, repressing our frustration with never-ending slings and arrows until, unrequited and unlistened to, we act up like pitchfork-wielding villagers in some Gothic horror, projecting our angst, our anger, and our fear of the unknown on some officious outsider.

On the drive home I find myself unable to drill down on my own emotional response. Do I feel merely inconvenienced at the proposed reductions, or something deeper—something like defeated or damned? Am I morbidly curious and also, maybe, a touch embarrassed for us, recalling in particular the moment when the USPS rep announced that nearly 5 percent of us had opened our postal surveys, reviewed them, and inexplicably stuffed them, unmarked, back in the envelope. What demos would do such a thing? And while we're surely entitled to laugh at our own stubbornness or stoicism in the self-effacing way we do, I can't help but begrudge the representative's apparent amusement at our idiocy. Doesn't she know that we are, after all, *the* iconic conscientious Americans, the ones who perennially lead the nation in rates of volunteerism and voter participation? Buffalo's response rate to the postal survey topped 65 percent—a greater turnout than in most elections. In the 2012 presidential elections approximately 57 percent of eligible voters in Iowa cast their vote—fifth nationally—with Minnesota and Wisconsin occupying the number one and two spots respectively. Today in Buffalo we bettered that already excellent rate of participation by nearly 10 percent. So why is it that so many of us left feeling judged and inept?

No one can return government-issued questionnaires like we can, as our census mail-in return rates demonstrate once every decade. The bureau's map of Census Mail Return Rates highlights a topography of Middle American compliance. Here in Scott County nearly 83 percent of citizens returned their census. Only one county in Iowa (Decatur) fell below the national average in rate of survey returns; only two counties in Michigan (Wayne and Marathon) fell below the national average; one in Wisconsin (Milwaukee) and none in Minnesota. Put simply, when Uncle Sam hands out homework, Midwesterners are America's most thorough assignment completers while, as the Census Bureau puts it, "lower mail return rates are common throughout the Sun Belt and rural areas of Appalachia and parts of the Western U.S."—places where suspicion of the government and its motives run higher still.

Are rural and small-town denizens uniquely adept at such acts of citizenship-by-correspondence because so many of us are older and retired, blessed with a largesse of time (nearly 15 percent of Buffalo residents are 65 or older)? Does the citizenry here oblige the government because the government has, at least historically, reinforced its entitlement? Buffalo, like so many Middle American towns with populations under two thousand, is more than 95 percent white, begging the question: Does our reputation for civic-mindedness boil down to an ability to maintain a status quo that has historically enfranchised white landowners at the expense of others? Or, in its own small way, does the Battle of the Buffalo PO embody a conflict more human than historical—a universal protest by the dispossessed against further dispossession?

I'm tempted to cast today's community meeting as a truth-to-power protest, but even that characterization falls short of accurate. Sure, what I witnessed was a fight with the simmering potential to turn into something more menacing, but it had been a bureaucratic war of attrition, the USPS having predetermined the outcome (reduced hours), leaving us, the supposedly empowered citizenry, merely to pick our poison. Would we rather achieve the prescribed reductions by eliminating the post office entirely, shifting to a village post office, or reducing window/retail hours? As America's great middle-of-the-roaders we opted for the compromise rather than the go-for-broke option—reduced hours, please and thank you.

After dinner and dishes at home, I surf the Internet looking for the kind of context I hope will help me better understand the emotions I feel (indignation at what feels like government policies hastening the decline of rural and small-town America again) with a better understanding of the grim financial realities faced by a Postal Service badly out of step with a younger and more diverse America whose postal habits are probably more like my own. If given a choice I pay my bills electronically. And though I receive my mail six days a week via rural delivery, on busy days I can't be bothered to check the day's harvest of bills and junk. Truth be told I could forego the Saturday mail delivery the Postal Service has lately pitched as a cost-saving measure without any real disruption to my life. But I don't want to—my stubborn belief in demographic equity (why should rural and small-town residents bear the brunt of cost-saving measures?) trumping my belief in the collective belt-tightening and all-for-one-one-for-all fiscal prudence Middle Americans are known for.

On the *Daily Yonder* I read the views of postmaster Mark Jamison in western North Carolina, who points out that the provincial post office has long been a fruitful contact point between Americans and their government officials. He describes the occasional services he performs as postmaster—opening jars for those who can't, putting together bicycles for kids for Christmas, filling out money orders for elderly customers, and sorting out medical bills and customer service disputes—that go far beyond the call of duty. I'm wholly sympathetic to Jamison's points, though I have never seen my postmaster perform any such services. Like many Digital Age Americans I'm probably more likely to Google "how to open a sticky jar" than I am to motor in to the PO with my stubborn container of pickles.

And yet, for all the ways in which I am typical of those that love what the post office stands for but increasingly prefer not to affirm that mission with my hard-earned dollars, I have also borne witness to that singular relationship Jamison claims "goes far beyond a customer–vendor relationship." One particularly difficult winter my lane lay buried in snow for a week or more while, unbeknownst to me, a package waited for me at the post office in town. I recall looking out the window one frigid morning to see Chris, the local postmaster, careening his four-wheel-drive SUV toward my house, not via my snow-drifted lane, but via the cornfield immediately adjacent. I almost hugged him when he reached the door with my package, not because I approved of the dangerous gambit, but because he had cared enough to attempt it. At other times I've purchased rolls of stamps from Mark, my rural carrier, by simply leaving cash in the mailbox, thereby saving myself the trip. I like to think that if I didn't pick up my mail for a week or two, Mark might grow sufficiently concerned to check on me. How many anonymous corporate delivery drivers or couriers would do the same?

Or maybe it's better to ask how many should. In allowing me to purchase postal products by mail as an alternative to trekking into town, Mark has saved me a mere three miles (the roundtrip distance between my home and the nearest PO) and all of ten minutes travel time. Had I in fact journeyed to the brick-and-mortar storefront in town, perhaps I would have purchased additional USPS goods and services not available at my mailbox. Maybe I'm selfishly holding on to full window hours and six-day rural delivery not because my life requires such services, but because, like that sweet old lady or gentleman in town, having people wait on me makes me feel valued for once. Perhaps the fact that the post office is saying it no longer has the time and resources to dote on me and millions of other small-town Middle Americans is a good thing, a necessary move away from an unsustainable form of codependence. Still I can't help but worry over the fact that they'll soon be available fewer hours to answer my bell.

The situation isn't much better six miles north of Buffalo in the town of Bluegrass, Iowa, population approximately 1,500, which USPS will soon add to its list of locations under review for reduced hours. Bluegrass is classified as a Level 18—a small to midsized PO managed by postmasters paid at an executive administrative level. Like many post offices of its ilk it very likely operates in the red. According to USPS figures the Bluegrass Post Office reports annual revenue at just over $157,000, which only sounds impressive until one subtracts the annual cost of the leased building (around $15,000) and the salary of the postmaster (postmasters in the area average around $70,000 per year). Add in the cost of utilities and other necessary overhead, and annual revenue is reduced to something closer to $50,000. And because Level 18 post offices usually need several postal clerks and rural delivery carriers in addition to a salaried postmaster, the final numbers predict a sizable loss, even excluding the cost of inventory on hand. And, I remind myself, both Bluegrass and Buffalo boast geographical advantages many small-town post offices would surely die for, what with the ninetieth largest metropolitan area in the United States looming less than fifteen miles beyond their respective city limits, and the spillover wealth and mobility such proximity provides.

The more I ponder the question the more I realize that what to do with a Postal Service on life support amounts to an ethical dilemma. Should the zip code in which a citizen lives determine the level of service offered them by their government? In a world of de facto geodemographic discrimination does rural and small-town America need the equivalent of a *Brown vs. Board of Education* ruling to mandate that government services (social services, health care, postal services, and the like) be equal to those received in better endowed portions of the United States, where higher levels of educational attainment and resulting per capita income make supplying services significantly more profitable? I learn that roughly 30 percent of the residents in Buffalo, for example, have completed some college coursework, but a deeper dive into the data shows that just under 4 percent hold a bachelor's degree while just under 8 percent have obtained an associate's degree. Compare those numbers to, for example, Bettendorf, one of the four eponymous Quad Cities less than fifteen miles away, where approximately 30 percent of residents hold a bachelor's—more than seven times the rate of educational attainment in Buffalo. Bettendorf's median household income, in excess of $75,000, exceeds Buffalo's by approximately $30,000 per household per year. Bettendorf's $30,000 income advantage could buy the average family there roughly 60,000 more stamps per annum than an analogous household in Buffalo. So the question of whether or not a rural or small-town PO should close or downsize due to lack of profitability might reasonably be viewed as a moral question: should customers with less education, and less money, be penalized for representing less profit potential?

To address this and other inequities a group calling itself Iowans for Post Office Services wrote the U.S. Postmaster General in the summer of 2011 to point out that the smallest ten thousand post offices in the nation made up less than 1 percent of the USPS budget. The letter, written on behalf of more than forty communities, including Onslow, the PO whose potential closing had spurred my participation in the community meeting in the first place, hoped to appeal to the USPS's sense of demographic fairness. "Unlike large cities, rural communities face great hardships with the closing of their Post Offices because residents do not have the luxury of going to another retailer that sells stamps or accepts packages," it read. The letter, cosigned by then Iowa governor Terry Branstad and Lohrville, Iowa, mayor Donny Hobbs, asserted the Postal Service's particular responsibility to elderly customers who received vital medications by mail, the kind of customers for whom the post office served as the "primary connection to the outside world." The slow death of the PO in rural communities, the letter implied, would all but kill quality of life for citizens in graying towns like Stratford, Iowa, where fully one quarter of the population was sixty-five or older.

For his audacity in resisting the closing of Lohrville's post office, the Postal Commission solicited from Mayor Hobbs more than twenty pages of written testimony as part of a 2011 congressional hearing on the USPS Retail Access Optimization initiative whose implementation had already resulted in the shuttering of hundreds of rural post offices. As part of the proceedings Hobbs is compelled to offer written, on-the-record responses to the Postal Commission "interrogatory" as well as to deliver congressional testimony under oath while subjecting himself to rigorous oral cross-examination. The interrogatory, published as public record, reveals a contentious back-and-forth in which representatives of the Postal Commission repeatedly ask Hobbs for research and studies to back up claims of his post office's indispensability until, late in the hearing, the exasperated mayor replies, "It would be highly irresponsible for me to spend any of my town money contracting for research and survey work when I can just go down the street and talk to my citizens. I need not study the academic literature to understand what a rural town's identity is. I know it; I experience it every day; and I live it."

However, Hobbs could and did cite in his favor the statistics derived from USPS's own data on mail volumes in Lohrville, which showed that more than two thousand first-class letters, sixty-three priority parcels, and fifty-three money orders had been dispatched during the two-week period encompassed by the study. When divided by the town's population of slightly more than 350, the numbers worked out to one piece of mail or transaction per day for more than half of the town's total population. Asked by representatives of the Postal Service "whether the residents of Lohrville value their elderly neighbors sufficiently to volunteer to conduct postal transactions for them or to make visits to the Post Office in periods of high heat, snow, or ice" if the nearest post office were relocated to Lakeville (10 miles west) or Farnhamville (8 miles east), Hobbs bristles at the implication that his town's denizens don't care enough about their elders to help them make a twenty-minute roundtrip to a relocated post office. He points out that the town's younger residents are hard-working people who already have their hands full with work and family commitments and, further, that the bureaucrats comfortably ensconced in Washington, D.C., have forgotten the severity of midcontinent winters. "Driving 30 miles across country on country roads is not like driving in a city or a suburb," Hobbs reminds them, adding that residents of Lohrville can find themselves snowed in for days at a time and unable to make the lengthy trip to a neighboring town to collect vital correspondence: "Again, this is a good example why the Postal Service was created, is maintained, and remains relevant and why I am doing everything I can to keep my Post Office open."

In the end Mayor Hobbs and Governor Branstad prevailed in their fight, arguing successfully for a six-month moratorium on closings while staking out a position embraced by U.S. senators from rural states on both sides of aisle. Still, despite the stoppage of planned closings, the USPS succeeded in reducing hours at thirteen thousand small post offices across the country from 2012 to 2015, with thousands of postmasters losing their jobs. Lohrville and Onslow, Iowa, two of the post offices flagged for potential closing, found their hours reduced to four per day, Monday through Friday, a partial victory for undersized, underresourced communities fighting more radical reductions or the complete privatization of the Postal Service. Still, Middle America took it on the chin, suffering not just further reductions in government services but a painful public airing, via congressional hearings and in the popular press, of its most insolvable demographic challenges.

Meanwhile the city of Buffalo continued to face challenges that, taken collectively, felt to many like an existential crisis, including the proposed closure and consolidation of its elementary school in 2018 and, in 2017, serious injuries sustained by its beloved police chief Terry Behning after twenty-year-old Logan Shoemaker, high on meth and attempting to elude police after a first-degree robbery in the nearby Quad Cities, ran over Behning while driving a stolen garbage truck in a case ultimately prosecuted as attempted murder.

By comparison with the fifteen surgeries required to get the heroic police chief back up on his feet, the potential closure of a town's school or post office, or both, may not seem like death blows, though the one-two punch can feel like civic erasure. The problem facing Buffalo and small towns like it is not so much the government's reasonable request for one-time belt-tightenings in times of fiscal trouble—such sacrifices as practical-minded communities like these have often made and will make long into the future—but the never-ending nickel-and-diming that feels to some like slow, inexorable demise.

LIFE AND DEATH IN OZ

On paper I am in central Kansas to give a presentation on those brave souls who first settled these far-off Great Plains, but my real purpose is to put my finger to the allegedly limp wrist of north central Kansas, to examine the body, habeas corpus, for signs of life.

Like much of the region known as the "Big Empty," portions of central and western Kansas are experiencing such profound depopulation that they have taken a page from the Homestead Act and begun to offer free land to a new generation of hoped-for homesteaders. The youth out-migration problem here is so pernicious and long-standing that it's now been battled by multiple generations. As far back as 1966 editors at the state's leading newspapers, including the *Lawrence Daily Journal-World*, owned the problem by name in a column entitled "Our Brain Drain." "It has been obvious for some time," the editors wrote, "that Kansas has been financing the education of business and education leaders only to lose them to other states."

In 1966 Kansas finally had the numbers to back up the anecdotal evidence of Brain Drain in the form of a data set from the then-director of the

Center for Regional Studies at the University of Kansas. At the time nearly a quarter of out-migrators left Kansas for nearby Missouri, prompting David Huff to opine, "with lack of opportunities, college graduates have to go elsewhere. Not only is the state losing human resources with potentially high economic values but it is also throwing away an investment that amounts to millions of dollars annually." Forty-some years later, in 2008, the same story was told by NPR's Noah Adams, whose intro intoned, "Young professionals continue to flee places like Iowa, South Dakota, Nebraska, Kansas." Four years before the NPR story hit the airwaves, the book *What's the Matter with Kansas?* by Thomas Frank had become a national bestseller.

I have come to Kansas seeking answers for how to bring a rural town back to life. Specifically, I have come to meet up with the good folks of Tescott, Kansas, population approximately three hundred, whose creative city burghers have offered free land to families willing to build a home on the city-owned lots next to the K–12 school the town has fought to keep. Weeks before my visit, I dialed up the city homepage to find the biggest bolded type reserved for a link reading "FREE LAND." Eventually, I had clicked my way to the eligibility requirements, which state simply that "you must have at least one child age 18 or younger that will be enrolling in the Tescott Public Schools or is preschool age with the intent to enroll upon entering school." The photo of the single, 1,400-square-foot prebuilt "Home for Sale" is dated January 2008. The home is well equipped with niceties such as vaulted ceilings, fireplace with oak mantle, open oak staircase, and ceiling fans throughout. The listing price is just over $169,000.

In advance of my visit I had managed to contact Tescott city officials, though it hadn't been easy. City Clerk Joanna Schwindt's belated reply struck an apologetic chord; the city offices were open on Mondays and Thursdays only, her computer had died and, she informed me, "almost everyone is out harvesting wheat, or has a chore that is connected to the harvest."

Living outside a farm community of less than five hundred people myself, I understood, but something also told me that Joanna wasn't overly keen to talk about the free-land program, though eventually she had opened up enough to relay the basics, writing, "A part of the vision is to encourage growth in our community and enrollment in our schools.

The free land has not attracted any younger families." Still, Joanna had indicated a bright spot in describing another tract of land with lots for sale rather than for free. "That area," she explained, "has proven to be more desirable and there are three new homes built at that location."

I gathered from Joanna's somewhat down-in-the-mouth e-mails that the free-land offer had generated a surfeit of speculative phone calls and e-mails, but not much follow-through. "It may be the economy has played a part in the lack of participation in the Free Land Program," she speculated. "There are established homes available in the area that can be purchased and many people looking to build may decide to purchase a home that is already complete." If I wanted to know more, she would put me in touch with a retired banker in town, Hal Berkley, who had served on the city's Economic Development Board.

Tescott is a dot on the map in the north central part of the state. Its relatively remote geography has proven challenging in the past but, by Great Plains standards, far from insurmountable, as it lays just a half-hour commute northwest of Salina, a major regional center with a population of approximately fifty thousand. Tescott is well served by state and national roads. Kansas Highway 18 runs west–east on the north side of town, roughly a mile and a half from the downtown business district, giving would-be commuters a straight shot into Manhattan, Kansas, eighty miles due east. Interstate 70, accessed via the interchange eight miles south of the city limits, takes residents to the state capital, Topeka, in less than two hours.

It's early June when I visit. The cottonwoods are green, and the wheat is tall and golden and ready for harvest. Unlike the Scottish Highland–like swells of the Flint Hills I drove through to get here, the land on which the town sits is dishpan-flat, and firmly in the death-grip of the Jeffersonian grid. Most of the town exists within the flood plain of the Saline River, which wends a serpentine path though the good loam just south of town. *Cutler's History of the State of Kansas* positively gushes concerning the original tilth of Ottawa County, describing it as "one of the best counties in Central and Western Kansas, having a rich soil, desirable location, being most admirably watered, and possessing a good supply of timber." Historically, this is a farming community, one where families root down deep and keep the land generation after generation. All that is changing, however, and town banker Hal Berkley, whose ancestors from Germany helped settle this place, has picked me up in his air-conditioned truck to take me on a tour of the efforts made by the community to retain and recruit young people in a town whose population struggles to reach three hundred.

Together we turn into an unnamed, unpaved street with a single new ranch home, roughly one dozen raised foundations, and some grass burning up in the Great Plains summer sun. The parcel before us looks as macabre as any new housing development still in its forlorn, unloved, and unlived-in phase: just scorched earth scraped mercilessly flat by earth movers and dozers. Utility boxes and sewer access egresses await the hoped-for influx of neohomesteaders.

Though he lives in one of the many single-story ranch homes in town, Hal speaks like a farmer, deep and slow and considered. He's a big man, sturdily built, and rural Kansas through and through. He's also smart as a whip. He uses words like *animosity* without even pausing and yet still pronounces *school* with an infectious drawl that makes it sound like two complete syllables, *scho-ewl*. School turns out to be the first subject he wants to talk about as he explains how a conservative town like Tescott decided to jump on the free-land bandwagon sweeping portions of rural Kansas. Rather than submit to a consolidation resulting from declining enrollment (graduating classes hover around a dozen here) the tiny yet proud municipality joined with Bennington, Kansas, formed a district, and operated K–12 at both places, bringing the nearby small towns of Culver and Glendale, the latter located eight miles south on Interstate 70, in on the arrangement. The logical thing, my host admits, would have been to have a single shared campus in the center of the county, at Minneapolis, but the towns in question just weren't ready for it, he explains: "There was so much animosity among the people, and we knew if we did that we would die."

Prior to the partnership with Bennington, enrollment in Tescott's school had "slipped a bit," as Hal puts it. The idea for a free-land giveaway represented a recognition of shared vulnerability felt by town and school, the latter of which offered up the free land. The town in turn raised the lots above the flood plain as required by law, and put in electric, water, and sewer. And yet for all this there were no takers. Marquette, Kansas, forty miles south, started their free-land program well before Tescott and, Hal says, got rewarded with a bump in their school-age enrollment. Tescott's timing wasn't quite so fortuitous, as its initiative coincided with the housing downturn of 2007 and 2008. The Great Recession was hard on Tescott and towns like it. With an ever-shrinking percentage of the workforce engaged in agriculture, not even record high wheat prices in March 2008 could keep the city's poverty rates from eclipsing 15 percent.

Given Ben Winchester's and Randy Cantrell's research on Brain Gain across the small-town rural Midwest, it's natural to assume the economic fates of undersized rural towns across the region would be more or less akin to one another: If Redwood County, Minnesota, and others like it in Winchester's and Cantrell's respective home states of Minnesota and Nebraska are experiencing an influx of better-educated, higher-earning thirty- to forty-nine-year-olds—the "Brain Gain" thesis Winchester had argued so passionately and convincingly during our time together in Lamberton, Minnesota—one would imagine Tescott to be the beneficiary of a similar demographic bump. A closer look, however, shows that it and its neighbors in north central Kansas face a far steeper climb. At just under six thousand residents, the population of Ottawa County is little more than a third of Redwood County, Minnesota. Poverty rates in Hal Berkley's city are nearly double those in Lamberton, and the percentage of residents with a bachelor's degree or higher, hovering around 13 percent, lags several points behind Lamberton and about twelve percentage points behind the nearby Salina, Kansas, micropolitan area. Comparing the community's economic indicators to those of Salina, to whom it loses many of the young people who want to remain within a half-hour drive of home, creates a clearer picture of why the town's talented young don't typically choose to root down here. Thirty- and forty-somethings able to buy into the housing market thirty miles down the road will find median home values in Salina twice what they are in Tescott, with the bonus of shorter commute times and a bump in median household income of nearly $8,000 on average. The village's reliably conservative politics may dissuade some progressive young people from staying or relocating, as the Republican presidential nominee has won close to 80 percent of the Ottawa County vote in recent general elections.

Tescott faces daunting climatological and environmental challenges as well, relative to other small rural towns elsewhere in the region. Located near the edge of the comely upland region known as the Smoky Hills, the soils are rockier here, and thinner than they are in the heart of the

Corn Belt. The approximately sixteen inches of rain that falls on average during the growing season registers several inches shy of the eighteen to twenty inches needed to produce the highest-yielding corn, making the area better suited to wheat than more profitable corn and soybeans. And while wheat prices here topped $10 a bushel (twice the forty-year average) near the height of the recession in the summer of 2008, soybean farmers farther north in Iowa and Minnesota were netting over $16 during the same period for their chosen crop. Agricultural land values are lower on average here, too, than in the upper Midwest. As commodity prices peaked in 2008 and 2009, Ottawa County farmers could expect to get around $3,000 per acre for their land on average, considerably less than the $4,000 per acre farmers in Redwood County, Minnesota, might net. Hemmed in by the Saline River flood plain to the south and more rugged hills to the north, the town's topography presents would-be homebuilders with environmental contingencies that can be costly to address.

With still no takers for the free land in sight, Hal put up the money himself and built the first home—the one I'd seen for sale on the city website—with local business partner Tom Weatherd, figuring that a family with school-aged kids would be more likely to be the first settler in the neighborhood if the house had already been built for them. Even that incentive failed, however, and just as suddenly the challenge turned from how to entice families with children into the district to simply breaking even on a selfless investment. Hal lowered the price on the home he'd built on the free lot multiple times but, he reports, "We never even had any lookers to speak of."

North of the highway, on higher ground that provides for a sweeping view of the surrounding hills, the city of Tescott had better luck, selling lots for the bargain basement price of $8,000 to help cover their losses on the unclaimed free land south across the highway and nearer the school. Three houses ended up being built on the for-pay cul-de-sac lots north of town on the pleasantly named Pheasant Court. At the time of their construction, they were the first new homes in town in some seventeen years.

"So we did get things stirred round a bit," Hal tells me, though the takers on the $8,000 lot were not exactly of the school enrollment–building age the town's burghers and boosters had wished for. "This is a retired farmer," he adds, pointing to a nice new home with ambitious rock landscaping. "It didn't bother him that there's cattle right here in the feedlot in the wintertime." Hal and his fellow citizens also stirred things up with the addition of the John Hutchinson Nature Trail dedicated in 2011, whose namesake passed away the year prior. The short yet handsome path runs through pines and other softwood trees north of town, its entrance marked by a plaque that reads: "John proudly served his community for twenty-five years. He was always looking to the future and for ways to improve Tescott for community members."

Hal's equally passionate dedication to his hometown's health and well-being explains why it was ultimately a difficult decision for him to take lemons and make lemonade, offering the free-land house he had built to his daughter and her twins, though that workaround still left him short of the overall objective, as his daughter and her children were already living within the school district. "It didn't add any more people to our town like we wanted it to," he concedes. At first blush the failure of the free-land program is a bit of a mystery in a town the census claims has right around 150 housing units and close to 90 percent occupancy—conditions that suggest the makings of a potential housing shortage. But nearly 35 percent of those units are rentals, and the majority of residents here cannot hope to afford a sticker price of more than $150,000 on a new home even if it does come with a gratis lot and other perks.

Still, in addition to the three houses built on the for-pay lots, a house was moved, whole-hog, into Tescott from Salina and set on a foundation elevated above flood stage, making, technically, for four new homes built within the city limits over the space of roughly two decades. Prior to Tescott's implementation of the free-land program, Hal reckons the last new house had been built by the Federal Emergency Management Agency (FEMA) around 1993, after another of the floods that episodically deluge this low-lying land.

After taking a look at Hal's "no-lookers, no-takers" house sitting somewhat forlornly among the free-land lots, we cruise slowly down Main Street. My host points out the creek, a tributary of the Saline River a half mile south, that periodically floods the town all the way to the highway, and the beauty shop building that was built new after much wrangling with FEMA, which ended up changing the rules midstream in the building process. We ease past the nondescript Bank of Tescott that Hal ran for many years prior to his retirement, past the abandoned IGA grocery store that Hal, too, once bought along with a few partners in order to try to save it. Despite putting $10,000 in for his share, the patient was too long gone to be saved, leaving the townspeople of Tescott to drive sixteen miles to the county seat, Minneapolis, to get their groceries.

The commercial buildings here are functional rather than pretty—mostly beige brick and steel siding of the kind you find on machine sheds and pole buildings in farm country. The number of cars and trucks parked diagonally on Main can be counted on both hands, including one or two out front of a bar/restaurant called Some Beach, Somewhere (known locally as "The Somewhere.") The Somewhere sports a galvanized steel, hoop house–styled roof in the shape of the ubiquitous hog houses that once dotted the fields in places like this one. To illustrate its "Some Beach" namesake, some person, some time, had the idea to paint the mostly windowless façade in pastel beach colors that have long since faded along with the initial whimsy. The Somewhere is the town's heartbeat, a place where a dozen or more of the its most avid boosters meet for coffee and conversation in the morning in an event Hal calls "the big thing in town."

My host and I roll to a stop in front of a small, handicap-accessible building beside a small park created in the space where another downtown building has been razed. Turns out this peaceful little park with its pretty pergola and park benches and raised perennial flowerbeds is Hal's "retirement project" for his community. The same community spirit, and the need for additional office space, compelled him to buy the building adjacent to the park, on whose north-facing wall his granddaughter painted a mural of the town's shepherd-founder backdropped by a streetscape of frontier Tescott. Hal's Hang-out, he calls it, and when he got the key to place he turned around and made copies of it to hand out to locals, hauled some exercise equipment in, brought in a coffee maker and decks of cards, and turned his newly purchased office/man-cave into a kind of complimentary community center.

Still, there aren't enough entrepreneurs with Hal Berkley's vision and means in town anymore to carry on benevolent philanthropy on this scale, and several of the buildings we've passed, including the Somewhere and the defunct grocery store, have lately been for sale. The Somewhere was offered up at around $40,000 not long ago, Hal tells me, but, again the story was the same: no takers, so the owners pulled it off the market and continued to serve the coffee klatch in the morning and the dinner and beer crowd in the evening as if the thought of pulling up stakes had never crossed their minds.

A town, like a body, is under a certain de facto obligation to exist. Once incorporated a town typically self-perpetuates via taxes and levies, such that no matter how dire things get, it maintains a legal instrument by which it can ensure its own survival. Thus the relative legal rarity of dis-incorporation, even in hard-pressed rural regions fighting for their life.

And yet no town can persist without a quorum of citizens, a critical mass of denizens capable of performing the increasingly complicated role of governance in the Digital Age. There exists a threshold of viabil-ity, a tipping point that explains, for example, why one sees many small towns of four hundred to five hundred people across agrarian Middle America, but relatively few with populations under two hundred. In Kansas, Tescott is considered a "third class" city. Under state law, when a city incorporates, it becomes a city of the third class. However, min-imum standards for incorporation have tightened considerably since Tescott's frontier-era founding, and these days a city must generally have either three hundred inhabitants or three hundred or more platted lots served by water and sewer lines to be considered viable for incorpo-ration. By today's standards Tescott City would barely qualify for city status, an on-the-bubble marginality felt acutely by many of its current residents. According to practice, once a city is incorporated in Kansas, it continues to be a city even after falling below the minimum required to become a city, even if the minimum is later raised. A city can disin-corporate, but if citizens decide to reincorporate at a later date, then new minimum requirements must be met. Satisfying those new require-ments would be a difficult if not impossible task for Tescott given its present difficulty in drawing new residents, even with the enticement of free land.

In 1861 and 1862 becoming a city simply required that two-thirds of a town's or village's taxable inhabitants sign a petition for incorporation to be taken to the county probate judge for a rubber stamp, given the pressing need for warm bodies. Horace Greeley once said of the settlement craze, "It takes three log houses to make a city in Kansas, but they begin calling it a city as soon as they have staked out lots."

Back at Hal's Hang-out on Main we examine memorabilia in a building that functions more like a family reliquary and shrine than its intended use as an exercise room. Hal's only sister is an avid genealogist, and she's filled the room with artifacts of the family's genius for survival—haunty antique cribs in dark wood and baby buggies that belonged to their ancestors, black-and-white framed photos and photo montages of long-dead, unsmiling kin, and spiral-bound books that tell the family's proud history. Several feet are required to encompass the length and breadth of the family tree as depicted on a poster hung on the wall.

It's a history well worth telling. The atmosphere is heavy with the past here, and more than a bit like a morgue or mothballed museum. The Berkleys came to Kansas from Germany in the 1830s and, like many German émigrés to the rural Midwest and Great Plains, made their living at farming. Hal's father went off to college and was asked back to town to become the Bank of Tescott's resident bookkeeper in 1923, earning $25 a month and lodging above the bank so long as he would keep the books and the furnace well-stoked. Hal shares with me old bank ledgers showing that the local savings and loan had $59,000 to its name in 1923. Now, he tells me, it holds assets worth three hundred million, demonstrating that at least some in Tescott and nearby communities have managed to thrive.

My host hands me a heavy, almost biblical tome called, appropriately enough, the Book of Hal, prepared especially for him, about him, by his sister, and documenting all the important events in Hal's life and the lives of his ancestors. There are photos from Hal's graduating class from Tescott, all nine of them, in 1951—a fortuitous bunch that suffered its first death in 2012 to set a school record for class longevity. Over half of the class stayed within twenty-five miles of home. Here is a picture of Hal's first new car, a 1951 Chevy Fleetline he bought brand-new for a mere $1,705 before heading off to the University of Kansas in Lawrence, where all his brothers and sisters, save one, earned their college degrees. The Berkleys were (and are) a profoundly professional people; among Hal's six brothers are two who attended law school and another who attended medical school. All of Hal's children have remained relatively close by: one son sits on the board of a bank in Topeka; another farms just outside of town; his daughter is living in town in the house her father originally built to entice modern-day homesteaders to set up shop opposite the school.

For all the achievements it dutifully inscribes, the quasi-biblical Book of Hal also demonstrates what makes it difficult for some newcomers to love a place like this one with the same dogged determination. The Berkleys have done well by Tescott, and Tescott by them. In farm country, where access to capital is a practical necessity, Hal's clan had the benefit, in addition to their native intelligence, work ethic, and savvy, of access to money via their connection to the bank. Their word is as good as their bond here, because their reputation is a known and bankable commodity. But in a town so focused on its past, a free-land émigré, if indeed they were to materialize, would likely lack roots and probably money, two indispensable commodities if one hopes to do business. And if they are nonwhite, the lack of belonging may be felt even more acutely in a town where, according to the 2010 census, 309 of the 315 residents were white.

After our time at the Museum of Hal, we return to the question at hand, what to do about declining population in a town where not even a land giveaway has helped reverse the specter of demise and depopulation. Optimistically, the community bonded to build a suite of new classrooms and a gymnasium around 2010, though declining enrollments couldn't possibly have justified the outlay. Glendale, a town ten miles due south, has just one or two kids of school age to offer the Tescott district, Hal tells me; the same is true in Ada, which supplies just two or three children to the school in nearby Minneapolis.

And still eleven of the twelve free lots given by the school to attract families sit empty at the time of my visit, and Hal and the town's board have tried everything to sweeten the deal: brochures, online ads, even a $1,000 incentive offered to a local modular home dealer for the referral of any "homesteader" who would build their modular home on one of the lots on offer. All of which leaves Hal Berkley and the other restive members of the town's cognoscenti feeling an urgency they've not quite felt before.

Still there is much life here if one defines life as energy and vision. The town's infrastructure, including its school, is in good shape; the necessary FEMA modifications to downtown businesses have been made, and the reserves are still strong at the bank. In the life, death, and life again cycle of farm towns on the Great Plains, Tescott is still fighting for its life, but for the moment its diagnosis, thank goodness, isn't terminal.

Leaving Hal's office we pass the old grade school where as a boy he attended first through fourth grades, and which now serves as a museum spearheaded by his sister. The old grade school got a new roof and fresh coat of white paint for the town's 125th, an occasion whose custom logo evoked the image of a sturdy sign not unlike the welcome sign I'd passed on my way into town. The logo produced for the burg's birthday showed three pillars: "Family," "Community," and "God" and the accompanying slogan "Still standing strong."

"It's a nice place to live," my host tells me after a prolonged period of silence has passed between us in his pickup truck. "I like a small town, you know; you can drive around and not worry about running anyone over. Your kids can play in the street. We never lost one playing the street . . . stuff like that." He pauses, thinking over what even to him must sound like a lukewarm endorsement. He tries again. "You see, it's our church. It's slowly losing its members. And the young people are gone, and unless you get young people back in you're not gonna have anything."

Not long ago Hal had gone out to the old family farm to watch his grandson cut wheat with a thirty-foot-wide head on his combine. In Hal's day the head was six-feet wide and it took five times as long to cut the crop. As efficient as it's become, farming just doesn't require as many laborers as it once did. Tescott, too, once had a cheese factory located just across the tracks from where we sit in the truck, chewing the fat. Tescott cheese was known far and wide in these parts, becoming in essence the town's calling card. Then people quit milking, my host explains, and government regulations did away with milking cans: "Milking can tie you down and no one wants to be tied down anymore." I ask him if there's any way the town could be restored to its former glory, and he sighs heavily before answering, "Only if we get something that would produce a job in this area. I don't see much to bring the young people back. It's just too easy to run into Salina." He pauses again, considering his next words carefully but deciding to say them anyway. "I think that we're in trouble. I hate to say it."

Unlike many of today's young people, Hal always wanted to come back, even when he was away at college in Lawrence. "I always tried to get home. But then again I had a job to come back to," he recalls. Postcollege Hal moved in with his brother, who ran the bank in Stockton an hour or so west on Highway 18. "You just got to have work," he says in a tone that tells me that's just about his final word on the subject.

And well timed, too, as we've arrived back in front of the handsome home he's raised above the flood plain, complete with a decorative foot bridge over a drainage ditch. He invites me to follow him inside, and we walk into a home packed to the gills with Berkleys—gathered on the backyard patio with coolers, talking in the kitchen over ice water, playing in the generous yard—sons, daughter, grandson, granddaughters. Hal has taken most of his afternoon to show me around town and not once mentioned that the day had otherwise been set aside for a family gathering. The Berkleys graciously offer me a tall glass of water, while family photos are passed around and introductions are made. Every three years Hal's seven siblings and their kids gather together with extended family—124 attended the reunion this year, though today I am meeting just the Berkley side of the larger clan. And yet the house is so full with them it's difficult to find an unoccupied corner of the kitchen in which to stand. Married for more than six decades, Hal and Eleanor have welcomed four children and eleven grandchildren.

There is genuine warmth and energy here, as well as charity, generosity, mercy, understanding, and good old-fashioned hospitality. Though most of the family will leave Tescott today or tomorrow when the reunion is over, and the Berkley's shady street will grow ghostly quiet again, this limb of the family tree is strong at least, and full of life.

Exhuming the Regionalist Body

It's an almost unthinkable place to find a memorial stone for the man who is arguably the Midwest's most forgotten Regionalist poet—hard beside a gloriously backwater bar and grill, the F. B. and Company, with a line of Harleys parked out front and, out back, a pasture golf course, the aptly named "Back Nine," best tackled drunk.

Jay G. Sigmund

> Who of the goodness of his living and beauty of his
> writing gave back to the people of the
> Wapsie Valley that joy which they had
> given him.
>
> 1885–1937

I've made the short trip from my hill farm to pay homage to the home village of the writer Ilya Tolstoy hailed as "an American Chekhov and Maupassant," a man who published over 1,200 poems, 125 short stories, and

over 25 plays all while mentoring Regionalist writers and painters—Paul
Engle, Marvin Cone, and Grant Wood among them—until their legacy far
eclipsed his own. As of his untimely passing in 1937 at the age of fifty-one,
Jay Sigmund had authored at least six volumes of poetry and four books
of short fiction, an output made doubly impressive by the demands of his
day job as an insurance executive in Cedar Rapids, Iowa.

Today, Jay Sigmund's Waubeek amounts to a ghost of a town, an unincorporated huddle of weathered buildings hugging the south bank of the
Wapsipinicon River. Even Internet searches come back mostly empty save
for the place's coordinates, roads, and time zone. The usually reliable
Roadside Thoughts: A Gazetteer for the United States and Canada notes
somewhat sadly, "As far as we can tell, Waubeek has not been included
in past Census counts, so there is no population information." And yet
Sigmund grew up here, and later made a summer home in Waubeek in the
midst of a successful insurance career.

I seek out the Sigmund memorial stone hard beside the local watering
hole in part because I've made it a personal goal to exhume and resurrect
the forgotten literary voices of my native Midwest. Rather than simply
deny or decry the amnesia that so often flourishes in no-nonsense, work-
first agrarian cultures like mine, I want to acknowledge that forgetfulness,
meet it head on, and set about counteracting it by reintroducing writers
of my native region in what amounts to a second chance at the right-
ful appreciation due the deserving dead. Lately I've taken to calling Sigmund "America's most forgotten Regionalist," and at my own readings
I've begun handing out copies of a Sigmund literary anthology for free,
encouraging the lucky recipients to go forth and read a lost voice that once
proudly sang a shared heritage.

So, though I'm chagrined to find Sigmund's stone as badly neglected
as his literary star, I am not surprised. You see, Jay Sigmund died by his
own hand. In 1937, at the age of fifty-one and at the height of his literary
powers, the man known as the Bard of the Wapsipinicon River died of a
gunshot wound (later ruled accidental) on the river he loved so dearly and
whose praises he sang in his widely published poetry. He had been hunting rabbits when he apparently slipped, his gun discharging into his leg,
all but tearing away the limb. Doctors amputated the very next morning;
still the blood loss was heavy, and they could not save him. Some half
dozen years earlier the Bard of the Wapsipinicon River had had a finger

amputated after a horrific auto accident on his way to serve as a sort of master of ceremonies at Grant Wood's famous art colony, Stone City. Sigmund's crash-up ultimately inspired one of Wood's darkest and most Gothic paintings, *Death on Ridge Road*, and foretold the poet as a man potentially marked by death.

John T. Frederick, who published many of Sigmund's works in his journal *The Midland*, captured his friend's exceptional ability to reconcile both dark and light in an essay entitled "The New Realism," wherein he writes, "He [Sigmund] had also a deep sense of the tragic reality which often underlies a surface seemingly dull and prosaic." William Rose Benét commented likewise on the overarching tone of the poet's work in his 1931 review in *The Saturday Review of Literature*, matter-of-factly declaring, "Mr. Sigmund deals in tragic materials." The tragic reality underlying Sigmund's work as both writer and an insurance man in many ways came to define the Middle American Gothic, since it was Sigmund who so powerfully influenced the aesthetic of Wood. And with age the poet's cultivation of a fatalistic bloom only grew.

It wasn't just that Sigmund died by, or at least at, his own hand that brings me to his memorial stone, but his uniquely keen sense for life's doppelganger, its darker side. The Spanish poet Lorca would say the poet who presents such a simultaneous appreciation for life and death—life in death—possesses duende, and so, too, does the region from whence the poet divines and distills their tragic sense. That Sigmund, like Wood, found the duende in an agrarian Middle West better known for its sobriety and stability feels all the more remarkable. Of his own native country, Lorca writes: "Spain is, at all times, stirred by the *duende*, country of ancient music and dance, where the *duende* squeezes out those lemons of dawn, a country of death, a country open to death." Sigmund, too, sensed the dark currents of history running underneath his native region. Inspired by Sigmund's work, Carl Sandburg wrote, "Iowa is humanly as tragic and mysterious with the fate of man as was Greece, Rome, and the soils that produced the cultures of the Elizabethan or the Victorian eras." The duende, as Lorca conceived it, brought with it a sense of fatal premonition, of death's ability to draw nearer then farther, like a moon waxing and waning.

Eerily, only eleven days before he accidentally took his own life, Sigmund had drafted a "Literary Will," addressed to his disciple, the Regionalist writer Paul Engle. "The sudden and unexpected death of two or three friends here of late has made me realize the uncertainty of life," Sigmund wrote. He asked Engle to serve as his literary executor after his death, "to run over the things I've scribbled off since 1921 and see that any of them worth preserving (if such there be)" were looked after. Sigmund had no reason to anticipate his own death. An insurance man well-versed in actuarial science, he must have known his risk factors were low: a physically active middle-aged man, happily married, fully employed. And yet something in his life—the duende perhaps—tugged at his ear, convincing him of the necessity of choosing an executor despite no outward sign of impending morbidity.

Sigmund's death-sense was as sharp as the plowshares that cut his native soil and sent the field mice scurrying each spring, so much so that personal friends and literary patrons could, looking back at his later work, consider his final literary efforts to be his swan songs—verses containing intimations of his own demise. Sigmund contemporary D. H. Lawrence, dead at forty-four from tuberculosis, notes the essential irony of death's timing, reminding us that each year we pass "the anniversary of [our] own death," and Lawrence's life followed his own keen death-sense. His last work, the aptly named *Apocalypse*, attempts a kind of spiritual ethnography and linguistic etymology of the term "apocalypse," which comes from the Greek *apo-kalypso* meaning to reveal, to unveil. "Unlike prophecies which warn, chastise or reward an individual or a group on given conditions," writes literary critic Shirley Bricout, "an apocalypse is an unconditional prediction of coming events which will unfold at an undisclosed moment, no matter what mankind does or doesn't do."

At times the poem or song can serve as a rehearsal of a future requiem, an artistic vehicle for a fate the artist can do little or nothing to forestall—*swan song*—signifying the final song, gesture, effort, or performance before a death real or metaphorical. Shakespeare's swan song, his "last" play in many respects, was *Henry VIII*, a drama whose cannon-fire special effect ignited the thatched roof of the Globe Theatre in June 1613, burning it to the ground along with Shakespeare's "lost" play *Cardenio*. The loss of the theater and the script marked a double tragedy, explaining why *Henry VIII* is still viewed as a jinx if not a curse. The last poems of Lorca himself, father to the Theory of the Duende, are shot through with tragic circumstance. In August 1936 Lorca was dragged through the streets of Granada, Spain, to face death by firing squad. Among the last poems, the most important, said the *New York*

Times, were "a long lament, all of the valor and violence of a people . . . caught and interpreted." The imagery of bullfight, the reviewer noted, had been "heightened to become images of death." In "Lament for Igna-cio Sanchez Mejias," published in *Lament for the Death of a Bullfighter and Other Poems*, the dying bullfighter sees death approaching as the horns of the beast drawing perilously close, then:

> Across the ranches
> Went a breath of secret voices
> By which the herdsmen of the pallid mist
> Called to their heavenly bulls.

The last poems of Lorca serve as an exemplar of the Gothic principle he outlines in his Theory of the Duende, one divined from a tragic place, Andalusia, Spain, in a tragic time, the Spanish Civil War. The poet explains the mysterious connection between place and the duende as something beyond mere mysticism or fatalism. In his lecture-cum-essay "Play and the Theory of the Duende" the maestro writes:

> In every other country death is an ending. It appears and they close the cur-tains. Not in Spain. In Spain they open them. Many Spaniards live indoors till the day they die and are carried into the sun. A dead man in Spain is more alive when dead than anywhere else on earth: his profile cuts like the edge of a barber's razor. Tales of death and the silent contemplation of it are familiar to Spaniards. From Quevedo's dream of skulls, to Valdés Leal's pu-trefying archbishop, and from Marbella in the seventeenth century, dying in childbirth, in the middle of the road, who says:

> The blood of my womb
> Covers the stallion.
> The stallion's hooves
> Throw off sparks of black pitch . . .

to the youth of Salamanca, recently killed by a bull, who cried out:

> Friends, I am dying:
> Friends I am done for.
> I've three scarves inside me,
> And this one makes four.

Sigmund's Middle American Gothic was every bit as death-illuminated as Lorca's poems of Spain or Flannery O'Connor's Christ-haunted stories from America's Deep South. His day job, after all, was to preside over a company that sold life insurance to common-sense people afraid of suffering prematurely their ultimate fate. Just as it was a preacher's job to understand the spirit, it was an insurance man's job to calculate risk, life expectancy—to weigh the pleasure and possibilities of the now against the negative potentialities of an imagined future.

"No one sees all sides of human nature as the insurance salesman," Raymond Klass wrote in the *Cedar Rapids Republican* in a tribute to his lost friend. "He has seen a man insure his $400 automobile against fire and theft, the car which could be replaced, and then refuse to insure his own life in favor of wife and children. . . . He has seen a farmer insure his hogs for his own benefit and then refuse to insure his wife and babies. He has been frowned upon by the wife in taking the application and later met with the tears of gratitude as he brought in the amount of the policy in favor of the beneficiary. . . . In other words, Jay G. Sigmund has seen the human side of human nature."

Surely, Sigmund's wellspring of duende sprung not just from his unusually morbid profession, but from the haunty backwater place where he was born: Waubeek, Iowa. By the 1930s Waubeek's initial rush of settlement-building and blacksmithing had ground to a somewhat deadening denouement in less than half a century. Shortly after its establishment in 1855, Sigmund's home village already boasted an active mill, one of the finest stone buildings in the county, and a busy trading post—the three-story limestone structure that would become the F. B. and Company bar. By the turn of the century, notes the *History of Linn County*, the slumbering village still had four stores, a post office, a creamery, two churches, good schools, and fine stone quarries. Still, it had fallen badly behind the times even then, the authors feel obliged to note, commenting that the rural enclave had no railroad and "[had] made no advance for the past twenty years." Here the editors swerve, one presumes out of mercy or grace, opting not to inventory Waubeek's faults or failures for posterity: "It is not necessary to enlarge on this [the town's] history. It is doubtless a history of many other townships, but we as citizens have a local pride."

Serving witness to such economic and cultural decline may not advance the cause of prideful historians dutifully penning the history of their rural community, but it did much for Waubeek as a wellspring of art, at least according to Grant Wood, a close friend of Sigmund who visited his friend's summer residence there many times. By the Great Depression, the march of progress that had largely bypassed Sigmund's river town had left it ripe for the artist of *American Gothic*. In Wood's only book, *Revolt against the City*, the maestro opines, "I have been interested to find in the little town of Waubeek, near my home, farmer-descendants of the folk of New England fishing villages. Waubeek has not changed or grown much since it was originally settled, because it was missed by the railroads and by the paved highways. The people of this community have kept as family heirlooms some of the old whaling harpoons, anchors, and so on which connect them with the struggle which their ancestors waged with the sea." Wood believed that the "misfortune" of the people of Waubeek was the artist's gain, for it opened up a largely untouched, untapped vein of what he viewed as authentic "farmer material" needing "interpretation." Wood viewed Sigmund as representative of this preserved-in-amber ethos, a remnant interpreter of such bygone people, writing, "My friend and fellow-townsman Jay Sigmund devotes his leisure hours to the writing of verse celebrating the kind of human beings I have been discussing. He is as much at home in Waubeek—perhaps more so—as in the office of his insurance company."

Sigmund's champions, reviewers, and blurbists seemed, too, to sense something altogether different about the Bard of the Wapsipinicon and the strange, backwater place that had nurtured the dark seeds of his unorthodox talent. Unable to classify him as mere sentimentalist writing nostalgia about the past (he was, after all, writing about the heirloom people of the present that only seemed like the past to the rest of an urbanizing nation), some interpreted his difference as redolent of the future. Each time Newberry Prize–winning author Charles Finger wrote in praise of the poet's work, he seemed to fast forward to the inevitable day sometime in the future when Sigmund, resting in peace, would be properly esteemed. Finger argues that Sigmund's greatness is missed by the present generation, yet certain to be redeemed in the sweet by-and-by: "The fact is that Jay G. Sigmund . . . seems to have an eye on readers of the future." Writing in *All's Well* shortly after the publication of Sigmund's book *Least of These* in 1935, Finger made his literary soothsaying even more poignant, insisting, "Someday, when historians of the future cast

about in newspapers and magazines for material to enable them to recon-
struct ways of life in the Middle West, and are disappointed, someone may
exhume Sigmund's books from among my collection, and great will be the
joy of the discoverer."

Carl Sandburg, too, sensed in Sigmund the dark, roiling waters of the
duende, and it was Sandburg, in part, who helped introduce the Regionalist poet's work to editors in Chicago, where Sandburg worked at the
Chicago Daily News until 1932. The *Daily Tribune*'s "A Line o' Type or
Two" column functioned as a sort of poetry bulletin board: scribes from
around the Midwest sent in their verse, pithy epigrams, and witticisms,
and occasional questions on craft for discussion and publication. As 1936
turned to 1937, Sigmund increased his productivity, as if some new and as
yet unvoiced urgency had taken hold of him, spurring his creative output.
The poems he wrote in that season demonstrate, sometimes quite literally,
what Wallace Stevens called the "mind of winter." On February 9, 1937,
arrived "Sonnet for a Zero Night," whose stanzas capture the coming of
winter in a killing freeze and the chilling nihilism of the season:

By the sharp wind that whips across the knoll—
Why plan a crop with winter in this role?

By August of that year Sigmund's mind of winter had hardened further,
his tenderness and sensitivity shaded by a darker impulse and a growing lament. The Bard's penultimate poem in the *Daily Tribune*, entitled
"Return After a Decade," bespoke personal sea-change, its closing cou-
plet reading: "Ten years have run their sands through— / There's change;
so much of change." The following week Sigmund wrote in again, this
time with a poem entitled "Hunter's Blood" whose very title proved
eerily predictive of the fate he would soon suffer in the hunting grounds
along the Wapsipinicon River. "The earth things are in peril," Sigmund's
speaker observes on his nature walk. Overhead, fledgling hawks circle,
awaiting their first kill, and where once the poem's speaker protected the
rabbit's den, now, overtaken by some darker impulse, he wishes "these
young hawks luck," effectively abandoning his overwatch and surrender-
ing to the predator its chosen prey. Fatalism, married with world-weary
submission to an unseen fate, haunt what turned out to be Sigmund's
final poems.

Ironically, the speakers in Sigmund's poems succumbed to a Gothic world view even as the literary reputation of their author soared. In the April 25 edition of that same year, the *Daily Tribune* followed up with a lengthy article entitled "Iowa College Out with New Chapbooks" heralding Cornell College's publication of Sigmund's book of poems *Heron at Sunset*. Writer John Evans wrote of the collection: "His [Sigmund's] spontaneity raises his verse to the level of poetry. The vacuity of retirement, the surge of spring, the terror of the trapped, the depression of autumn, the futility of senility, the loneliness of winter, all these simple but poignant emotions are aroused in the reader, not by the artifice of cadence, but by the art of creation." In his introduction to the volume, Cornell College professor and series editor Clyde Tull offered, "Mr. Sigmund's work is characterized by fine sincerity, a thoroughgoing sympathy for the small town and country folks he portrays so vividly in his stories and verse, and a quiet mastery of technique that attracts little attention to itself but gives pleasure to the discriminating."

On October 22, 1937, eager readers opened their *Chicago Daily Tribune* to find a morbid headline: "Jay G. Sigmund's Last Poem" allegorically entitled "Early Fall Evening." The fine print below the verse read: "The poem above . . . was the last received by *The Line* from Mr. Sigmund, celebrated poet of Cedar Rapids, Iowa, whose career was ended by a hunting tragedy." Sigmund had already been dead four days as *Tribune* readers digested his last poem with what must have been a mix of profound regret and dread at his violent end. Moved, they mailed in their eulogies, among them a short poem entitled "Lines to Jay G. Sigmund" that appeared in the space in "A Line o' Type or Two" lately reserved for the Bard of the Wapsipinicon. The official cause of the October 19, 1937, death was a "hunting accident" in which, as literary critic Clarence Andrews put it, "he [Sigmund] was accidentally wounded by a blast from his own shotgun as he hunted near his home by the river."

In a prefatory note to the posthumous Sigmund tribute collection, *Select Poetry and Prose*, Paul Engle remembers getting the awful news: "[The painter] Marvin Cone drove out to Stone City October 20, 1937, and told me of Jay Sigmund's death. It was a dark day, rain coming up in flurries. I was chopping wood. We stood and looked down at the Wapsie, flowing with an autumn brown. I had been walking along it the day before, at the same hour when Jay was lying in the field calling for help in the empty air." Upon hearing Cone's news, Engle could think of nothing better to do with his sadness than to write an elegy, which he titled "Jay G. Sigmund," and which concludes,

> We knew him too, we were his friends
> From the farming country around
> The Wapsie land where he lived and worked
> We know the feel of that ground.
>
> We will die different men because
> We knew him face to face.
> Let us bury him now with his weather and his crops,
> And say—He belongs to this place.

The *Cedar Rapids Gazette*, Sigmund's hometown newspaper and a long-time supporter of his work, broke the news to the city under the headline "Cedar Rapids Poet Is Shot While Hunting; Leg Amputation Fails to Save Life of Businessman and Writer." The October 20, 1937, obituary opened, "Jay G. Sigmund, Cedar Rapids poet, and one of the Midwest's most prominent writers and lecturers on literature, died in a local hospital at 9:10 p.m. Tuesday following amputation of his left leg after a hunting accident near his summer home in Waubeek Tuesday afternoon." The article detailed how the fifty-one-year-old Sigmund had lost his footing while following a wounded rabbit in the pastures near his summer home and had accidentally discharged his shotgun into his leg below the knee.

The *Gazette* covered Sigmund's well-attended funeral under the headline "Extols Sigmund's Life and Writings . . . Father Campbell Speaking at Funeral Service Refers to Businessman-Poet as Complete Personality." Campbell, emphasizing Sigmund's well-rounded character, reminded mourners that "a saint is a whole person—a complete personality, so I place him [Sigmund] with the saints." Indeed, the diversity of the estimated five hundred attendees, reported as a mix of "members of the local insurance agents association . . . as well as representatives of the various art, literary, and civic groups to which he [Sigmund] belonged," testified to the size and diversity of the author's audience. Father Campbell, the article reported, said he "hoped the farmers and townspeople of Waubeek . . . would raise a monument to the memory of the man who lived among them, wrote among them."

Appropriately, given that Sigmund had left his home on the fatal day to ramble in the woods along the Wapsie River, those speaking at the funeral focused on his enduring legacy as a naturalist-poet. Among those offering eulogies, Sigmund's neighbor John Wagor remembered fondly Sigmund's love of nature. Fred Poyneer called Sigmund a "student of the outdoors" and a man who "knew the spirit as well as the technical side of nature." Perry Buxton of the *Wheatland Gazette* celebrated Sigmund's ability to "take the smoke of autumn or the flight of a hawk and interpret it for us." Dr. H. M. Gage, president of Cedar Rapids' Coe College, urged grievers not to focus on the words coming from the rostrum but on themselves. "This is what Jay would have wanted," Gage said, looking out over the diverse crowd. "Just folks with all their folkishness."

While no statues were erected in Sigmund's honor by the farmers and laborers of his home region, as the reverend might have hoped, Sigmund's literary friends and boosters did erect a small stone memorial in Sigmund's hometown of Waubeek, the one I have come to see—the one that reads: "Jay G. Sigmund who of the goodness of his living and beauty of his writing gave back to the people of the Wapsie Valley that joy which they had given him." In Cedar Rapids, Coe College marked the poet's passing by publishing a limited-edition collection entitled *The Hawk that Haunts the Sky*. "In tribute to Mr. Sigmund's interest in young writers and his friendship for the Writer's Club," the dedication to the in-memoriam volume read, "we here reprint several of his favorite poems." Two years after his death, in 1939, Sigmund's friend and fellow writer Paul Engle made good on his executor's promise, compiling and publishing a selected works. Sounding a cautionary note about the downbeat, minor key played in some of his mentor's most poignant verse, Engle warned, "The purpose of a poet is not to write about something beautiful, but to make a beautiful thing of his poem. To that end, an unpleasant thing is as good as a pleasant. . . . Furthermore, it is in many horrible and depressing moments in life that an intensity of feeling is produced. It is one hope of the poet that his poems too will produce an intense mood, so he draws on heightened emotion wherever it is found."

Engle's introduction makes an unusually good case for his friend's cultivation of a distinctively Middle American duende, no less authentic or heightened in its tragic sense than Lorca's or Shakespeare's. Engle's words remind, too, that the player of what Lorca called the "dark notes" of the duende is no less an artist; in some ways, they are truer for their fidelity to minor chords. Much as Sigmund loved farm country, Engle maintains that he refused to romanticize it: "He knew how bitter and grinding a job the farmer has, how sometimes no amount of sweat or hard work will make up for bad luck or bad judgment. He understood how farms are lost, go out of the family, and every treasured household thing sold by the clanging voice of the auctioneer. He knew that moonlight came to a farm, and debt, too."

Inside the crumbling limestone building that has for decades housed Waubeek's only watering hole and community gathering spot, I am at a loss as to what to do with myself after my memorial stone visit. It's late afternoon on a beautiful day—not quite happy hour, and far too bright and balmy and beautiful to hole one's self up in a bar agonizing over the tragic death and forgetting of a native son.

I shoot some pool, make small talk with the bartender, who doesn't remember Sigmund. I am trying to explain to myself as much as to the tender my presence here, which must strike him as anomalous. I've come alone, ordering nothing but a Coke, and the modesty of Sigmund's memorial stone and legacy here has left me in a bit of a sour mood. I sink the eight ball in the corner pocket and lean the stick up against the wall, wandering out to the deck to look upon Waubeek's modest, muddy river, the Wapsipinicon, that flows just beneath.

Why have I come here—to deepen my sense of indignation at the historical slight dealt a dark-horse writer who came to his calling too late in life, and died too early, and, as a consequence, is too little remembered for the breadth and depth of his achievements? Or have I come because in Sigmund's own fatalism I sense a whiff of my own or perhaps that of our shared agrarian region's, the way that Sigmund might have heard the leitmotif of his own future on the wind, rattling in the space between the words like so many loose barn boards?

In the end the Bard of the Wapsipinicon's memorial stone came to rest beside the river whose lore he helped immortalize, beside a bar/general store whose roots here reach as far back as his own. More recently, Sigmund's home county historical society has honored him with a lane named in his honor in the memorial park adjacent the bar and grill. The county historical society, too, has created a digital exhibit leading latter-day

Sigmund discoverers on a digital "expedition" to this very place, as part of the hoped-for rediscovery of their forgotten cultural heritage.

Jay Sigmund would no doubt be pleased by such developments. He might sit, unnoticed, on a bench nearby, whittling cherry wood with his one good hand, watching the city folk come in cars unaccustomed to the patina of gravel dust. He would be pleased to see them turn down Jay Sigmund Lane just off Boy Scout Road and head back to their comfortable, mobile lives full of excited news of their journey. He would pen a poignant story about them, no doubt, wistful if not a bit sad. In it he would note the wry irony of how changing fashions can bring such fine, caring folks as these into the countryside to properly acknowledge, four score years later, the life and work of an ordinary man, a man who quietly did extraordinary work in the most ordinary of extraordinary places, wanting nothing more, by and by, than to be remembered for it.

10

DREDGE

A Middle American Gothic

Weeks after his father's passing, the farmer's son still stews in the cemetery where his kin sleep beneath their heavy black blankets.

Cock an ear to the cemetery where the Union dead lay buried and you can hear over the hills the drone communion of commuters on the highway, a few miles yon, as the crow flies. Their route of choice is named for a martyred president buried in springtime, while the Judas trees bloomed in some distant capital city. They're good solid men, coiffed and clean-shaven aerospace engineers with solid degrees and coffee mugs of stainless steel to speed them on their journey to the smokestacks of cereal town. Their obituaries shall read *in-flight entertainment systems* and *precision targeting weapons*.

If you're Somebody you'll get a school named after you or a community center. If you're Really Somebody you'll get an airport or a superhighway, so great is our appreciation for unrestricted movement, for ease of travel. Road noise is our adulation. We love you moving on.

In the dream he is having he is a hopelessly slow bipedal hominid chased by a banker then a black-suited bossman—the usual agrarian bogeymen. Then, just as they are about to overrun him, he transforms into a wolf, loping crazy on all fours.

His father was a pistol; he's a son of a gun.

Two years shy of his fortieth birthday, a Midwesterner named James B. Hill filed a patent for a machine to dredge the hell out of his native state. He named the contraption Buckeye Traction Ditcher and, boy howdy, could it ditch. It ditched the entire Great Black Swamp, an unfathomably large miasma snaking its way from Indiana to Ohio. Once the gargantuan machine had gorged itself its young inventor took it to Louisiana, where it simmered and stewed and eventually drained the devil out of that state, too.

The devil, as everyone knows, is in the details. It is also in the treacherous logic by which a man attempts to drain his own personal swamp.

The same year the farmer-professor's father won his home county's award for combating the scourge of soil erosion, the Farm and Rural Life Poll found two-thirds of the farmers in the Fatherland felt the nation had some seriously dirty water, while just 20 percent reckoned the water on their own farm was polluted. "There was a strong tendency among respondents to view the problem as much worse the farther it was from home," the study's authors concluded.

What can a man mired in the early middle of a life spent in the midlands of a great middling country really know about the art of living but what his parents taught him and the serendipitous happenstance of his own incomplete education. The rest is pure divination.

Folk wisdom: A man who is lost moves in circles, like water before a drain.

Down on Jungletown Road, his friend-of-a-friend, Rosalie, claims the sober bottomland farmers and inebriate river rats thrill to the sight of wildcats prowling the backwaters. Everywhere the professor has ever traveled in these sprawling midlands the big cat claws at the imagination. And yet he has never, not even once, met a soul who could produce one. The panther, he can only surmise, is a myth of necessity or convenience, like Santa Claus.

In his late twenties, in what he now calls a "youthful indiscretion," the farmer's son purchased a second home, a modular in the mountains priced less than a top-of-the-line pickup truck. He blames the acquisition on an almost Transcendentalist desire for wildness. For reasons he could not then fathom it took him six months to overcome the fear of telling his father of the ecstatic transaction.

The plot of ground he chose positively burned with panther-rumor, there in the leafy hollers along the spring-fed river off Bat Cave Holler Road. Once closed, his eyes pictured the big cat limber and cool, wearing a coat of crushed velvet, midnight blue, eyes lit up like a demon in some cartoon.

Before James B. Hill got hold of it, the Great Black Swamp was so thoroughly mud-gumboed even the Michigan and Ohio militias couldn't make it to the front lines to fight the Toledo Wars. First rule of warfare: to come to grips with incipient murkiness one must baptize themselves in something murkier still. *The fog of war*, the professor's professor—a political philosopher of some renown—once called it. No one is a greater circumambulator.

For the record the Great Black Swamp doesn't exist anymore. Its study is now confined to that slippery euphemism "historical geography."

The inventor of the superduper ditcher that drained the Great Black Swamp, James B. Hill, shares the farmer-professor's birthday. Hill was working as a drainage-tiler-of-a-nobody when he made his big discovery, like Einstein, slaving away in the patent office dreaming of the calculus of personal improvement.

Hope and the future for me are not in lawns and cultivated fields, not in towns and cities, but in the impervious and quaking swamps. —Thoreau

Finding his early machines bogged down by mud, Hill dreamed up some boss wheels that could travel over muck and sand, sans sinking. He called his whimsical method "apron traction." It gave the army the idea for modern tank wheels, the swamp being an uncanny simulacrum of war.

When the original Buckeye tiler himself grew old in the miasmic swampland he had drained in his good old salad days, he turned his inventor's acumen to ciphering out the inscrutable genetics of cross-pollination, and damned if he didn't invent a corn hybrid bearing his name, Hill's White Cob Yellow Dent.

I want a good Middle American swamp named after me when I'm gone, may I rest and burble in peace.

Hill wouldn't let a goddamn wetland stand in his way. Once decamped to the Sunshine State, he cooked up an amphibious vehicle to travel through the swamps of Florida to grease the wheels of lucrative drainage deals struck with bigwigs hoping to drain a topography already at or below sea level. The Big Idea was to turn a peninsular swampland of dubious character into a promised land for Corn Belt émigrés, a place with the kind of fatal allure Middle Americans would be all too happy to leave their settled homes for.

The American Society of Mechanical Engineers designated Hill's original Buckeye Traction Ditcher as "International Historic Mechanical Engineering Landmark" in 1988. It's in the hall of shame/fame.

To businessmen in the Deep South *Buckeye Traction Ditcher* just about screamed Yankee. The steam-breathing, soil-draining, path-making contraption needed a new name, something familiar to the poor crackers paid peanuts to drain Tallahassee or pump down Okeechobee with it. Call it The Tractor instead, he said, and they did.

He who conquers his swamp conquers the world.

In Wildness is the preservation of the World. Every tree sends its fibers forth in search of the Wild. The cities import it at any price. Men plow and sail for it. —Thoreau

Hill and his first wife produced ten children themselves, naturally. Near his death the old ditcher crowed of having spawned in excess of one hundred descendants across Middle America from Ohio down to Louisiana.

Claiming one man and his machine could save an entire people from the thoroughly malarial nature of their low-lying state is stuff fit for snake-oil salesmen or faith healers, some said. When the trustees in charge of the improvement plan grew restive in the capital, Hill's engineers were pressed to write in with their personal testimonies. They said they had seen the machine work miracles, by God. Pay the man, they said—pay him anything he asks.

The historical geographer considers the possibility of copious offspring sired from a potent admixture of Hill's innovative whimsy with the long-simmering swamp gas inhaled while astraddle his infamous Buckeye Ditcher. In any case the historical caption is the same: Hill Spreads Seed.

The part of the Great Black Swamp that sprawled across the Ohio state line into Indiana is called the Limberlost. According to the *History of Jay County*, Limberlost was the namesake of an especially agile hunter by name of James Miller, who, while tracking his prey along the banks of Limberlost Creek, got himself powerfully lost. Every so often he would blaze a tree to prevent himself from running around in circles. That's where his friends found him, their "Limber Jim," and commemorated one man's supreme lack of direction with the forever-name: *Limberlost*.

At the turn of the century an author wrote a book about a poor girl who lives on the edge called *A Girl of the Limberlost*. The book made its author, Gene Stratton Porter, famous, and wound up on the silver screen in 1924, 1934, and 1945. The real star, though, was the Great Black Swamp. It positively shone.

Though she would later come to live in it and to love it, Porter herself called the marsh a "treacherous swamp and quagmire, filled with every plant, animal and human danger known—in the worst of such locations in the central states."

There's kind of dancing lights there sometimes, but I supposed it was just people passing along the road with lanterns. Folks hereabout are none too fond of the swamp. I hate it like death. I've never stayed here a night in my life without Robert's revolver, clean and loaded, under my pillow, and the shotgun, same condition, by the bed. I can't say that I'm afraid here at home. I'm not. I can take care of myself. But none of the swamp for me!
—A Girl of the Limberlost

The Indiana State Museum maintains that the marsh received its name from Limber Jim Corbus, who went hunting in the swamp and never returned. The familiar local cry was "Limber's lost!"

For the farmer drainage makes good business sense. What would you do if you had a perennial pool of standing water in your place of business? Live with it?

"Dear Sirs: – In accordance with your recent request that I inform you in regard to the work of The Tractor, I beg to submit the following conclusions which I have arrived at after a careful and convincing test of The Machine.

It has operated satisfactorily and successfully. . . .

It is a question of either using this Tractor on the interior . . . or abandoning the same as impracticable without its use." —*Minutes of the Trustees, Internal Improvement Fund of the State of Florida*, 1910

The family of the farmer's son wanted their scion buried between his own mother and his father, in the middle of the commemorative arch commissioned in iron. Thirty inches between graves is what you need, minimum, the Boneman claims, speaking with his shovel, his arms outspread to charade the requisite breadth. Still, in the end there isn't enough space, not in March. Bury the blessed patriarch in the family's first-choice location and the whole grave wall might collapse on account of the natural swampiness of springtime.

The lord almighty is hiding you all right done you ever dout it this money of yourn was took for some time las nite but it is returned with intres for god sake done ever come to the swamp at nite or late evnin or mornin or far in any time sompin worse an you know could git you–A FREND. —*A Girl of the Limberlost*

The central portion of the farmer-professor's immaculately drained state was known by its original settlers as the "Thousand Lakes Region" for its bogs and fens and plentiful pothole wetlands. They arrived to a land veined by cataracts bordered by rushes and burning with panther-rumor. In a lifetime of years the pioneers managed to destroy 90 percent of the state's wetlands, nearly doubling the national average for such destruction.

"Gentlemen: – I have seen The Machine in operation and have carefully examined it, and from my own personal knowledge I am satisfied that it is especially adapted to the work . . . and will not only make the survey [of the interior] . . . practicable, but will greatly reduce the cost of the work. I therefore recommend its acceptance and the payment of the amount due." —*Minutes of the Trustees, Internal Improvement Fund of the State of Florida*, 1910

Gene Stratton Porter designed a fourteen-room Queen Anne rustic log cabin in the Limberlost in 1895. In eighteen years spent living in the swamp she wrote six of her twelve novels and five of her seven nature books, including the best seller *A Girl of the Limberlost*. The Porters lived in their Victorian cabin until the swamp was tiled away to nothingness in 1913. She found herself drained of inspiration.

Online you will find a vigorous debate between Bonemen who dig by hand and Bonemen who've mechanized their undertaking. The question anymore isn't whether to dig the grave with a backhoe or spade, but what kind of backhoe to dig with. If in doubt, the Middle Western idiom applies: go big or go home.

"Here's the thing, Junior. You could git yerself a 40–50 horse John Deere with a backhoe attachment. BTW, you'll want a backhoe with turf ties and a ten-foot dig depth and sufficient breakout force. Personally, I like the Werk Brau quick couplers and buckets for grave-digging, but that's just me." —An Internet Sage

Somewhere in our well-drained midlands a county clerk muses to his hometown newspaper about our rising epidemic of seasonal loss and estrangement, "Maybe it's after winter, women saying 'I can't take this fool anymore,'" he said. "Maybe it's 'I don't like what you got me for Valentine's Day' or maybe it's 'You got your girlfriend something better than you got me.'" Around here, even our elected county officials prefer dark humor.

The perpetrator is a man, this we know in advance. In the Fatherland we accept the theme of man as ultimate spoiler. He rapes the soils. He poisons the fields then slices them through to the bone. His hands are perpetually dirty. He buries the past then quietly simmers. We watch him fill up with darkness, like a swamp.

Daylight Savings Time, as any farmer, Boneman, or ditchdigger knows, is an invention of urban self-interest. The earliest British promoter of DST, William Willet, didn't care to have his rounds of golf cut short by the nuisance of darkness. Ditto for Woodrow Wilson, a Princeton professor who likewise enjoyed a good walk spoiled. Citified men endeavor to forestall the darkness; they have no Gothic interest, no love of swamp in them.

Say what you want about Ohioan Warren Gamaliel Harding, but, like any God-fearing farm-reared Middle American, he knew enough to call Daylight Savings Time "a deception." He knew a quagmire when he'd stepped into one. He preferred that his darkness arrive early.

Presidential scholars consider Harding possibly the most corrupt president in history, despite the biblical promise of his middle name.

A Democratic leader of the time, William Gibbs McAdoo, once called Harding's speeches "an army of pompous phrases moving across the landscape in search of an idea." I call them the product of a particularly miasmic state.

Harding shared his middle name with a Pharisee and a teacher of the Apostle Paul. The book of Acts portrays him as a man of great ethical stature. With a name like Gamaliel, it's no wonder that Harding's most zealous backer, Harry Daugherty, got behind his backslid friend, of whom the best he could later say was: "Well, he looked like a president."

Vis-à-vis the relative wisdom of the backhoe versus the back-breaking spadework left the living, some Internet sage opines, "Grave digging, that's a dying business," and some old grump writes back. "OH COME ONE, WHOP WANTS to be digging graves at the young age of 18, I'd rather clean bathrooms."

We may suppose the Internet sage meant "who" rather "whop," but it's hard telling. Dig all you want, it's still inferential at bottom.

"If you knew of a great scandal in our administration," Harding once asked his upright Quaker Secretary of Commerce Herbert Hoover, "would you for the good of the country and the party expose it publicly or would you bury it?" Hoover, the son of an Iowa blacksmith, predictably urged his boss to dredge the secret up, bring it to the light.

On the last day of the month the farmer's son, his father now dead and buried, officially receives his letters of legal appointment, which mean that he has all but become his father, legally speaking. They arrive from the estate attorney whose high-rise office in the nearby cereal town overlooks the crooked river that has beget two five-hundred-year floods in a mere ten years, thanks in part to the underground tilling revolution brought about by James B. Hill.

The legal letter is sent him in a Dupont™, Tyvek® "Protect What's Inside"™ envelope, Survivor Quality. Made in the United States, Tyvek is your basic polyethylene, the professor is given to understand, a plastic whose toxic polymers last infinitely longer than the average American marriage ending in divorce, which stews and simmers along for eight years on average before it takes on water, spilling its secrets.

Fold flap over line. Lick. Deposit into darkness.

At night in the days after his father passes on, the farmer's son imagines himself wading through a quagmire holding a messenger bag of unknown contents above swirling, sulfurous waters. From the fetid bank, watching him, Fear wears a black coat and burns with panther-eyes.

You will know a man by the marks he leaves when he is lost. This is what his father told him.

Part III

Resurrections

11

GHOST PLAYERS

"When darkness falls on that giant screen you'll all see a movie I'm betting every single one of you has seen at least once before, and some of you ten, fifteen, twenty times before," legendary sportscaster Bob Costas tells the faithful who have gathered tonight "to attempt to capture what remains of our youth," as he puts it. "But you've never seen it quite like this . . . in centerfield, on the Field of Dreams. This is going to be a special." Tomorrow Costas will take to the field with others for a celebrity baseball game to mark the twenty-fifth anniversary of the *Field of Dreams* film. Tonight he has gathered three of its stars, Dwier Brown, Timothy Busfield, and Kevin Costner, to talk about what the movie means to them, and to us, two and a half decades later.

Viewed from the lawn chair where I sit, the screen idols hardly appear to have aged since I threw my own *Field of Dreams*–themed high school graduation party, turning our farm's back pasture into a manicured ballfield. The square-jawed Brown still looks the spitting image of a youthful John Kinsella; Busfield, who played Mark in the film, has grayed only slightly since he played Annie Kinsella's heartless banker brother. Costner, bronzed from a weekend playing baseball in the sun with his three kids, is still and forever the boyishly handsome Ray Kinsella. I'm not sure whether to attribute their collective preternatural youth to Hollywood glamor, plastic surgery, or good clean living, but their agelessness feels almost miraculous to me, as if the intervening twenty-five years had never happened. We've come to worship under a timeless summer sky—periwinkle with high wispy clouds that have put us all, stars included, in something of a time warp. Gazing across the verdant green ballfield dotted with hundreds of moviegoers, Busfield can't help but wax nostalgic.

"You know [in the film] Kevin plays this guy from the sixties. And when I look out here it feels like what it was like in the 1960s when people would pour out onto the fields." Sitting beside Busfield, Brown waves his arms languidly above his own head, charading a kumbaya moment something like Woodstock or the Summer of Love. Busfield struggles to find the words for what he feels, though the wellspring of his epiphany is clear.

On this night the air is heavy with nostalgia, as it so often is on summer evenings when people come together to celebrate the few things that are unchanging in their lives. "I think we all at times wish we had a perfect relationship with our parents as they die," Busfield says, summing up. "Nobody wants that fractured relationship and the haunting that Ray goes through."

Hence we've come like pilgrims, from all points on the map, for a celebration with a single-minded purpose, namely the adoration of a movie that itself takes us back a generation to Ray's father, John—the ghost whose thwarted dreams animate Ray's desire to build the field that will bring his father back to life.

Costner, dressed casually in a button-down plaid and jeans, listens thoughtfully before offering his own assessment of the film that was a surprise nominee for an Academy Award for Best Picture in 1989. "*Field of Dreams* is really our generation's *It's a Wonderful Life*. It's a movie that ranks and doesn't seem to fade," he says to a round of applause. Costas asks Costner how such a cinematic miracle could come to pass— how a screenplay rejected by multiple Hollywood studios could become an enduring classic in less than a generation—a movie that, as he puts it, "echoes down the corridors of time."

The movie star prefaces his answer by motioning out to the infield, where families play catch and run the bases in the twilight. "You know, I'm really glad that people are out in the field playing catch and not paying attention to what we're saying because that's appropriate. I mean who really cares. The mayor is going to run for office, and so is the governor . . . so what!" The crowd hoots and hollers. The mayor, the governor, even Denise Stillman, the controversial new owner of the field she hopes to turn into a profit-making sports complex—each had earlier taken a turn at addressing the crowd, a poor microphone having conspired to make their commentary sound like so much static. The governor had read a lengthy proclamation declaring an official Field of Dreams Day in the state, while the mayor of Dyersville, Iowa, the beatifically named Jim Heavens, had vouched for the cultural and economic value of the field to his city of approximately four thousand. Each of the night's dignitaries had to sought to name and to leverage the spiritual force that has brought thousands of people to this sacred ground, this sanctum sanctorum, for the anniversary weekend, not to mention an estimated seventy thousand visitors annually. The precise attraction to this place is an alchemy Costner still struggles to name twenty-five years later.

"Sometimes we see things and we respond to them," he muses, comparing the movie to the Empire State Building or the Golden Gate Bridge, something that moves us viscerally even on first viewing. "We're going to bundle up now. We're going to get our own lawn chairs. Maybe the fireflies will come. . . . I'm going to go get my coat. I imagine you're going to get your coat. I'm going to get really close to the people that I love. I'm going to think before the movie starts about the people who made a difference to me in my life. I'm going to sit in a little cornfield in Iowa. These lights are going to go out. And we're going to watch a movie. And I don't think there's anything more American or any bigger miracle than this move that was made . . . here on this field. . . . For those who aren't here, they don't really know what they're missing."

This weekend's twenty-fifth anniversary celebration, timed to coincide with Father's Day, represents a chance for us, the movie's disciples and defenders—the fellowship of the Field—to experience communally the spiritual satisfactions of an intensely personal cinematic experience. For the moment we don't care about the film's many detractors, movie snobs who find it too allegorical, too Midwestern, or simply too corny. We've come to nourish our souls in the company of others who have likewise come to associate the film with peace and renewal: the crisp clapboard house with its long curving verandah, the upright picket fence, the Easter-green grass, the handsome boy-next-door movie star who might as well be Jimmy Stewart or Cary Grant, the storyline and setting so powerfully elemental they've draw us here like homing pigeons.

Like religion, baseball "insists upon the idea of a rural and Edenic unspoiled origin," its pastoral preoccupations being "beginnings, origins, and the myth of the garden" writes sports scholar Gregory Erickson. When we round the bases we literally and figuratively come home. In baseball the "past is always part of the present." The hero in American literature is often a loner, Erickson points out, needing to find their place—their way home—akin to a single lonesome batter facing an entire team arrayed to stop him. Much like Western religion, baseball places profound emphasis on a kind of personal salvation achieved via return—coming back to home base—to the original force that animates us and gives our lives meaning.

On this night we, the Field's devoted followers, seek paradox: achieving personal salvation together.

In the film's opening sequence Ray Kinsella stands utterly alone and apart in his cornfield, suspended in a spectacularly Gothic circumstance: presiding over the slow and painful death of a family farm that he is ill-equipped to manage. Ray is a thirty-eight-year-old transplant, a misfit estranged from his home (New York), and struggling with a profession he knows little about. He is displaced from the progressive politics and hippie lifestyle he had lived while in college in Berkeley, California, and alienated from the voice inside that tells him something crucial is missing in his life. Naturally it's then, when his existential and spiritual angst is at its greatest, that the voice reaches him, not on some windswept moor in Europe, but in a Middle American cornfield, whispering the enigmatic prophecy, "If you build it, he will come."

Ray is circumstantially stuck and powerfully haunted. Abandoning the family farm to foreclosure would be akin to abandoning his family, and given his love for his wife and daughter, abandonment is not an option he is willing to consider. He confides to his wife, Annie, that he believes the "he" in the whispered prophecy may be his father's life-long fascination, the tragi-heroic Chicago White Sox outfielder Shoeless Joe Jackson.

Unable to sleep one night, Ray confesses to his wife his feelings about his father:

> I never forgave him for getting old. By the time he was as old as I am now, he was ancient. He must have had dreams, but he never did anything about them. For all I know, he may even have heard voices, too, but he sure didn't listen to them. The man never did one spontaneous thing. Annie, I'm scared that's what growing up means. I'm afraid that's happening to me. And something tells me this may be my last chance to do something about it. I want to build that field. Do you think I'm crazy?

Fortunately for Ray's psyche, Annie doesn't think her husband is completely crazy, though she teases him good-naturedly that if he keeps hearing voices the locals may soon be burning him at the stake. At other times she jokingly offers to visit him at the funny farm when inevitably they lock him away in a garret. The neighbors feel that Ray would be better suited to an asylum than a failing family farm. When he heeds the voice and plows under his corn (and his profits) to build the field, dubious and distrustful drivers-by gather on the gravel road to stand in judgment, shaking their heads in disbelief. In the original screenplay writer Phil Alden Robinson describes the naysaying gawkers as "look[ing] at one another as if to say, 'Could it be Communists?'"—the word connoting not only the Communist witch hunts of the 1950s but also, no doubt, Ray's and Annie's rabble-rousing Berkeley politics.

Ray's field soon becomes his cathedral, his confession, his rosary, and his penance. He spends hours raking it, grooming it, and watering it with the faith of a supplicant, assured of the knowledge that if he doesn't get the field—his Hail Mary—just right, whatever spell it might cast will fail. The Romantic nature of Ray's radical vision helps free him from the fatalistic thinking that has him convinced of his incompetence as a farmer, father, and financier. If he can somehow reproduce the transcendent image in his mind's eye with absolute fidelity, he believes something good is bound to happen.

Here the story deftly pivots to its core theme: faith in the unseen. Before he begins to build the field, Ray experiences a premonition of a "dreamlike image of a baseball field at night" and the ghostly silhouette of a man with his back turned to him. The setting for the haunt is a dreamy half-lit Midwest awash in the darker pastels of the threshold-hour after the sun goes down and before the moon rises. The scenes are a nocturne given ethereal substance by the spooky mists hanging over endless cornfields that simulate the hereafter.

My favorite ghostly character in *Field of Dreams* is Archibald "Moonlight" Graham, the onetime right fielder for the New York Giants turned local doctor in Chisholm, Minnesota. It's Moonlight Graham for whom the haunty voice in Kinsella's head whispers, "Go the distance," which Ray interprets to mean "Drive to Chisholm, Minnesota." In the film Ray asks the aged small-town doctor if he could make any wish what it might be, and Doc Graham replies:

> Well, you know I . . . I never got to bat in the major leagues. I would have liked to have had that chance. Just once. To stare down a big league pitcher. To stare him down, and just as he goes into his windup, wink. Make him think you know something he doesn't. That's what I wish for. A chance to squint at a sky so blue that it hurts your eyes just to look at it. To feel the tingling in your arm as you connect with the ball. To run the bases—stretch a double into a triple, and flop face-first into third, wrap your arms around the bag. That's my wish, Ray Kinsella. That's my wish. And is there enough magic out there in the moonlight to make this dream come true?

Maybe it's because I grew up with men and women like Doc Graham—self-sacrificial, good of heart, true of purpose, and haunted by dreams of roads not taken—that his words still send shivers down my spine. Doc Graham is my grandfather, sacrificing a life of travel for the gravity and rootedness of the farm; he's my grandmother, trading a promising career as an artist and musician for the less glamorous but no less worthy calling cards of mother, grandmother, and farmer's wife. In each case unyielding ties to the past, to family and to the land, prevented the pursuit of more glamorous lives. And though such trade-offs are surely more a part of the human condition than a strictly regional inheritance, it's fair to say that these what-might-have-been stories resonate more deeply in places where duty trumps mobility, and where economic limitations and conservative cultural mores constrain self-realization. Perhaps this is the definition of a haunt—the psychodynamic, psychoactive space between what the haunted wants (or wanted) to be, and what they are (or were) in actuality.

In real life Moonlight Graham played only one inning of one game on June 29, 1905, before being sent back down to the minors. He died in

Chisholm, Minnesota, in August 1965 at age eighty-seven. He spent the blink of an eye in the major leagues, and forty full years, from 1919 to 1959, serving as the doctor in the Chisholm schools. He died a strictly local rather than national hero, known for giving free exams to the poor children of the Iron Range miners who could come to his office on Saturdays to have their eyes checked free of charge. In the film Doc Graham seems full of life as he takes his midnight constitutional down the deserted streets of Chisholm wearing his flat cap and wielding his cane. Only wisps of gray smoke, a soundtrack in a minor chord, and the deserted streets remind us that Ray is, in fact, visiting a dead man—a real-life ballplayer who died in 1965. It's a time travel scene, moving back ten years before the novel on which the movie was based, *Shoeless Joe*, was even a glimmer in author W. P. Kinsella's eyes. To live in a small community like Graham's Chisholm, Minnesota, is to be keenly aware of time past and passing, of the spirits of forebears forever floating in the cornfield mists or lingering just around the next bend. The idea that the actions taken in this life can ease, and sometimes exacerbate, the pain of the departed ("ease his pain; go the distance") amounts to something more than mere parable.

Accompanying Ray on his quest to Chisholm is writer Terence Mann, played by James Earl Jones. A cynic when Ray kidnaps him from Boston, Mann eventually agrees to accompany Kinsella and a youthful Graham back to the Field of Dreams, so that the doubting writer might see for himself the Romantic vision our hero has fashioned from his acres of Midwestern corn. Once on the field Mann transforms from writerly misanthrope into bright-eyed boy again, imbued with innocence and clairvoyance. When the town banker, played by Busfield, arrives at the farm demanding Ray sign the foreclosure papers, it's Mann who quietly gives our hero faith, speaking his premonition:

> Ray, people will come, Ray. They'll come . . . for reasons they can't even fathom. They'll turn up your driveway, not knowing for sure why they're doing it. They'll arrive at your door as innocent as children, longing for the past. "Of course, we won't mind if you have a look around," you'll say. "It's only twenty dollars per person." They'll pass over the money without even thinking about it; for it is money they have and peace they lack.
>
> And they'll walk out to the bleachers, and sit in shirt-sleeves on a perfect afternoon. They'll find they have reserved seats somewhere along one of the baselines, where they sat when they were children and cheered their

heroes. And they'll watch the game, and it'll be as if they'd dipped themselves in magic waters. The memories will be so thick, they'll have to brush them away from their faces.

People will come, Ray. The one constant through all the years, Ray, has been baseball. America has rolled by like an army of steamrollers. It's been erased like a blackboard, rebuilt, and erased again. But baseball has marked the time. This field, this game, is a part of our past, Ray. It reminds us of all that once was good, and it could be again. Oh, people will come, Ray. People will most definitely come.

Later, when Shoeless Joe invites Mann out into the cornfield, the scribe faces an irrevocable decision that's part Faustian bargain and part Jimmy Stewart *It's a Wonderful Life*: whether to forsake a fraught and frustrating existence (life) for the allure of the unknown (death) and concourse with angels. When Mann contentedly crosses the first-base line and strides out onto the field, the mechanics of his departure from the world of the living follow the rules of the established ghost story, wherein a clear delineation exists between the moonlit, nocturnal realm of the spirits and the daytime, sunlit world ruled by the living. Mann must choose either to reside among the living or to depart with the team of ghost players into the Cornfield Beyond, but he cannot have both. Moonlight Graham, too, faces a similar threshold moment, in reverse, when he crosses the first-base line from field to sideline in order to treat Ray's injured daughter Karin. In so choosing he resumes his mortal form, transforming before our eyes from a wide-eyed major league prospect full of youthful immortality back into an aging and benevolent doctor.

If Mann is the movie's liminal writer-shaman, and Moonlight Graham its sacrificial Christlike figure, we, the viewer, are surely aligned with Ray or Annie as our proxy—needed in this life, accountable to something or someone, vehicles for something greater than ourselves that we little understand but nevertheless choose to serve on faith. We're the receptacles for voices that guide us, instruct us, and madden us in their inscrutability.

"If you build it, he will come," the voice in the movie tells Ray of the fantastic ballfield he's contemplating, and come they have in real life, in numbers that drew the attention of Chicago-area real estate investor Denise Stillman, whose Go the Distance Baseball LLC bought the 193-acre Don Lansing farm on which the Field sits in 2013 for $3.4 million with the goal of turning it into a youth baseball sports complex of the kind that had been built in Cooperstown, New York. Initially, it seemed the Stillmans were godsend buyers, ensuring as part of the acquisition that the Field would remain rather than be plowed under for corn and soybeans, as had happened to a portion of the outfield in the past. In addition to preserving the ballpark, Go the Distance would construct something it called All-Star Ballpark Heaven, a youth baseball complex with twenty-four fields and sixty clubhouses arrayed around the centerpiece property. "There are as many reasons people come to the field as people who come to the field," Stillman told the *Los Angeles Times*. "It's a place of healing, a place of acceptance."

Almost immediately, however, Stillman and Go the Distance found themselves playing defense against folks who wanted the field left exactly as-is—as a mom-and-pop shop lovingly maintained on a shoestring budget by a Heartland farm family with no tickets, no turnstiles, and no attempt, other than a small gift shop, to cash in on the faith of those making pilgrimage. A group of about twenty Dyersville area locals calling itself the Residential & Agricultural Advisory Committee LLC, or RAAC for short, filed suit to stop the rezoning of the property in district court, blanketing the town one Sunday morning with anonymous leaflets headlined "Save Our Town." Among other insinuations, the "Save Our Town" letter alleged that local restaurants and hotels would begin catering to high-dollar out-of-town visitors and neglect the needs of regular customers; the city, in its eagerness to encourage growth at any cost, would throw its citizens under the bus in pursuit of the almighty dollar. Already the Stillmans had been incented with a reported $16.5 million sales tax rebate, and a $15 million Midwest Disaster Area Bond Allocation. RAAC accused the Dyersville City Council of using the Stillmans' purchase as a reason to make a land-grab, voluntarily annexing land between the city limits and the Field of Dreams, thereby turning the historically rural landscape into a de facto exurb subject to the dominion of the city. The Stillmans, in turn, filed countersuit for libel against RAAC for what they considered the group's false propaganda detrimental to their project.

Shortly thereafter an anonymous moderator in town created the Save the Field of Dreams Facebook page as a place where citizens clamoring for a referendum or a public vote could air their opinion, as well as the growing number of Field of Dreams supporters across the country suspicious of the All-Star Ballpark Heaven development plans. The ensuing conflict was no longer limited to locals versus outsiders but fundamentalists versus what might be called secularists. The fundamentalists wanted to see the town of four thousand avoid selling its soul to the highest bidder, while the secularists didn't care as much where the money came from, so long as it helped stimulate economic development and better quality of life in the undersized industrial and agricultural community. In the view of the fundamentalists the Field's real value lay in the penitents who found solace there that they could find nowhere else. Once the temple had been co-opted by commercial or corporate forces, they argued, that spirit would fly from the place like a choir of frightened angels, perhaps never to return. It wasn't that people in general would stop coming but that once the Field was turned into a commercial enterprise, purists would lose faith.

Once the Save the Field Facebook page was up and running, defenders of the Field weighed in from all across North America. Many, like Laura Grzyb of Regina, Canada, bore personal witness to the quasi-religious experience. "Part of what makes it so amazing to visit is its remoteness," Grzyb posted in March, months before tonight's anniversary weekend showing of the film. "Even the drive as we arrived was perfect. The small farms and huge corn fields, winding gravel roads we took . . . all added to the magic of this place. If this development goes ahead it will lose this magic. I love the look of the development and it is a great thing for baseball in your region . . . but not here in this magic place. Please."

From Green Bay, Wisconsin, Ken Crain posted this assessment: "Another case of big-city, greed driven 'developers' destroying something for the almighty dollar." Protecting the sanctity of the field, its forever "feel," must be paramount, Crain insisted, concluding: "This development will crush what Field of Dreams is, but people like the Stillmans don't give a crap about that sort of thing. It would be nice if they would just stay in Chicago instead of planting their cancer in the middle of Heaven/Iowa. People like them make me sick."

From New York City, Yankee fan Joe Martell echoed Crain's sentiments, opining at length:

The whole allure and "magic" of the Field of Dreams is that it is a baseball field built in the middle of a cornfield. Surrounding it with 24 baseball fields, along with parking, concession stands, bathrooms, meeting rooms, etc., does not take away from this allure and magic, it totally destroys it! The Field of Dreams becomes just another field immersed among many. Something that is common and can be seen in any city, in any state throughout this country. As the Terence Mann character states in the movie: "This field, this game: it's a part of our past, Ray. It reminds of us of all that once was good and it could be again." Enough said!

Andy Long weighed in from Ohio:

I don't think you need to be from Dyersville to be passionate about the future of this place. I'm from rural Ohio and have only passed through Iowa once in my life, but this place means a lot to me. My father taught me baseball and we spent many a lazy summer night listening to Cincinnati Reds games on the radio. He passed away last fall and as this is my first baseball season without him, I long for one more catch with him. I won't, sadly, but a visit for the first time to the Field in its glory will help me find closure. It isn't just a baseball field. It's a national treasure, and we should keep it preserved as is.

Brenda Harrington agreed that the field should be a nationally protected site, though her choice of words was decidedly less diplomatic: "I am so tired of the greedy a-holes out there destroying beautiful places like this one."

Perhaps sensing that they were losing the public relations battle for All-Star Ballpark Heaven, Stillman and the *Field of Dreams* movie site took to Facebook to defend themselves, but even that attempt at redirecting the conversation backfired when it was discovered that several thousand "likes" that had suddenly appeared on the Stillmans' site had originated in Istanbul, suggesting that Go the Distance LLC had paid for the appearance of support.

Increasingly, the battle over the Field as holy ground assumed a Gothic dimension. A letter to the editor of the *Des Moines Register* concluded its appeal with, "As for proposed All-Star Ballpark Heaven, please. That monstrosity is to the spirit of the FIELD OF DREAMS story as performance-enhancing drugs are to bubblegum." Meanwhile, Save the Field advocate Michael Collins exhorted his fellow conscientious objectors, "Go the distance to the homes of the owners of the Go the Distance LLC and take your pitchforks and torches. Leave the damned field alone!"

Go the Distance LLC had unwittingly unleashed a perfect storm of grassroots protest, bringing the battle to an agrarian region known for its resistance to change. It was one thing for locals to abide the abandonment or razing of a seldom-used or crumbling brick-and-mortar historic building, but quite another to face the prospect of living in perpetuity with a once sacred site turned into a commercial zone. The devil had slouched into Bethlehem, the Field's most ardent preservationists claimed, as they mobilized for a conflict that felt very much like a real-life representation of the on-screen conflict between the heartless banker played by Busfield and the idealist-dreamer-Romantic played by Costner. In the script the bank that threatens the Kinsellas with foreclosure stands as the story's only true evil, an antagonist far more dangerous than the scandalous Chicago Black Sox players the film depicts as existing in a kind of purgatory. In Romantic fashion the script posits true sin as a hero who fails to listen to their own voice or fails to act on the dictates of their individual conscience. RAAC and the Save the Field of Dreams Facebook page had been created as vehicles of a community conscience with an almost Gothic mandate: drive the usurping elites away from this place, with pitchforks if necessary.

With its plans to take the movie's lasting legacy to the bank, Go the Distance LLC had unwittingly piqued supporters of America's most traditional sport, a national pastime whose devotees are seemingly hardwired for nostalgia. In baseball, generational memories can be overlaid, and records compared, because the basics of the game—wooden bat, rawhide ball—have remained pure in the eyes of the game's followers. "[Baseball] breaks my heart," former Major League Baseball Commissioner Bart Giamatti writes in his book *A Great and Glorious Game*, "because it was meant to foster in me again the illusion that there was something abiding, some pattern and some impulse that could come together to make a reality that could resist the corrosion."

Little wonder that enthusiasts would make a devil of the limited liability corporation that proposed to turn a sacred field into a money-making venture, for in changing it from a fated ballpark blessed with a unique brand of homegrown mysticism to a for-profit complex, they ran afoul not only of baseballers' need for the illusion of guilelessness but also their need to protect something in their lives as pure and uncompromised. "I need to think something lasts forever," Giamatti opines, locating himself among the mainline of the game's sentimentalists. "It might as well be that state of being that is a game; it might as well be that, in a green field, in the sun."

Almost from the beginning life has been imitating art where the Field of Dreams is concerned. Like Ray Kinsella in the film, the farm's original owners, the Lansings, had been family farmers caring for land that went back one hundred years. The eventual visit from the Hollywood location scout came as a bolt out of the blue, shocking them until they, like Ray Kinsella, realized they had something special. Once the farm had been turned into a set and the completed movie nominated for an Academy Award, the "they will come" prophecy Terence Mann issued Ray Kinsella in the film happened to the Lansings in real life. In fact, the family felt so strongly that the Field, like the movie, should be kept "small, simple, serene" that they eventually bought out their more commercially inclined neighbors, the Ameskamps, who owned left and center fields. Now, in fighting against the Field's development, RAAC and the moderators of the Save the Field Facebook page fancied themselves conjuring the fighting spirit of Ray and Annie Kinsella, who in the film protest against the banning of books and other attacks on free speech in their community in addition to building the Field and defending it from would-be infidels like the town banker bent on repossessing the property.

Meanwhile, the flesh-and-blood Ghost Players who played ball each Sunday when the Lansings owned the farm wondered whether they, like Shoeless Joe Jackson's Black Sox in the movie, would lose their venue with the change in ownership. Some of the Ghost Players were locals with a passion for the game and a willingness to dress up once a week in the historic Black Sox uniforms. But others were former ballplayers drawn here by a dream, like Moonlight Graham and Ray's father in the movie. One was Ron "Hank" Lucas, a sixty-five-year-old upholsterer from Holy Cross, Iowa. In 1967, Bill Plaschke of the *Los Angeles Times* reported, Lucas signed with the Dodgers and pitched one summer for their rookie league squad before an accident at the meatpacking company where he worked ended his baseball career. "My career was finished before I ever got a chance," Lucas told the *Times*. "This field gave me another one." Frank Dardis, another of the Ghost Players who appeared in the movie in 1988, kept coming back, unable to get enough of the feeling the Field imparted to him. "After all these years it's still amazing, you walk out of the corn and you can hear a pin drop, we still get goose bumps," he told the press. "You hear people crying. You see people turn to each other. This is one place where families aren't afraid to say, 'I love you.'"

Until the Lansings sold their dream to Go the Distance LLC, the Ghost Players had functioned like a sort of Knights Templar—serving as custodians of the field, quite literally, and defenders of the ideals it stood for. Now, however, the regular Sunday appearances of the Ghost Players have ceased, as if the team itself had disappeared into the corn, unwilling to play ball until the true spirt of the place returned.

On a makeshift stage consisting of potted palms and a picket fence Denise Stillman is playing master of ceremonies as if no bad blood runs between herself and the community. The majority of the out-of-town visitors arriving for the weekend's twenty-fifth anniversary celebration are blissfully unaware of the conflict, knowing little to nothing of the battle playing out in the courts. With Costner and his costars recalling the magic of that summer of 1988, Stillman and her opponents are, to their credit, willing to temporarily put aside old grudges for the sake of tonight's birthday party.

Costner and Busfield and Brown, as if by some powerful Hollywood witchery, may have cheated Father Time, but I, sitting in my folding chair, have changed mightily from the 135-pounds-dripping-wet pipsqueak who brought his first-ever serious girlfriend here on their first long-distance outing together away from the prying eyes of parents. In the intervening years I've lost my father, fallen in love, had my heart broken, and learned to fall in love again. I'm thicker about the middle and through the face, my mien now my father's at my age, but grayer. And yet while I look more and more like him with every passing day it's my mother whose spirit I conjure on this movie anniversary night, a survivor's spirit that could dream a dream and stay with that dream until it had—good or bad—come to pass.

Maybe I should be ashamed at the giddy anticipation I feel being here twenty-five years later for an evening of feel-good celebrity worship, of indulging in movie make-believe, but I feel no such call to judge. I'm simply grateful that this spot still exists and that it's here to receive my return. My knock may be different, but the door still opens. Maybe it's because I grew up on my own green peaceful place steeped in history that I do not feel an urgent need to extract peace from the evening's pastoral vision. Or maybe I have, like so many others, simply taken this humble holy ground for granted, since it is, comparatively speaking, in my own backyard.

On this Father's Day weekend the press is reporting the case of a terminally ill father who spent the day playing catch with his adult sons before readying himself to watch the movie on the inflatable screen in center field. Afterward in the guest registry the father wrote, "I can die now," and his son, right below him: "My father can die now."

Like any mecca this is a place not for the spiritually complete, if such a thing exists, but for the broken looking for a home, in the original sense of the word *nostalgia—home* coupled with *sickness*. And maybe it says something about the brokenness of men, or our human need to heal, that we are said to be the intended audience for the movie's object lesson: the necessity of easing the pain of those we have wronged or slighted, everything the voice tells us to do that we have thus far resisted. In that sense the Field of Dreams is a place of last resort at the same time that it is a place of new beginnings. It's a church with bleachers instead of pews.

Before the stadium lights go down and the opening credits roll Costner's voice drops to a whisper. He intimates that women more than men understand the core message at the heart of the film. "When we talk about *Field of Dreams* we talk about men crying, and sometimes crying uncontrollably, and it's a movie about the things that go unsaid between fathers and sons. But I think . . . what has made this movie universal is women. . . . Women came to the movie and didn't care about Gil Hodges or the men coming out of the corn. The theme women got when they watched *Field of Dreams* with men is that they looked at them and said, 'You fix this!' You call your dad and you fix this silliness. You reach out to your son and fix this silliness that's keeping you apart."

And maybe that, in the end, is the whispered voice both sides of the nightmarish Field of Dreams controversy would do well to listen to—the one reminding the wounded hero in us to listen, to heal, and, ultimately, to mend.

12

Cornfield Cathedrals

You won't find Foxfield Golf Course on any official map. It doesn't advertise. It's run by two unpaid employees, a father and a son. There's no director of marketing, no blow-dried golf pro with a silver spoon, no fleet of fancy mowers grooming the course within an inch of its life. Golf's bureaucrats with their impossible-to-reach standards and half-cocked formulae were never allowed a foothold here.

Some say this cornfield mecca never really existed, apart from some inexpensive business cards printed once upon a time. And yet I played it, day after day, adapting my game, polishing my strokes, learning my chops. The meadowlarks, the hand-stitched yellow nylon flags, the dandelions, the bee trees, the farm apples, the island green surrounded not by deep blue water but by barnyard gravel, the two-hundred-yard forced carry over a fourteen-foot-high wall of field corn to a distant barn topped with a windsock. Foxfield was my Nirvana and Valhalla.

Alas, Foxfield is no more. Not long ago I paid my final respects, pulling over on the gravel shoulder back home in farm country to let the car idle while my memories settled. The first green, atop the knoll 221 yards out, had been plowed under, the rotting elms and ashes and Scotch pines bulldozed, the land pressed back into service growing commodity crops.

What remains is a memory of how soulful life in such a far-off place as this can be—how right—and the realization that for its ultimate meaning an outdoor game, played among an outdoor people, depends on the evocativeness of the environs, the worthiness of the stadium.

Theologians, mystics, literary theorists, and quacks insist we become pilgrims only when we realize what we lack. "A pattern emerges," author Paul Ellie observes, "one that seems to fit Dante and Chaucer . . . and the present day alike. A pilgrimage is a journey undertaken in light of a story. A great event has happened; the pilgrim hears the reports and goes in search of the evidence, aspiring to be an eye-witness." Me, I'm seeking to drink from that inimitable Kool-Aid of my youth, before the snake slithered across the fairway, before Tiger Woods hit the fire hydrant. I want out of a life of Walmarts and sweatshop-forged 9-irons and decadent country clubs that surely qualify as cultural and spiritual malaise. I want back to the home farm, to the spirit-filled work and play that pervaded there.

Last year, for the first time in my life, I played just twice. Seen one overcrowded, nondescript, weekender's golf course, you've seen them all, the cynic in me decided: the two hot dogs nobody wants spinning endlessly on the rotisserie, the Snickers bars and Planter's peanuts and expired Rolaids on offer behind the counter, the cheap Scotch at the bar on hold for a hole-in-one or a blindside tragedy before it can be liberated from the bottle. Like Limbo, we don't celebrate enough here in the overlooked, underrated middle of the country. We play it safe and take our bogeys, blithely chirping "it could have been worse." These days the Saturday grind at the nearest municipal course in the nearest city can feel like a six-hour slog through Gomorrah.

After thirty-odd years of such middling Middle Americanism, of Protestant work ethic and prudence bordering on Puritanical, I'm ready to be a true pilgrim, to do what pilgrims do: travel across the burning sands in search of a mecca.

A year ago I would have phoned my father on the farm to tell him I would be stopping by to see him on my westward journey. But my father, bless him, passed away last March, just a few weeks shy of the Masters golf tournament we watched religiously together. I got the call to come in the darkest, most godforsaken hour of morning, and a week later his spirit had flown. In our blind stumbling grief at the moment of his passing, searching desperately for a way to mark his passage into that paradise beyond this one, my mother, sister, and I, keeping all-night vigil in his hospice room, opened a Florida orange—a love of his on par with golf. We might instead have opened a sleeve of Topflites in his honor, so great was his admiration of, and existential angst about, the four-letter game.

It's my father I'm thinking of now as I make final preparations for my trip, and the course we built together in our back pasture. He was only a few years older than I am now when he decided to "chase the dream" in the late 1980s. Every morning in those drought years, in between back-breaking jobs on the farm, he'd practice his game in the scant shade offered by our aluminum-sided pole building. As a teen I'd awake to the thwack of a 5-iron and see him there, his Marlboro burning on the ground, working out some unseen kink in his swing. I'm still not sure what his quest was back then—the mini-tours, the professional circuit, or maybe just the perfectionist goad of the game itself—but whatever it was, he must have felt it as acutely as the longing I feel for him now.

When finally I arrive at the farm I find the door to the shed we once used as our clubhouse firmly locked. I know better than to expect to see Dad zealously spraying weeds in the barnyard, or resolute behind the wheel of our John Deere tractor pulling the gang mower behind. Still, I half expect to see him, so profoundly does his spirit permeate this place, *our* place. Instead, in his absence a slow fire smolders in a burn barrel burned down to ashes. Today, after a prodigious rain, the grass is a monstrous, nitrogen-fed green. I have never seen the pastures look so lush. I pop the trunk and grab a club for what will almost surely be my final swings on the sacred soil of our home course—Foxfield G. C.—the "club" that consists of the pasturelands and ribbons of grass running through our family's 160-year-old, 500-acre heritage farm. In the eighties, when I took up the game under my father's tutelage, he named the course Foxfield after the elusive fleet-footed spirit that made its den in a ditch bank on our land's western boundary. The name stuck. Later he would have business cards made up, cards he would present in earnest to hollow-eyed night clerks at discount hotels in hopes of scoring a corporate discount during the few budget Christmas breaks we took in search of affordable winter golf.

Foxfield forever flummoxed the good folks behind the desk at the Motel 6 and Howard Johnson's, but it was real enough to us. At its peak it sported flags of yellow nylon sewn by my aunt Patricia, a small-town tailor. It boasted flagsticks welded by my father out of old scrap iron. It featured Kentucky bluegrass and rye sown and mown to tee-height by an honest-to-god reel mower, the "Turf King" Dad salvaged from a local junkyard run by a neighbor family aptly named the Rottmans and, with plenty of elbow grease and swearing, snake-charmed back to life.

Beyond our five-hundred-acre fiefdom, however, Foxfield remained a myth. As teens my golfing peers joined country clubs, while I made Foxfield's dozen pasture acres my adolescent proving grounds. I was both intensely proud of the homely, homespun course Dad and I had made and secretly ashamed of it; so much so that when my high school golf coach, impressed with my tee-to-green game, asked where I was a member, I swallowed my tongue. I realized how much like a bumpkin I'd sound when, inevitably acknowledging the telltale weaknesses in my game, I'd be forced to admit that I'd seldom had the privilege of practicing on "real" putting greens. In Foxfield's alternate reality, a shot hit within a club's length of my aunt Patricia's homemade flags was considered "good" or "in." Putting was a practical impossibility on the hardy rye-bluegrass mix planted at cornfields' edge. No matter how closely we cut it, generations of cumulative thatch made the shorn surface something closer to the stiffest military buzz-cut than the soft, even knap of tournament-ready bent grass.

This coming spring, the ground where I learned to love the game, the ground where I am now searching for a playable lie in the unmown grass, will be pushing up corn and soybeans again instead of swallowing up golf balls. Thus I've come to pay my respects on my way out West, the way you give a horse one last free-spirited romp before putting them out to pasture.

I choose a 9-iron and fall easily into my stance in the pasture east of the house where my great-grandparents' home once stood before it was burned to the ground. Just like that I am thirteen again, aiming my junior 5-iron at the old grove of ashes and elms that once stood where I now aim, back before my father bulldozed them, too, to produce this perfectly green expanse. I pick a particularly brown stalk of corn—nearer to harvest than the rest—and swing. It's a beauty, arcing high into the endless prairie sky, right at its target. I turn for a moment in hopes Dad might be watching from the window, as he used to after he'd gone inside to drink whiskey and read *Time* magazine, and I'd swing on into twilight.

My return shot back to the car is as bad as the shot out was good. The wiry, overgrown rye grabs my club, rolling it over. The shot, a low, weak flub, dives left. I find the ball nestled like an Easter egg in the preternaturally tall bluegrass a mere ninety yards distant and opt to walk it back in. I've four more hours to drive on the first leg of the journey to Omaha, Nebraska, where my friend Celeste promises she has a surprise awaiting me. Already, I've lingered too long.

I say goodbye, and thanks, to Foxfield in a voice barely above a whisper, throw my 9-iron—Dad's 9-iron—in the trunk, and pull out of the drive of the home club headed toward Nebraska in search of what lies beyond.

After a four-hour Autobahn I meet Celeste in the Omaha gloaming at the Summer Kitchen Cafe just off Interstate 80. Celeste grew up golfing in and around Papillion, Nebraska. Now, she's a freelance graphic artist. She slides into the booth across me wearing a black bow in her blonde hair, like something straight out of the Jazz Age.

"I've got something for you," she says after our meals arrive—a grilled cheese and soup for her, artery-clogging panini and fries for me. She opens up a folder and retrieves three sheets of loose-leaf sketchbook paper.

"Gods for your journey," Celeste says, passing them to me across the table. She beams, pointing to the first illustration of a girl in a pleated Easter dress bending over a delicate short-iron shot. "That's Chip. . . . She's all about finesse. Most of the gods of golf are men. You need a girl." Celeste points to a caption underneath the second god of golf she's drawn, an imp turning cartwheels in front of very serious linkster, poised midswing. *Distracting unsuspecting golfer into missing a shot*, the caption reads. "That one's Duff," she says.

"And last but not least . . . Bogey," she adds, pointing triumphantly to the final mug in the apocryphal trinity she's sketched for me. I follow her finger to a penciled-in big man bent painfully over a midiron shot, his bulbous rump stuck into the air. Another gentleman, equally portly, stands beside him in a waistcoat, knickers, and tie, his hand stuck insolently in his hip pocket. He looks like a mixture of William Howard Taft and Boss Hogg from *Dukes of Hazzard*.

"Double Bogey?" I ask.

"Yep," she says. "May they accompany you on your journey."

Nebraska's forgotten Sand Hills present the first of several gigantic sand traps west of Omaha. From Interstate 80 you can see them some thirty miles north, looming larger than hills but lower than mountains. I am destined now for Giltner, Nebraska, a burg that on its nascent web page advertises a pasture golf course somewhere on the outskirts of town.

The water tower in Giltner, as in many of the Middle Western farm towns time forgot, looks like a shiny metallic golf ball balanced atop a slender tee. Passing parched dryland corn in a region that was once called the Great American Desert, I'm yearning for golf of the kind I'd blissfully played with my father growing up. On what passes for Main Street I spot a man shuffling into the town's post office and follow so close on his heels I'm worried it'll seem to him like a stick-up. The last thing I want to do is scare off this precious human resource.

I wait in respectful silence for a moment before venturing a tentative *how-are-ya?*

"Surviving," he says, spinning the combo on his postal box. He doesn't look up.

"Sometimes that's all you can ask for," I say, and mean it. I live just outside a farm town like Giltner, a town where people struggle mightily. It's not the highly vocal kind of economic complaint that shows up on the front page of the *New York Times*. It's slow, grinding, proud rural poverty that asks little of the world around it and gets suffered in the kind of stoical silence many urbanites assume went the way of the dinosaur. "You don't know where Chapman Street is, do you?"

"Can't say I do," he says. "You might check over at the . . ." He lifts his seed-corn cap and scratches thoughtfully at the few hoary hairs underneath, clearly trying to think of a place in town where there'd be folks milling around on a Saturday morning. "Well, why don't you head on over to the fillin' station and see if they know."

At the filling station the guys seem glad for the distraction unexpectedly washed up on their shore. They offer enthusiastic directions to my destination—on a gravel road, past a grove of trees, across a bridge, onto the blacktop, all the way to the *town* of Chapman about fifteen miles distant, not to Chapman *Street*, as I had originally thought.

"No good way to get to Chapman," one of the gas-station guys opines. "Whatcha lookin' for anyway?"

Peace, I want to say. *Longing. Be-Longing.*

"A pasture golf course," I confess, bracing for some good-natured ribbing, but receiving none.

"There's a Pump 'n' Pantry in Chapman," the man tells me. "If you get lost again, ask 'em there."

After several wrong turns I eventually pull into a potholed dirt lot beside an aluminum-sided farm building with a sign sporting a cartoon cow, the words "Pasture Golf," and a phone number. The land here, river bottomland, is dry and sandy, flat as a putter head.

I'm sitting on the back bumper eagerly donning my soft spikes when I spy a woman speeding toward me in a golf cart—the owner, I figure, come to issue me a hearty Great Plains welcome. I pay her coming only casual notice, chomping at the bit to get my clubs out of the trunk.

She skids to a stop in an unholy cloud of dust, offering a "Can I hep ya?" But her tone isn't exactly Chamber of Commerce.

My voice, when I find it, comes out unexpectedly John Wayne. "I'd love to play some golf, ma'am," I tell her.

A chicken runs between where she stands, beside her cart, and me. "Course's closed," she says firmly. We're at twenty paces, she and I, a distance better fit for gun-slinging than interpersonal communication. "Closed this past May. . . . Economy went bad. She pauses to point toward what was once fairway to an anemic stand of dryland maize. "We planted corn."

"I've driven a long way to get here," I venture on the heels of a long, painful silence. "Any chance I could play a hole?"

"We got weeds coming up through the old greens . . ." She trails off.

"Just one hole," I ask, feeling desperate.

She's sizing me up like an opponent in a game of Texas Hold'em, no doubt weighing the insurance risk of having a stranger tromping around on the edge of her cash crop. I can tell I look too young to her—too little salt in my pepper—to merit the potential liability. How can I possibly explain that I grew up playing my way around cornrows exactly like these, that for me they're part of the breadcrumb trail leading back to the game, and to my father.

"Can't do it," she says, finally.

The encounter badly bursts my pasture golf balloon, the trend that was to take golf back to its shepherd-humble roots and away from high-dollar, high-maintenance elitism and exclusivity. I'd banked on the fact that a golfing mecca might just as well exist down a rutted washboard road in the Great Plains as at the end of Magnolia Lane in Augusta, Georgia, or 17-Mile Drive in Pebble Beach, California, in the same way that, in a better world, one ought to be as likely to find a drop-dead gorgeous Donna Reed living in a farmhouse at the end of a gravel road as loitering with her mocha frappé at a suburban Starbucks.

Callaway, I console myself, once returned to the boiling cockpit of the car to search my map for a consolation source of pasture golf. Callaway, Nebraska, an hour and a half distant, is barely big enough for its own dot on the atlas. Alas, there's no phone number to call at the course, no way to prevent another rock-road goose chase ending in existential frustration. One of the quirks of pasture golf is that there's usually no paid staff, no set hours. You take your chances. So when you're already on a road rally across the great inland desert in search of a true unadulterated golf mecca, an hours-long crapshoot of a detour strikes you as eminently justifiable.

In an attempt at due diligence I work the phone to the Broken Bow Country Club. Broken Bow, Nebraska, is twenty miles and a world away from woebegone Callaway. In any case theirs is the nearest golf-related phone number I am able to find. When a woman named Lita answers I ask her if she's confident the course in Callaway still exists. "I hear about it every once in a while," she says, and I can't help but wonder if *once in a while* means, as it often does in my home region, anytime since the Bush administration. "Yeah, I'm pretty sure it's still open," she adds, talking herself, and me, into the course's existence. "You know it's got sand greens, right?"

The road to Callaway, thirty miles of twisting, brokeback country road that turns from gravel to pavement without warning, takes me into the heart of the Sand Hills—a depopulated expanse of warped, twisted, grass-covered knobs, cottonwood bottoms with coulees of trickling water, and bluffs of sand held down by something that looks like gorse. These aren't just dunes, they're mega dunes—badlands—as tall and wind whipped as anything along the shores of Lake Michigan.

I roll the windows down as I tour the tiny town of Callaway. I am surprised to discover the little burg of a few hundred souls out here on the edge of the prairie better provisioned than many bedroom community suburbs back in Chicagoland—complete with library, historical museum, community center, and a grocery that oddly trumpets the fact that it's open Thursdays. No Carnegie library with Corinthian columns here, just an ignominious agricultural, aluminum-sided pole building to shelter the books and the part-time town librarian. It looks like home.

When a few minutes later I roll into the gravel lot of the pasture course on the outskirts of town I am so thoroughly jangled from the dry dusty car ride that I fairly burst out of the car into the High Plains sun. From somewhere in the distance I hear the strangely welcoming sound of an internal combustion engine—a mower perhaps. I see flags fluttering, an old steel shed open to reveal a half dozen carts, and a sign that reads "out-of-town golfers $5.00 all day" on the side of an *American Gothic*–styled building that looks like it might have been a schoolhouse or country church in a previous life.

I slide my Honest Abe into the honors-system envelope, carefully feeding it into what looks like a recommissioned safebox. And I am off, like the shepherds of yore, in search of a rabbit hole. If the gods of golf are in heaven, and if indeed their pantheon is as large and diverse as such an inherently capricious game demands, then the gods must make their home, at least part of the year, in this purer representation of the shepherd's game. Surely, the angelic keepers of the sport's original flame would fly in here as often as they would in the sea-swept, coin-endowed cathedrals along the Coasts.

My first swing with Dad's old 2-iron is a pull-hook left into the high rough. I arrive to find the ball sitting down in a tractor tire–formed crater, from which I do well to advance it eighty crooked yards into still more tall-grass prairie. A romp into grasshopperland, a lost ball, and a few recovery shots later, I make my sand green debut.

When I finally do manage to sink a twelve-foot putt on the seventh green, I'm practically euphoric, though no one witnesses my triumph. I find one married couple, a dozen head of healthy-looking bovines, and at least as many golf balls mangled by the mower in my nine holes at the Callaway Golf Club. The couple proves good-natured (it's impossible to be any other way navigating the vagaries of pasture golf), the cattle docile, and the reclaimed golf balls plentiful. I ask the local couple what the protocol is for married golf on sand greens: Who smooths and who rakes? (Their marital advice / Zen koan of an answer: "It's give and take.")

My last drive turns out to be my best and longest, hit to within forty yards of the pin on the 309-yard ninth hole. When I arrive I am chagrined to find the ball sitting down in a depression of soft sand. I'm tempted to improve my lie, play "winter rules," until I hear my father's voice, unbidden, telling me to "play it as it is, not as you wish it to be."

I forego my par but keep my integrity.

Driving solo across America's high lonesome plains in an economy car without cruise control requires a pilgrim's devotion. The scant few golf courses you pass en route look like they'd sooner give you a horsewhipping than offer up a birdie. And if you happen to lack air-conditioning in your vehicle, as do I, the trip through the Great American Desert turns out to be positively hallucinogenic. At one point, in a heat-induced haze I imagine my long-deceased grandfather riding shotgun beside me in his bib overalls; another time I swear to seeing a dead ringer for Zsa Zsa Gabor as I pass through yet another town on the edge of the prairie.

Still, you're not alone. Make this trek in the late summer and you run into pilgrims and has-beens and hallucinogens of all sorts, all in search of a dream. Interstate 80 is the route of choice for neohippies en route to the Burning Man festival in Black Rock Desert, Nevada, crammed into their parents' cast-off Subarus and Volvos while the older longhairs still roll in their vintage VW buses and Westfalias. They don't wear flowers in their hair in the Google age, but they do put flowers on their bikes, and bikes on the back of their cars, and paint-swirled, Van Gogh-esque designs on the back of their buggies alongside the ubiquitous symbol of the Burning Man himself, a towering effigy that goes up in mad, orgiastic flames each summer to culminate the annual festival devoted to "radical self-expression."

Here and there, these seekers and peaceniks and conspiracy theorists have taken black rocks and arranged them along the roadside, against a backdrop of beige desert sands, into countless peace symbols and smiley faces and names of long-gone lovers and legends. Seeing this organic rock graffiti makes me glad to be part of the unhinged wagon train heading west in search of some El Dorado. Mine is the sublime solitude and unforgiving, soul-measuring examination offered by the kind of pasture golf I once played with my father on the farm; theirs the delicious, nihilistic flames of Burning Man. We all seek Nirvana, and we've all lit a fire under ourselves to find it.

When, on my way back to work and my "real life" awaiting me in northern Illinois, my check engine light comes on in Elko, Nevada, and I limp into a Motel 6 for the night, I'm not sure whether I am in purgatory or hell. And when I receive the next morning a $1,000 estimate for repairs, I smile gamely at the mechanical delay and compare my impulsive cross-Plains vision quest to thirty-six holes of golf played on a hundred-degree summer day. It turns out to be more about raw determination bordering on lunacy than it does about any particular talent or transcendent vision.

"Golf is a paradigm for life," my father used to tell me when, as an occasionally angsty teen, my faith in the game, and in myself, would be broken. Even then I had a hunch he was right. The road, by my father's logic, is little more than a concrete ribbon of fairway, the 1,600 round-trip miles between where you are now and where you dream to be. The intense heat is something, like any purifying fire, to be sought after, gutted out, and ultimately used to summon the angels of our better natures. The thoughts of family and former lovers that come to you, unbidden, during the long lonely drive must be allowed to pass, Zen-like, in favor of existing in the moment of your making. You may be alone out here on the inward nine, literally and figuratively leaking oil, but you are headed home, back toward the house.

And when finally you arrive home on the night of the fourth day, when God created Pebble Beach, Augusta National, and the Nebraska Sand Hills, and said it was good, you arrive under a wildly clairvoyant moon-man burning through a gauze of cottony midcontinent sky seen as if viewed through the illuminated rice paper of a Japanese lantern.

In the wee hours you drive into this or that ubiquitous suburban village where you earn your otherwise unremarkable living, and where you have left the porch light on for yourself in anticipation of your return—like candles lit and left by the faithful to light the path home for the restless blessed dead. Down darkened streets you cruise, past shuttered, highbrow boutiques and darkened big-box stores, toward this handsome place of your workaday existence, a place where the gods of commerce reign supreme. Slipping the car into park you opt to leave the clubs in the car overnight, easing out of your over-the-road life on a seeker's still shaky limbs before falling gratefully into bed.

Your father taught you to work toward such a place in life—banker's hours, nice work if you can get it, roof over your head; your father taught you to abhor such a place, with its easy and godless complacencies. Your real home, lest you ever forget it, or get uppity, is a place of common birds and common songs, of common trees that do not flower for show or on call.

You, you unremarkable pilgrim, you beautiful lost soul, you fallen angel, you were never trained to bloom, but you will.

13

DOVESONG

A Middle American Dirge

The mourning dove's funerary dirge debuts to mixed reviews. She's full-breasted as an opera singer, her bosom a too-human sort of pink. Man and wife roost on opposite sides of the windy barnyard and coo to one another the reedy, melancholic tunes soon to turn summer afternoons wistful. *I am pretty sad, pretty sad, pretty sad for you*, they croon, and the tenor of our days turns gray to suit.

The April afternoon warms into the low 80s, the flies stuck like glue to the sugar water weeping from the newly cut maples.

I would end it if I could, laments the grief-stricken farmer's son over and over, hand-wringing until his sweetie gently calls him Love and coos, Turn on some music if the dovesong bothers you.

If thy right hand offend thee, cut it off.

We're thirsty for the season's first color, for purples and blues. Only a splash of violets underfoot, yet we'll make a tincture of it, like the monks do. It'll do to soothe the pain, or stop a tumor dead in its tracks. Eat the roots and make a stew. Decorate tombs.

For the first time in nearly a century open season has been declared on the dove. Amendments fail to outlaw the lead bullet or set the kill zone back from our homes. The chief executive signs the bill in the company of lobbyists from the NRA. These five ounces of meat with wings are purported to bring seven million dollars into governmental coffers. Our governor is a man of God, we are reminded upon passage of the controversial bill.

Forty-one of fifty states favor open season on the dove of mourning, making them, in effect, sitting ducks.

"I would give some violets, but they withered all when my father died." —Ophelia

Rosemary for remembrance; fennel for flattery; columbine for ingratitude; daises for faithlessness. Violets for constancy of devotion.

The beautiful soul the farmer's son laid to rest had made his wishes known in advance. He'd wanted to be buried in a pine box, what our resident casket-making monks call "the Simple Rectangular Casket," no bones about it. "This model is frequently used as a presentation casket as well as a cremation casket," claims the glossy sales brochure. It's as good for a bed as it is for a bonfire. Screwdriver and keepsake cross included.

In the bright April afternoon the vultures, *Cathartes aura*, alight on the barn's bowing roofline, up near the sky-blue lightning rod with it blown glass bulb, and overwatch. They spread their wings to six, seven feet, easy, airing out underfeathers, carpal edges drying for imminent flight. The farmer's son shivers when the shadow passes overhead, a blight upon the sun, a pox upon us. He's got a grim job to do.

What does the dove say? *Perch-coo*, he croons, unmated on his conspicuous perch. Listen close and it's a soft *coo-oo* followed by two or three louder *coos*. He's a one-note wonder.

It's the ides of April and the farmer's son and his dear one, little dove, wake up to a surprise snowfall, great white flakes of it, falling from the sky in clumps, plastering the trunks of pines like so much wet confetti, decorating the ditch thistles like Christmas holly. By midmorning it melts, the damp bringing the red-breasted robins out to breakfast beneath the car.

We are slowly inventorying what winter has left us. We have:

A bar
A bank
A realtor
A mechanic
A gas station
A grain elevator
A Boneman
Two abandoned weight loss centers, one labeled "Curves," the other called "Silhouettes"
A homemade sign on Main that reads "Elvis Lives"

We do not have:

A doctor
A café
A grocery store
A newspaper
A butcher or a baker

We do have a chiropractor. We are a people with bad backs. We must go elsewhere for our internal medicine and our mental healthcare, or we do not go at all.

The town where Elvis lives has not grown in more than twenty years.

When this land was first settled, the pioneers recorded fourteen to sixteen inches of topsoil. By 2000 the average was six to eight inches. Experts predict the rest will be gone within our children's lifetime.

Would you believe the obscene Easter lily is still sending forth its phallic blooms and its vulvic pistil? Last weekend he peaked inside, watched the waxy lips ready themselves for the dusting of pollen.

If you stay long enough after a country burial you'll see the tent come down like a big top, the church-basement chairs snapped shut, and the faux velvet seat coverings folded up like so much cheap linen. You'll see the gravedigger and his sons, idling just out of view down the gravel road, drive right up to the side of the gaping maw and begin shoveling the dirt in, Bonemen all.

The trick is to set a little topsoil aside, near the back. That's saved to go on last, to grow the grass whose shocking green will aid in our forgetting.

The four grown Bonemen work in concert, the father and his sons: the alternating rhythm of their shovels penetrating the black dirt and the thump of the soil on the pine box sounds, from a distance, like the old field song:

> Oh, poor sinner,
> Now is your time
> Oh, poor sinner,
> Now is your time
> Oh, poor sinner
> Now is your time
> What are you going to do
> When your lamp burns down?

After years of felling trees by hand, the power of the chainsaw intoxicates him. The maples fall all too easily once he gets the knack of it, cutting the notch first in the direction of the fall, and on the tougher trees, throwing his Sweetie a rope to tug on. The oldest of the maples are nearly as old as he, and yet they'll come down in a minute. He thinks of the Lorax as the engine whines, but he tells himself he's not clear-cutting but thinning, cultivating, taking out the weak and the rotted and the diseased. He's playing God in the name of forestry, of husbandry.

Half of every pound of wood he cuts, the experts tell him, is pure carbon sink. Young trees soak up more. The old have lost their absorption, become a liability.

In the woodlands, flush with the power of the instrument his father forbade him, he feels himself becoming a monster, a creature. His blood is up. The trees are coming down.

His little dove says he seems distant, and he does, even to himself. There are things in his heart he cannot find the words for. How he might go the way of his father. How he might choose blackness. How he might look for the thing beyond the thing and go gently into that good night. He might.

And the Holy Ghost descended in a bodily shape like a dove upon him.

The clever grackle will soak bread in puddles of rainwater to soften it to taste. Flighty ventriloquist, he will make you think you are hearing the music of angels when you are in fact hearing musical complaint. He will use another bird's nest if the bird hotel is booked for the night. He will wipe the antiseptic secretion of ants, walnuts, lemons, marigold blossoms, mothballs, or chokecherries on his wings to kill off parasites. He's an alchemist of iridescence, a paragon of self-preservation.

The mischievous grackle can also mimic the sounds of other birds or even humans when it suits him, though not, it should be noted, as convincingly as the mockingbird.

In the afternoon, when he and his Sugar clear brush together, the red-winged blackbirds alight on the silver maples. *Agelaius phoeniceus*. Birds with crimson epaulets. Together they send up a throaty *check* followed by a slurry-whistle *terrr-eee*, until the trees ring. *Chit chit chit chit cheer teer teer teerr*. The couple watch them warily. An angry blackbird is prone to attack if provoked, but at a distance they're a welcome chorus.

"Oh, if I was a blackbird could whistle and sing
I'd follow the vessel my true love sails in
And in the top riggin' I would there build my next
And I'd flutter my wings o'er her lily-white breast
Or if I was a scholar and could handle the pen
Once secret love letter to my true love I'd send
And tell of my sorrow." —Traditional

The farmer's son and his little dove make a nest together alone on the disturbed prairie, overhead the globe of stars upset and pushing back.

On the way to meet his father's personal banker—the usual agrarian bogeyman—the farmer's son takes the backroads. He passes a place called Tamarack Stables, its equestrian jumps toppled by the wind, travels past Crock Angus and Jerri's Cut and Curl, to the new million-dollar homes with the golf carts parked out front, ready for the new season. Development is at his doorstep a half-hour drive from the city limits of cereal town. The new elementary school, paid for with bonds, stands on the north side. Only the playground equipment and the two small spruces in the lawn distinguish it from a prison, or a lab, or a government installation, or an office suite of corporate thinktanks. It's impossible to tell anymore at a glance, from the outside, what a building might house.

The country road bends west and he follows it, past the gray Presbyterian church with the sign out front that reads "It is holy to be forgiven," past the brown-brick Methodist church in town where his grandparents occupied the pews together for their commencement service in 1935, and where they married five years later, on a cold day in December, his grandfather's birthday, so they could remember.

Though he is not family, the funeral director takes care to use the proper noun "Dad" in the subject line of his e-mails, as in "A month after Dad's funeral . . ."

The debate over open season on the mourning dove heralds the coming of the culture wars. Readers weigh in. One says, "Good deal, something more to kill." Someone else says, "Glad to see another tasty option for the menu and the sport." And another: "Go find a tree, give it some love, and leave us alone."

The black-capped chickadee makes its visit to the cemetery early, saying *fee-bee*. It would eat from my hand if I would let it, this gentle angel that will lay me a half dozen speckled eggs in a perfect cup of woven grass, like an Easter basket.

Lately we have been uneasy with the words with which we name our professions, lest they suggest the macabre or draconian to the next generation. *Farmer* alone is verboten unless preceded by "organic," "sustainable," or "conservation." We prefer "funeral director" to "mortician" or "undertaker." A funeral director orchestrates funerals. Perhaps we should call him a "grief educator."

The dove is a pigeon with a public relations firm, detractors say.

Beethoven's last recorded words were "Pity, pity—too late!" as the dying genius was told of a gift of twelve bottles of wine from his publisher. The maestro died of a shrunken liver, likely caused by too much drink. A competing theory claims the great composer's last words were "Plaudite, amici, comedia finita est"—*Applaud, my friends, the comedy is over.*

Please, he says, motioning the farmer's son to sit in the soft seats in the lobby, *think of me as your wealth manager.*

The land that is his birthright will be sold to pay the father's medicals bills and settle the estate. The housing development that springs up like a cancer will be named for the nearest river, stream, or saleable natural feature. Lots will be bought by the well-coiffed engineers who commute to work in the nearby cereal town. Good men who will crow to their coworkers about owning a five-acre lot in something called Cedar View Estates.

Others say the dying genius shook his fist at the heavens in rage.

Unlike the width of the two-by-fours used to build the tract homes of Cedar View, the depth of graves has remained the same since the time of the pioneers. Six feet under still means something here. Death is immune to trends, our funeral director claims.

The farmer's daughter felt her breath catch when her beloved father went under. For a moment she was afraid she'd suffocate too, but then, she said, she imagined the dirt as a blanket for keeping warm, and she could breathe again.

If you slip into the timber to take a piss this time of year you won't find much green except *Sanguinaria Canadensis*, common names pain ease, snake bite, sweet slumber. *Sanguinaria* from the Latin *sanguinarius* meaning "bleeding." The bloodroot contains alkaloids not dissimilar in effect from the morphine they administered to his father, in hospice.

Deeper into the woods find hepatica, aka liverleaf, liverwort. Hepatica from the Latin *epatikos* meaning "affecting the liver." It was used to treat liver ailments, maybe even Beethoven's.

Tell me again what the dove says, Love, when he comes.

He says be grateful for the song you sing. He says be glad to count yourself among the living, like the red-wings full of words and chatter each spring, full of opinions large and small, of lamentations and love and blessing.

AFTERWORD

Life after Death

Today is my father's birthday, July 11, and I'm spending it looking out the window of a cabin on the edge of the Ventana Wilderness in rural Monterey County, California. Though the rustic cabin boasts no air-conditioning and nothing that can rightly be called furniture, I have landed in a fortunate place, a zip code populated by the winners in America's longevity sweepstakes.

Admittedly, I am a stranger in a strange land here, and custom requires that I keep my native fatalism in check, for Californians are America's eternal optimists, capable of turning the other cheek to the most Gothic and gutting realities. I am merely a guest in a place that prides itself, Dracula-like, in being forever-young. By comparison with my native Midwest, the obituaries run in the local newspaper, the *Pine Cone*, are long and almost incorrigibly joyful, crafted by survivors chock-full of joie de vivre. The prescribed formats, word counts, and typographies insisted on by no-nonsense newspapers in the Heartland are thrown out the window here in favor of anything-goes. Often causes of death are omitted entirely rather than covered up by the blanket euphemisms ("died of a sudden illness") preferred elsewhere. Obituaries need not include the pro forma picture of the deceased at the end of their life. Here a picture of the dearly departed as a death-defying, show-stopping, devil-may-care young man or woman replaces the standard near-to-death headshot. And why not? As a rule coastal Californians are not a subtle or verklempt people, and their over-sharing obits often run a full column or more in length.

This week the venerable *Pine Cone* runs reminiscences for Vicki, for Michael, for Hadley, Anthea aka. "Toni," and Patricia, aka. "Debbie," for Nita, Charlotte, and Marjorie. Marjorie tops the list of the longest-lived at 103 years old, born in the year of Woodrow Wilson's inauguration as president. Like many coastal Californians she was born elsewhere—Bozeman, Montana—acquiring a college education in an era when such a credential remained a rarity. Active interests and a surfeit of hobbies are the key to longevity here, and Marjorie is no exception. Current events, international outreach, and travel top this centurion's long list of avid pursuits. According to the Centers for Disease Control, Marjorie is one of fewer than 4,500 people out of any given cohort of 100,000 that might expect to surpass the century mark.

Here too is Charlotte, aged eighty-eight, a chanteuse who sang at the famed Fairmont Hotel in San Francisco, daughter of the writer Dio Dawo. She is described as a positive person with a joie de vivre that could light up a room. Her family celebrates her legacy as an accomplished tennis player, a lover of music and symphonies, and a generous contributor to the resurfacing of the local high school's tennis courts. Here too is Nita, born 1930 in faraway Miller, South Dakota, a traveler to Europe, Turkey, and Jordan, among other destinations throughout the Middle East.

Next comes Anthea, "Toni" for short, college-educated, born and raised two thousand miles away in Pennsylvania, later to find her call-ing as an executive assistant in La Jolla. Like many in these pages she's a devotee of Frank Sinatra and bridge games with her friends. Toni lived to the ripe old age of ninety-five.

Here is "Debbie," pictured in full sixties bouffant, blonde and bristling with life. Born in Daytona Beach, she found work as a Cover Girl and a Coca-Cola model for billboards appearing in Times Square. Those spots earned Debbie a trip to Hollywood for a screen test, where she acted in two stage plays before meeting a handsome navy pilot one night at a cocktail party; he proposed to her the very same night. After giving birth to their two sons, Debbie turned her talents to art, studying with Thomas Leighton and at the San Francisco Art Institute, and later devoted her leisure time to horse-breeding and foxhunting. She prided herself in being a member of the Daughters of the American Revolution.

And let us not forget the week's sole male deceased, Michael, a dead ringer for Charlton Heston, borne in Grosse Pointe, Michigan, a mortgage lender in San Francisco for Heitman Mortgage, builder of shopping centers throughout California and Oregon, a president of a seafood canning company, and executive at a well-respected winery. Many clubs proudly counted him among their members, including the illustrious Pebble Beach & Tennis Club, the Bohemian Club in San Francisco, and the International Order of Saint Hubertus, an elite Austrian hunting order. His glass, the obituary reports, was always half full.

In 2016 *JAMA* published a revealing study on longevity as it relates to places like longevity-endowed coastal Monterey. Its authors divided the metropolitan United States into one hundred distinct commuting zones, noting that the commuting zones with the highest life expectancies were clustered in California (six of the top ten), while the commuting zones with the lowest life expectancies were centered in the industrial Midwest (five of the bottom ten). In Monterey County, where Toni, Vicki, Debbie, and Marjorie were fortunate enough to have lived out their days, a forty-year-old woman can reasonably expect to live to be almost eighty-seven years old. Indeed, the average age of the women eulogized in the pages of this week's *Pine Cone* tallies an exceptional 94.5.

For those who believe in geodemographic parity and fairness the *JAMA* study's key finding—a nearly fifteen-year gap in life expectancy for men and an approximately ten-year gap in life expectancy between the richest 1 percent and poorest percent of individuals in the identified commuting zones—should be cause for alarm. Making matters worse for the geographically or professionally dispossessed, inequality and life expectancy have increased over time. Between 2001 and 2014, the study finds, life expectancy increased by 2.34 years for men and 2.91 years for women in the top five percent of the income distribution, but by only 0.32 years for men and 0.04 years for women in the bottom five percent.

As recently as a generation ago America acknowledged the importance of offering its citizens, regardless of where they hung their hat, something close to geographic parity when it came to the essentials in life—clean air, decent water, passable schools, access to basic health care, and a higher education—as part of the democratic ideal. Now, a growing number of observers wrongly regard life in Middle America as a self-inflicted health hazard or risk factor—something like smoking or drinking or drug-addiction—a dangerous lifestyle choice accompanied by grave conse-quences. One day soon one imagines the well-preserved coastal émigré attending the wake of his cousin back home in the Heartland may pause before his kinfolk's open casket and offer this dry-eyed and sober lament: "If only the poor soul would have moved."

Despite the added risks or alleged deprivations, I have no intention of moving, and no desire to deny the ultimate end, though I hope, like anyone, to forestall it as long as possible. While the rest of the nation sometimes begrudges the Heartland our abiding necromancy and fussy cult-of-the-dead, it's worth considering the many ways in which a culture that speaks to, and with, its deceased is a culture more timeless, by defini-tion, than that enjoyed by good-timers and death-deniers living elsewhere. It's worth attending to the wisdoms gleaned by and from a people prac-ticed at looking death in the eye, all the while considering the collective cultural and spiritual wisdom resident in a land of hoary heads.

These days Midwestern Fatalism is part catchphrase, part Internet meme, and part regional stereotype. Among the sunny bon vivants living elsewhere fatalism has come to signify a certain old-world, sky-is-falling world view, though I argue our particular mentality suits our climes. In the minds of many bicoastal sophisticates, old-before-their-time fatalists like me have one foot in the grave already. Still I maintain that to love life is first to know and to respect death. Honoring the dead helps remind me to celebrate my time among the living. When it's all said and done a region that understands its dying alongside its living, that honors its past and passing, is a region worthy of the eternal.

ACKNOWLEDGMENTS

Heartfelt thanks to the good people who made this book possible, most especially Hal Berkley, Beth Howard, Ross McIntire, and Ben Winchester, who gave generously of their time and insight.

Special thanks as well to the editors of the Sport Literature Association, who published an early version of "Cornfield Cathedrals," under the title "The Longest Drive," in *Aethlon* 33.2 (Spring/Summer 2016), and to *Wapsipinicon Almanac*, who published an early version of "Springtime on the Prairie," under the title "Growing Seasons," in fall 2014.